Fresh & Fast

Fresh & Fast

Inspired Cooking for Every Season and Every Day

Marie Simmons

Photography by Alan Richardson

Houghton Mifflin Company
Boston   New York

For information about permission to reproduce selections from this book, write to Permissions, Houghton Mifflin Company, 215 Park Avenue South, New York, New York 10003.

Visit our Web site: www.houghtonmifflinbooks.com.

ISBN-13: 978-0-395-97173-4
ISBN-10: 0-395-97173-X

ISBN-13: 978-0-618-44029-0
ISBN-10: 0-618-44029-1

The following recipes first appeared in *Bon Appétit* in slightly different form: Pureed Carrot, Potato and Ginger Soup (page 55); Potato and Garlic Soup with Prosciutto (page 58); Seafood Soup with Saffron-Tomato Broth (page 64); Pasta Primavera, Asian Style (page 96); Chicken with Broccoli Rabe and Bacon (page 114); Sesame Brown Rice Pilaf with Garlic and Vegetables (page 168); and Black Bean and Vegetable Burrito (page 181). Courtesy of *Bon Appétit*.

Library of Congress Cataloging-in-Publication Data

Simmons, Marie.
    Fresh and fast : inspired cooking for every season and every day / Marie Simmons.
        p.   cm.
    Includes index.
    ISBN 0-395-97173-X (pbk.)
    ISBN 0-618-44029-1 (pbk.)
    1. Cookery.   I. Title.
TX714.S576 1996
641.5—dc20   96-4351

Design by Susan McClellan

QUM 10 9 8 7 6 5 4 3 2 1

ACKNOWLEDGMENTS

THE THEME OF THIS BOOK TOOK HOLD when a friend and colleague, Maria Laghi, called me to say that one of New Jersey's largest newspapers, *The Bergen Record*, wanted to add a column to their food pages and suggested that I call and talk to them about writing it.

Today, seven years later, "Fresh & Fast" is a syndicated column appearing in 80 newspapers across the United States.

Along the way, I have worked with many wonderful and supportive editors: Rosemary Black, Charles Monaghan, Patricia Mack, Russ Parsons, Colleen Bates and Jim Burns. But I especially want to thank Maria for thinking of me when there were so many other talented cooks and food writers out there.

I have enjoyed writing this column from the beginning because it was never an assignment, but a blank page, almost a diary, where I could express what I thought about what I just happened to be cooking that week or that day, which was, and still is, both fresh and fast.

Thank you Barry Estabrook, Rux Martin, Cristen Brooks, Judith Weber, Alan Richardson, Anne Disrude, Betty Alfenito and Susan McClellan. Without your brilliance, *Fresh & Fast* would not exist.

CONTENTS

Introduction

IT'S DINNERTIME, AND MY KITCHEN IS A FRENZY OF ACTIVITY. Seasoned rice simmers on the back of the stove, while I chop some scallions and green peppers to stir in later, along with oil and lemon. Chicken cutlets marinate in garlic, fresh thyme, olive oil and lime juice, ready to be pan-seared while the rice cools. In a few minutes, the cooked chicken will be placed on some prewashed salad greens with a spoonful of the rice salad on one side of the plate and a few pieces of roasted red pepper on the other. Within 35 minutes of stepping inside the door, we're enjoying dinner.

Uncomplicated meals like this one—marinated chicken cutlets and Yellow Confetti Rice Salad (page 224)—which I can make effortlessly and share with my family at the end of the day, are an essential part of my busy life. I choose fresh vegetables and fruits, quick-cooking cuts of meat, poultry and seafood, and pasta, rice, beans and grains over ready-made products. Fresh ingredients not only taste better but are more convenient than most packaged "convenience" items.

Red-skinned potatoes, for instance, need no peeling and are perfect quartered and browned in olive oil and seasoned with crushed red pepper, rosemary and garlic. Chicken cutlets, quickly seared, transform a salad into a main dish; in a sandwich, they become a hearty, nearly instant meal. Fresh scallops are nature's gift to the world of fast food, taking only a minute or two to cook in a hot skillet. Nectarines, their tender skins left on, need only to be sliced and placed in a mint sugar syrup to become dessert.

Because I get as much pleasure from eating as I do from cooking, I sometimes choose to devote a little more effort to preparation for the sake of taste. For example, the taste and texture of fresh green beans or fresh broccoli more than compensate for the few extra minutes they take to trim. The juice squeezed from a lemon or lime adds much more sparkle than bottled. I have yet to experience any instant garlic product that can replace the robust flavor of real cloves in their papery wrappings.

Relying on fresh ingredients means that my cooking has variety because it is influenced by the seasons. When the weather is warm and sunny, I turn to cooling foods that complement the day and my mood: bright, robustly flavored dishes like Tomato, Sweet Onion and Fresh Mint Salad (page 218) or Chilled Fresh Corn and Buttermilk Chowder with Shrimp (page 49). When it is gloomy and gray outside, I begin a shopping list for a soul-warming bowl of Black Bean Soup with Roasted Peppers and Tomatoes (page 62) or Orecchiette with Broccoli Rabe, White Beans and Garlic-and-Red-Pepper Oil (page 111).

Sometimes, it is whatever looks most tempting at my local farmer's market that sets off the chain of events in my kitchen. At other times, I find inspiration in my crowded A&P. A Saint Patrick's Day sale on cabbage may prompt a zesty Cabbage Salad with Lemon and Olive Oil (page 216). Topped with Spicy Marinated Shrimp (page 160), it becomes a meal. Another night, a special on cod fillets may catch my eye, and I decide to have Cod with Roasted Tomato Sauce and Black Olives (page 153).

To make the preparation easier, I always keep enough staples on hand for simple dinners. My cupboards are stocked with nonperishable basics: a selection of pastas—ditalini, penne, farfalle and spaghetti—and a variety of rices—brown and white Texmati and Italian or medium-grain. Equally essential are yellow onions, garlic and olive oil.

My refrigerator drawers are always stocked with vegetables and fruits that I consider indispensable: carrots, celery, scallions, mushrooms, lemons and limes. I buy fresh herbs and keep them perky by standing them in a glass of water in the refrigerator. On another shelf sits a salad spinner filled with washed salad greens.

As much as I love fresh ingredients, there are some ready-made products that I couldn't get along without. Thawed frozen peas can be stirred uncooked into rice or lentil dishes. Frozen lima beans can be added to soup or served plain with a warm vinaigrette dressing. Canned Italian plum tomatoes make a terrific quick sauce for pasta. Canned chicken broth, especially the relatively new reduced-sodium kind, is a perfectly acceptable substitute for homemade. Canned beans are mainstays in my kitchen. Black beans, drained and rinsed, are delicious in a salad when mixed with diced tomato, cilantro, crunchy corn and a dressing of lime juice and oil (page 198). Cannellini beans are tasty in pasta when mixed with bitter greens or in a salad.

MOST OF THE RECIPES IN THIS BOOK can be made in less than 1 hour. Others take a little longer, because they benefit from chilling, slow simmering or slow baking. Nevertheless, these dishes are sometimes even more convenient than the quicker ones, because you can do other things while they cook. When a recipe does have a step that will involve extra time, such as marinating, or when it calls for another recipe as an ingredient, like roasted red peppers or leftover grilled lamb, I alert you up front so you can plan ahead.

Because I've learned to adjust my menu according to the time and energy I have, dinnertime is the best part of my day. Part of the secret to my enjoyment is that I make only what I feel like eating. From my mother, who is still a wonderful cook at the age of 84, I've learned that good food does not have to be complicated. A fine dish can materialize from four ingredients: spaghetti, melted butter, freshly grated Parmigiano-Reggiano cheese and toasted walnuts (the recipe is on page 102). Food is too important to be relegated to mere sustenance. Or as I like to say, life is just too short to waste on a bad meal.

APPETIZERS

FAST

Finger Foods

Soy Almonds 12

Curried Pecans 13

Toasted Pita Triangles 17

Fresh Goat Cheese with Basil and Lemon 19

Chick-Pea Puree with Lemon and Mint 20

Smoked Salmon on Black Bread with Sweet Butter 21

Bagna Cauda 22

Crostini 24

Toppings for Crostini 25

Roasted Eggplant, Olive and Red Pepper Spread 25

Olivada 25

Mushrooms with Sun-Dried Tomatoes and Herbs 26

Fork Foods (Antipasti)

Bruschetta with Braised Escarole with Garlic and Olive Oil 30

Bruschetta with Red and Yellow Tomatoes 32

Mozzarella, Sun-Dried Tomatoes, Olives and Basil 41

WHEN YOU HAVE MORE TIME

Orange-and-Fennel-Flavored Olives 14

Lemon-and-Garlic-Flavored Olives 15

Crisp Fried Eggplant Strips 16

Ricotta Cheese Spread with Lemon and Herbs 18

Roasted Garlic Puree 27

Soy Almonds

PREPARATION TIME: 5 MINUTES ✳ COOKING TIME: 3 MINUTES ✳ MAKES: 2 CUPS

ONE OF OUR DAUGHTER'S FIRST jobs was as a prep cook in a health food restaurant, where she made the soy almonds for an Asian pasta salad. She gave me the recipe, and now I keep a supply on hand at all times. You can also make this with walnuts or a mixture of nuts. If you like your nuts a little spicy (hot), add a drop or two of chili oil, available where Asian groceries are sold.

1	tablespoon vegetable oil
2	cups (8 ounces) whole natural (with skins) almonds
2	tablespoons soy sauce
¼	teaspoon hot chili oil (optional)

1. Heat the oil in a large nonstick skillet. Add the almonds and stir to coat.

2. Add the soy sauce and the chili oil, if using, and cook, stirring, over high heat for 3 minutes, or until the almonds are coated with the mixture and the skillet is dry. Transfer to a platter (do not use a paper towel; the almonds will stick to it) and cool.

3. Store in plastic containers until ready to serve.

Curried Pecans

PREPARATION TIME: 5 MINUTES ❀ COOKING TIME: 20 MINUTES ❀ MAKES: 2 CUPS

THIS IS A VERY OLD RECIPE that I learned to make 25 years ago, when curry was considered daring and exotic. These nuts are a bit old-fashioned, I admit, but I love to munch on them with a tall, cool drink. They are also great sprinkled over chicken salad, stir-fried green beans or a mixed green salad.

2 cups (8 ounces) large pecan halves
2 tablespoons unsalted butter,
     cut into small pieces
2-3 teaspoons curry powder
½ teaspoon coarse (kosher) salt

1. Preheat the oven to 350 degrees F. Spread the pecans in a large, shallow baking pan and dot with the butter. Bake just until the butter melts, about 5 minutes.

2. Remove from the oven and sprinkle with the curry powder and the salt. Stir to coat.

3. Bake, stirring often, until the pecans are toasted and coated with the butter and curry, 10 to 15 minutes. Cool; store in an airtight container in a cool place.

Orange-and-Fennel-Flavored Olives

PREPARATION TIME: 5 MINUTES ● MARINATING TIME: 1 TO 5 DAYS ● SERVES: 8

KEEP THESE ON HAND for a quick snack before dinner. I like the salty, briny taste of Kalamata olives, but any brine-cured black olive (Niçoise, Greta or Moroccan) can be used.

½ pound brine-cured (Kalamata) black olives with pits

¼ cup extra-virgin olive oil

4 garlic cloves, bruised with the side of a knife

3 strips orange zest (removed with a vegetable peeler), cut into julienne strips

1 teaspoon fennel seeds, bruised in a mortar and pestle or with the side of a knife

¼ teaspoon hot red pepper flakes

1. Place the olives on the work surface and bruise them lightly with the side of a large chef's knife.

2. Combine the olives, oil, garlic, orange zest, fennel seeds and red pepper flakes in a storage container with a tight-fitting lid. Shake to distribute the seasonings evenly.

PLAN AHEAD:

Marinate these olives 1 to 5 days before serving.

3. Refrigerate for 1 to 5 days, turning the container and shaking occasionally, before serving. Let stand at room temperature before serving. These will keep for up to 2 weeks.

● APPETIZERS ●

14

Lemon-and-Garlic-Flavored Olives

PREPARATION TIME: 5 MINUTES ● MARINATING TIME: 1 TO 5 DAYS ● SERVES: 8

I LOVE THE TASTE OF GREEN OLIVES, especially the big, meaty ones from Sicily and southern Italy. Bottled green olives from Spain are also very good but are a little saltier than the Italian ones. You might want to rinse them well to remove some of the surface salt before using.

½   pound green olives with pits

¼   cup extra-virgin olive oil

4   garlic cloves, crushed with the
     side of a knife

½   lemon, halved lengthwise and
     cut into thin slices

1   tablespoon snipped fresh thyme
     leaves, plus a few sprigs

¼   teaspoon freshly ground black
     pepper

1. Place the olives on a work surface and bruise them lightly with the side of a large chef's knife.

2. Combine the olives, oil, garlic, lemon, thyme and pepper in a storage container with a tight-fitting lid. Shake to distribute the seasonings evenly.

3. Refrigerate for 1 to 5 days, turning the container and shaking occasionally, before serving. Let stand at room temperature before serving. These will keep for up to 2 weeks.

> **PLAN AHEAD:**
>
> Marinate these olives 1 to 5 days before serving.

Crisp Fried Eggplant Strips

PREPARATION TIME: 10 MINUTES ● DRAINING TIME: 1 TO 3 HOURS
COOKING TIME: 20 MINUTES (FOR 2 OR 3 BATCHES) ● SERVES: 4

DON'T SKIP THE SALTING AND draining step, as it will draw out the moisture and help the eggplant fry up nice and crisp. These are delicious served before dinner.

1   large, firm eggplant
1   tablespoon coarse (kosher) salt
    Vegetable oil

1. Peel the eggplant and cut into ¼-inch-thick slices. Stack the slices in layers of two or three and cut through to make ¼-inch-wide strips. Toss in a bowl with the salt and transfer to a colander.

2. Set the colander in a bowl. Place a small plate on top of the eggplant and a heavy can on the plate to help squeeze out the excess moisture. Let stand for 1 to 3 hours.

PLAN AHEAD:

Allow 1 to 3 hours to drain the salted eggplant.

3. Rinse the eggplant briefly with cold water and transfer to a large kitchen towel. Roll the eggplant up in the towel and squeeze it as dry as possible. Repeat with a dry towel.

4. Fill a deep skillet about one-third full with the oil. Heat the oil until a piece of eggplant sizzles upon contact. Fry the eggplant in two or three batches, stirring occasionally, until golden brown, about 8 minutes per batch. Remove from the oil with a slotted spoon, draining off as much oil as possible. Blot each batch on a double thickness of paper towel.

5. Serve immediately. These look nice placed on a tray or shallow basket that has been lined with a printed cloth napkin (a solid napkin shows oil spots).

● APPETIZERS ●

16

Toasted Pita Triangles

PREPARATION TIME: 5 MINUTES ❀ BAKING TIME: 20 MINUTES ❀ SERVES: 4 OR MORE

THESE TRIANGLES SEEM OLD HAT to me, but they are one recipe that my students always make at home, again and again. They tell me I could have retired (or at least been a CEO of a large pita chip company) if I had only thought to produce these commercially. The truth is, I would much rather make a few at a time for family and friends.

Once again, necessity was the mother of invention. I often buy pita breads, make one sandwich and the next day discover that the rest are dry and hard. So I tuck the bag of dry pitas in the freezer and forget about it. Then, whenever I feel like it, I thaw them, cut them into pieces, brush them with olive oil and toast them in the oven. Now I have a very efficient production line for the preparation of pita chips. These keep very well. I store them in my bread drawer in a self-sealing plastic bag. Eat as is or use to scoop up salsa or dips. I like them with the Chick-Pea Puree with Lemon and Mint (page 20).

1   package pita breads (4-6)
¼   cup (approximately) extra-virgin olive oil
1   garlic clove, crushed through a press
    Coarse (kosher) salt

1. Preheat the oven to 350 degrees F.

2. Using kitchen scissors, cut the pita breads crosswise (through the folded edge), forming 2 circles of bread from each pita.

3. Combine the oil and the garlic in a small bowl; brush the rough side of the bread lightly with the oil-and-garlic mixture. Sprinkle with the salt. Stack the pitas and cut them into triangles. (This is much easier than trying to brush every little triangle.)

4. Spread the pita triangles in a single layer on 2 baking sheets. Bake, rearranging the pitas so they will brown evenly, until crisp and golden, about 20 minutes.

5. Serve warm or at room temperature.

Ricotta Cheese Spread with Lemon and Herbs

PREPARATION TIME: **10 MINUTES** ● DRAINING TIME: **4 HOURS OR OVERNIGHT** ● SERVES: **4**

ALL THE INGREDIENTS FOR THIS spread are either staples in the refrigerator or can be picked up quickly at the supermarket. Draining the ricotta removes excess moisture, resulting in a stiffer, more spreadable mixture, but if you are in a hurry, the recipe works just fine without draining the cheese or draining it for less time. If you have drained the ricotta for the maximum time, you might want to mold it as directed in Fresh Goat Cheese with Basil and Lemon (opposite page). Vary the fresh herbs depending on availability. Substitute dill, parsley, rosemary or oregano for the thyme—or use a tiny amount of each. Remember that the intensity of fresh herbs varies. Add small amounts, taste and then add more.

Note: To make long, thin strips of basil (called chiffonade), stack 3 or 4 large basil leaves, stem ends together. Beginning at the opposite tip, tightly roll up the leaves. Then cut the roll into very thin crosswise slices. Use these fine "threads" of basil as a garnish.

> **PLAN AHEAD:**
>
> Allow at least 4 hours for the ricotta to drain before making this.

1   container (15 ounces) whole-milk or part-skim ricotta

1   garlic clove, crushed through a press

1   teaspoon grated lemon zest

1   teaspoon fresh thyme leaves, stripped from the stem
    Pinch salt
    Freshly ground black pepper

2   tablespoons extra-virgin olive oil

4   basil leaves, rolled and cut into strips for garnish (see note)

1. Empty the container of ricotta into a strainer and place over a bowl. Cover and refrigerate for at least 4 hours or overnight. Discard the water in the bowl. Or to speed up the draining, drain at room temperature for 1 hour.

2. Combine the drained ricotta, garlic, ½ teaspoon of the lemon zest, ½ teaspoon of the thyme leaves, the salt and a grinding of pepper; stir until blended. Mound into the center of a shallow bowl or serving plate and drizzle with the oil. Sprinkle the remaining ½ teaspoon lemon zest and ½ teaspoon thyme on top. Garnish with the strips of basil.

3. Serve with crackers, Crostini (page 24) or raw vegetables.

Fresh Goat Cheese with Basil and Lemon

PREPARATION TIME: 5 MINUTES ● SERVES: 8

MAKE THIS SIMPLE, FRESH-tasting appetizer when you need something festive and pretty at the last minute. I prefer the mild taste, creamy texture and round shape of domestic goat cheese for this recipe, but you could use logs of French goat cheese (without the ash covering) found in many supermarkets. If using the log, form it into a disk by mashing it with a fork and then pressing it into a custard cup or small bowl that has been lined with a piece of foil or plastic wrap. Then invert the cheese onto a serving dish, peel off the foil or plastic and proceed with the recipe.

The flavors for this recipe can be varied. For instance, snipped fresh thyme or rosemary leaves (about 1 teaspoon of each) can be used instead of basil. Orange can be substituted for the lemon. If you have a grater with a scalloped shredding blade, use it to make thin pieces of zest; they will look pretty on the cheese. This is the place to show off your best extra-virgin olive oil.

2 tablespoons extra-virgin olive oil
1 garlic clove, crushed through a press
1 disk (about 3 ounces) fresh domestic goat cheese
1 teaspoon grated lemon zest
  Freshly ground black pepper, to taste
4 basil leaves, rolled and cut into strips for garnish
  Table water biscuits, Crostini (page 24) or raw vegetables

1. Combine the oil and garlic in a small bowl; stir to blend.

2. Place the goat cheese in a small, shallow bowl or on a serving plate and sprinkle with the lemon zest and pepper. Add the thin strips of basil. Top with the oil-and-garlic mixture. Let stand at room temperature so the cheese will be soft and spreadable.

3. Serve with crackers, crostini and/or raw vegetables.

Chick-Pea Puree with Lemon and Mint

PREPARATION TIME: 10 MINUTES ● MAKES: ABOUT 3 CUPS (RECIPE CAN BE HALVED)

THIS IS ONE OF MY FAVORITE DIPS. Canned chick-peas are pureed with fresh lemon juice, olive oil, garlic and cold water until light and fluffy. This also makes a wonderful sandwich filling.

The mint adds a fresh taste. Pick up a bunch in the produce section when it looks perky and is very fragrant. If good-looking mint isn't available, use fresh dill.

2	cans (15½ ounces each) chick-peas (ceci or garbanzo beans), rinsed and drained
⅓	cup fresh lemon juice
2	garlic cloves, chopped
½	teaspoon salt, or to taste
⅓	cup plus 1 tablespoon extra-virgin olive oil
3	tablespoons cold water
1	tablespoon *each* finely chopped parsley, mint and/or dill
	Sprinkling of cayenne (ground red pepper)
	Raw vegetables, Crostini (page 24) or Toasted Pita Triangles (page 17)

1. Coarsely puree the chick-peas, lemon juice, garlic and salt in the bowl of a food processor until smooth. With the motor running, gradually add ⅓ cup oil in a thin, steady stream. Then add the water and puree until the chick-peas are smooth and fluffy. Scrape into a shallow bowl and smooth the top with a rubber spatula.

2. Sprinkle the top with the herbs and cayenne; drizzle with the remaining 1 tablespoon oil.

3. Serve with vegetables, crostini or pita chips.

Smoked Salmon on Black Bread
with Sweet Butter

PREPARATION TIME: 10 MINUTES ❋ SERVES: 4

WHENEVER I WANT a particularly festive bite to serve with sparkling wine, I splurge on smoked salmon. Many excellent-quality brands are available presliced in 4-ounce vacuum packages. These little canapés take just a few minutes to assemble and look like a million dollars.

4   slices firm, dark Westphalian
        black bread or warm plain
        thin-sliced toast
2   tablespoons softened
        unsalted butter
4   ounces thin-sliced smoked salmon
        Fresh dill sprigs, watercress leaves
        or other small fresh herb or
        salad leaf

1. Spread the bread with a thin layer of the softened butter. Arrange the salmon over the buttered bread in a single layer, cutting the salmon to fit.

2. Cut the bread into 4 small squares. Garnish each with a tiny sprig of dill, a watercress leaf or other tiny herb or salad leaf.

Bagna Cauda

PREPARATION TIME: 30 MINUTES • COOKING TIME: 10 MINUTES • SERVES: 8

FOR YEARS, I HAVE BEEN MAKING this wonderful dip (*bagna cauda* means "warm bath" in Italian) of melted butter, olive oil, anchovies and garlic in a copper double boiler and bringing it along with an enormous basket of raw vegetables to holiday family meals. We all stand around the bagna cauda table and dip in with pieces of raw fennel, celery, carrot, scallion, tiny radishes with tops for handles, red and yellow peppers, zucchini and leaves of radicchio and Belgian endive. Keep the bagna cauda warm in a chafing dish or a little ceramic server set over a candle. This is a wonderful first course for a sit-down meal. (See photograph, page 39.)

Assorted raw vegetables,
    such as Belgian endive, radicchio,
    scallions, fennel, carrots, zucchini,
    red and yellow bell peppers,
    celery, tiny radishes

BAGNA CAUDA

¾   cup extra-virgin olive oil
½   cup (1 stick) unsalted butter
1   tablespoon finely chopped garlic
1   can (2 ounces) flat anchovy fillets,
        drained, blotted with paper
        towels, finely chopped

1. Cut the cores from the endive and radicchio; remove the larger outside leaves for the dip; reserve the hearts for salad or other use. Trim the scallions. Trim the fennel and cut the bulb into wedges. Trim the carrots and zucchini, then cut into thin diagonal slices. Halve the red and yellow peppers; discard the stems and seeds and cut into wedges. Trim the celery and cut into 3-inch lengths. Trim the tops from the radishes, leaving attached the small center leaves or stems to use as a handle. Store in plastic bags until ready to serve. The vegetables can be prepared up to 1 day ahead.

2. Make the Bagna Cauda: Heat the oil and butter in a medium skillet over low heat until the butter melts. Add the garlic and cook, stirring frequently, until tender, about 10 minutes. Do not allow the oil and butter to get hot enough to bubble. Add the anchovies and stir until dissolved and completely blended; whisk to emulsify the mixture.

3. Serve at once, keeping the bagna cauda warm in a chafing dish or a small serving crock set over a candle. Place the raw vegetables on a platter or in a basket alongside.

BAGNA CAUDA, LORENA STYLE

LORENA ALESSIO, AN ARCHITECTURE STUDENT from Turin, Italy, who lived with us during her graduate studies, taught me to serve bagna cauda as a sauce over cooked vegetables. This makes a delicious first course before pasta.

Serve the warm bagna cauda over a selection of the following: Oven-Braised Fennel (page 262; omit the Parmigiano-Reggiano), Oven-Roasted Sweet Onions (page 272), Oven-Roasted Beets (page 243; omit the gremolata), Mom's Roasted and Peeled Red Peppers (page 276) or Easy Oven-Roasted Red Bell Peppers (page 278), Oven-Braised Leeks (page 266; omit the vinaigrette), Oven-Roasted Asparagus (page 235; omit the vinaigrette) and plain boiled new potatoes.

Arrange the hot or warm cooked vegetable or vegetables on a large platter. Pass the serving dish of warm bagna cauda, and let each person "sauce" the vegetables on his or her plate.

Crostini

PREPARATION TIME: 10 MINUTES ❊ BAKING TIME: 5 TO 20 MINUTES

SERVES: VARIES; PLAN ON 2 OR 3 CROSTINI PER PERSON

CROSTINI MEANS "TOAST" in Italian. Made from crusty long or round loaves of Italian whole wheat or white bread, crostini can be prepared using several different techniques, depending on the circumstances.

During the summer, I grill the bread, turning until it is evenly heated and lightly colored. Traditionally, the bread is rubbed with the cut side of garlic and then drizzled with oil. This method is fussy and time-consuming. I just brush it, using a wide pastry brush, with a combination of approximately ¼ cup extra-virgin olive oil and 1 garlic clove that has been crushed through a press.

Another method for preparing crostini, especially when just a few pieces are required, is to toast the bread in a toaster oven, under the broiler or using a regular toaster designed to accommodate wide slices. While the toast is still hot, I brush it with the oil-and-garlic mixture.

When making crostini for a crowd, use this very efficient method: Preheat the oven to 350 degrees F. Select a large baking sheet. Arrange the slices of Italian bread on the pan. Combine ¼ cup extra-virgin olive oil (or more as needed) and 1 garlic clove crushed through a press. Brush the bread lightly with the oil-and-garlic mixture on one side.

Bake in the oven for 20 to 25 minutes, until the crostini are golden, turning and rearranging after 15 minutes so they brown evenly. This produces very crunchy crostini, almost crackerlike. They can be served warm from the oven or at room temperature. They keep well for several days, stored in self-sealing plastic bags in a bread drawer.

Toppings for Crostini

Roasted Eggplant, Olive and Red Pepper Spread

PREPARATION TIME: 15 MINUTES

BAKING TIME: 20 MINUTES

MAKES: ABOUT 1 CUP; ENOUGH FOR 16 CROSTINI

EGGPLANT, BLACK OLIVES and red peppers combine in an easy-to-make spread. Inspired by the Sicilian classic, caponata, my version is a lot less complicated in technique and taste. This spread will keep for several days in the refrigerator, so make it ahead if you are planning a party, or just keep it on hand for a quick bite.

1	medium eggplant (about 1 pound), peeled and cut crosswise into ½-inch-thick round slices
3	tablespoons extra-virgin olive oil
1	garlic clove, chopped
1	teaspoon red wine vinegar
1	tablespoon chopped pitted brine-cured black olives
1	tablespoon chopped red bell pepper
1	tablespoon chopped fresh parsley
¼	teaspoon salt, or to taste
	Crostini (page 24)

1. Preheat the oven to 425 degrees F. Brush the eggplant slices on both sides with the oil. Arrange on a nonstick baking sheet and bake until lightly browned on both sides, about 10 minutes per side. When cool enough to handle, cut into pieces. There will be about 1 cup.

2. Combine the eggplant, garlic and vinegar in a food processor and puree. Transfer to a bowl and stir in the olives, red pepper, parsley and salt.

3. Spread on crostini and serve.

Olivada

PREPARATION TIME: 10 MINUTES

SERVES: 8; MAKES ABOUT ⅔ CUP

FINELY CHOPPED BLACK OLIVES flavored with anchovy and garlic is a delicious spread for crostini. Tiny Niçoise olives have a wonderful flavor, but they are the devil to pit. Often, I use Kalamata olives, which are saltier-tasting than Niçoise. They are larger, and the flesh falls from the pit easily when the olives are bruised with the side of a large chef's knife. Make sure to select your best-tasting extra-virgin olive oil for this spread.

½	cup coarsely chopped pitted brine-cured black olives
5	tablespoons extra-virgin olive oil
½	teaspoon finely chopped garlic
¼-½	teaspoon anchovy paste
	Crostini (opposite page)

1. Combine the olives, 2 tablespoons of the oil, the garlic and anchovy paste in the bowl of a food processor. Puree until smooth. With the motor running, add the remaining 3 tablespoons oil in a slow, steady stream until the spread is smooth. Transfer to a bowl and refrigerate, covered, until ready to use.

2. Spread on crostini and serve.

VARIATION

Spread the olivada on Polenta Toasts (page 190) and top with a piece of roasted red pepper.

Mushrooms with Sun-Dried Tomatoes and Herbs

PREPARATION TIME: 10 MINUTES

COOKING TIME: 6 MINUTES

SERVES: 8; MAKES ABOUT 1 CUP

MUSHROOMS ARE A STAPLE in my kitchen. I enjoy the earthy, almost meatlike quality that they add to dishes. As often as not, I serve them as the main event, rather than simply as an ingredient. This mushroom spread goes together very quickly. If you don't have both fresh oregano and thyme on hand, use dried and chop them with the fresh parsley. This technique rehydrates the herbs with the parsley juices and helps bring out their flavors.

2 cups chopped or sliced white button mushrooms

¼ cup chopped onion

4 tablespoons extra-virgin olive oil

1 garlic clove, crushed through a press

1 tablespoon chopped fresh parsley

½ teaspoon fresh thyme leaves or ¼ teaspoon dried

½ teaspoon minced fresh oregano leaves or ⅛ teaspoon dried

¼ teaspoon salt, or to taste
   Coarsely ground black pepper, to taste

2 tablespoon rinsed, drained, finely diced oil-packed sun-dried tomatoes
   Crostini (page 24)

1. In a medium skillet, cook the mushrooms, onion and 1 tablespoon of the oil over medium heat until lightly browned, about 5 minutes. Add the garlic, parsley, thyme, oregano, salt and pepper; cook for 1 minute. Cool slightly.

2. Transfer to a food processor and puree until smooth. With the motor running, gradually add the remaining 3 tablespoons oil. Transfer to a small bowl and stir in the sun-dried tomatoes.

3. Spread on crostini and serve.

Roasted Garlic Puree

PREPARATION TIME: 5 MINUTES ● COOKING TIME: 1 HOUR ● MAKES: ABOUT ¼ CUP

I HAVE ROASTED GARLIC every way possible. The objective is for the garlic to soften and turn a pale straw color. It should not brown, or it will turn bitter. As it slowly cooks, the natural sugars caramelize and the flavor mellows, becoming almost sweet.

Roasted garlic has a number of uses in the kitchen. I like it spread on bread in place of butter or as part of a sandwich, stirred into salad dressings or combined with cooked pasta. It is great added to mashed potatoes, stirred into soup or pureed beans or used as a topping for grilled fish. It is also delicious pushed under the skin of chicken breasts before they are roasted or broiled.

I have two ways of oven-roasting garlic. In the first, I roast the whole heads for 1 hour and then peel them, either all at once or as they are needed.

In the second, I roast peeled garlic cloves in olive oil. This is a great method if you are lucky enough to be able to buy jars of already peeled garlic in the produce section of your super-market. (Do not be tempted to buy the small jars of chopped garlic in olive oil; they might seem convenient, but this is one product that sacrifices too much flavor for the sake of time.)

2   garlic heads, or more
     Extra-virgin olive oil
     Salt and freshly ground black
        pepper

1. Whole heads: Preheat the oven to 350 degrees F. Rub the outside of the heads of garlic to loosen the papery skins. Place the garlic head on its side and cut off the points of the cloves ½ inch below the tips. Arrange the garlic cut side up in a dish just large enough to hold the heads comfortably. Drizzle each with about ½ tablespoon of the oil.

2. Cover the dish with foil and bake for 30 minutes. Uncover and turn the garlic cut side down. Roast for 30 minutes more, or until the cloves are soft. Let cool at room temperature.

3. Separate the individual cloves of garlic. Pinching the garlic at the stem, press on the clove and squeeze the softened garlic out into a small bowl. Mash with a fork. Each head will yield about 2 tablespoons pureed garlic. Add salt and a grinding of black pepper. Stir 1 teaspoon oil into the puree, if desired.

4. Refrigerate, covered, until ready to use. The garlic puree will keep, tightly covered and refrigerated, for up to 1 week.

Peeled garlic cloves: Roast as directed above, except preheat the oven to 325 degrees F and add enough oil to the pan to almost cover the garlic. An added bonus with this method is that you can use the roasted garlic-flavored oil to flavor the mashed garlic puree, as a dressing on salads or drizzled over toasted Italian bread.

ANTIPASTI MAKE A MEAL

NOTHING MAKES ME HAPPIER than an assortment of antipasti eaten as a meal. Some of my favorite dishes are cannellini bean salad, roasted red peppers, greens—usually braised escarole with garlic and lemon—and grilled mushrooms. When I serve them with fresh mozzarella cheese, some sun-dried tomatoes, intensely flavored black olives and crostini, I think I am dining in heaven.

Although there are quite a few elements in this menu for the cook to contend with, either some or all of these dishes can be made ahead, and they are all very easy to prepare. The peppers can be prepared in minutes and then left to roast slowly in the oven while the greens and mushrooms are cooked and the mozzarella, sun-dried tomatoes and olives are set out. The greens can be quickly cooked and set aside until serving time, and the crostini can be made ahead using the oven method. One of the advantages of antipasti is that they are delicious served either warm or at room temperature.

As the dishes are prepared, I line them up along the center of the table to be admired before we sit down to eat.

Mom's Roasted and Peeled Red Peppers *(page 276)*

or Easy Oven-Roasted Red Bell Peppers *(page 278)*

Braised Escarole with Garlic and Olive Oil *(page 30)*

Oven-Roasted Asparagus with
Shallot-Mustard Vinaigrette *(page 235)*

Pan-Grilled Mushrooms *(page 268)*

White Bean and Fennel Salad *(page 226)*

Mozzarella, Sun-Dried Tomatoes, Olives and Basil *(page 41)*

Warm Toasted Italian Bread

Bruschetta with Braised Escarole with Garlic and Olive Oil

PREPARATION TIME: 15 MINUTES ● COOKING TIME: 15 MINUTES ● SERVES: 4

THIS HEARTY BRUSCHETTA topped with garlicy escarole is easy to serve as an antipasto on individual plates at the table. It also makes a great lunch alone, on an open-faced sandwich or with a bowl of soup. Try spreading the toasted bread with a thin layer of Roasted Garlic Puree (page 27) and then topping it with the escarole. To serve as part of an antipasto platter or a vegetable side dish, see the variation below.

TOAST

8   diagonal slices (½ inch thick) Italian bread, preferably whole wheat
    Extra-virgin olive oil

GREENS

1   large head (about 1½ pounds) escarole, trimmed, washed and leaves stacked and cut crosswise into ½-inch lengths
1   tablespoon extra-virgin olive oil
1   small garlic clove, crushed through a press
¼   teaspoon crushed hot red pepper flakes (optional)
    Salt and freshly ground black pepper
1   lemon, cut into 8 wedges

1. Make the Toast: Toast the bread over a grill, in a toaster or under the broiler until lightly browned on both sides.

2. Arrange on a serving platter and brush lightly with a little oil.

3. Cook the Greens: Meanwhile, cook the escarole in plenty of boiling, salted water, uncovered, until tender but still bright green, 8 to 10 minutes. Drain well.

4. In a skillet, combine the oil, the garlic and the red pepper flakes, if using. Heat over low heat just until the garlic begins to sizzle, about 1 minute. Immediately add the escarole and stir to coat with the oil and heat through. Season with salt and pepper to taste.

5. Using tongs or a fork, place a mound of the escarole on each piece of toast. Arrange the lemon wedges between the bruschetta. Squeeze a little lemon juice over each bruschetta before eating.

VARIATION

Prepare the escarole as directed in steps 3 and 4. Mound on a platter and serve as part of an antipasto platter with Mom's Roasted and Peeled Red Peppers (page 276) and Pan-Grilled Mushrooms (page 268). Or mound in a serving bowl, garnish with lemon wedges and serve as a vegetable side dish with fish, poultry or meat.

Bruschetta with Red and Yellow Tomatoes

PREPARATION TIME: 15 MINUTES ● COOKING TIME: 10 MINUTES

SERVES: 8; MAKES ABOUT 24 BRUSCHETTA

THIS POPULAR RESTAURANT appetizer is so easy and refreshing that I make it all summer long. I first tasted bruschetta in Apulia, a region of Italy known for its sun-ripened tomatoes and robust, fruity olive oil. There, the oil is drizzled on bread that has been toasted (usually on an outside grill), and a wedge of tomato is smeared on the bread so it absorbs the juices. In my rendition, the bread is toasted, then brushed with olive oil and garlic and topped with a mixture of chopped tomato, olive oil, garlic and basil. These bruschetta are very pretty if a chopped yellow tomato is tossed in with the red.

- 4 tablespoons extra-virgin olive oil, or more as needed
- 1 garlic clove, crushed through a press
- 1 loaf Italian bread, cut into 3/8-1/2-inch-thick slices
- 2 cups diced ripe tomatoes (half red and half yellow, if available)
- 2 tablespoons chopped fresh basil Coarse salt, to taste
- 12 whole basil leaves for decoration (optional)

1. Combine 2 tablespoons of the oil and half of the garlic in a small bowl; set aside.

2. Grill the bread on a hot grill until lightly toasted on both sides. (Or, if you prefer, toast under the broiler or in a toaster oven.) Brush the toast lightly with the reserved oil-and-garlic mixture.

3. Combine the tomatoes, remaining 2 tablespoons oil, remaining garlic and salt in a small bowl.

4. Arrange the basil leaves, if using, on a large platter or tray. Top each piece of toasted bread with a rounded spoonful of the tomato mixture, making sure that the tomato juices drip onto the toast. Place on the basil leaves and serve.

Chilled Fresh Corn and Buttermilk Chowder with Shrimp *(page 49)*

Oven-Roasted Asparagus, Pan-Grilled Mushrooms and Oven-Baked Potatoes
(pages 235, 268 and 284)

34

Grilled Sea Scallop Brochette, Greek Style *(page 158)*

Pasta Primavera, Asian Style *(page 96)*

Pan-Grilled Smoked Turkey, Fontina, Bacon and Avocado Sandwich *(page 72)*

Penne with Roasted Vegetables *(page 106)*

Bagna Cauda *(page 22)*

Melon and Berries with Lime Sugar Syrup *(page 313)*

Mozzarella, Sun-Dried Tomatoes, Olives and Basil

PREPARATION TIME: 10 MINUTES ❋ SERVES: 4 AS A SINGLE ANTIPASTO; 6 TO 8 AS PART OF A MENU

MOZZARELLA, either commercially prepared or fresh, lends itself to any number of salad variations. This recipe features overlapping rows of sliced cheese, fresh basil leaves and sun-dried tomatoes. Sun-dried tomatoes are a good alternative when fresh tomatoes are not at their peak. Or you might try this salad with pieces of roasted red pepper instead of the tomatoes. Tuck other fresh herbs—especially thyme or rosemary leaves—in between instead of the basil.

My favorite form of mozzarella is fresh, which more and more Italian delis now carry. I like to buy it when it is still warm and juicy and use it the same day (the texture firms up once it is refrigerated). But any mozzarella will do.

10-12 slices (8-10 ounces) mozzarella, either fresh or commercially prepared

10-12 sun-dried tomato halves in olive oil

10-12 large fresh basil leaves

½ cup brine-cured black olives (Kalamata are good)

Extra-virgin olive oil, to taste

Freshly ground black pepper (optional)

1. Arrange the mozzarella slices and sun-dried tomatoes, slightly overlapping, on a platter.

2. Tuck a basil leaf randomly between the slices.

3. Garnish the platter with the olives. Drizzle a thin stream of oil over the dish. Add a grinding of black pepper, if desired.

Fresh mozzarella is available smoked and in salted and unsalted forms. I like the lightly salted best. Sometimes, I alternate slices of smoked and unsmoked on the same platter.

SOUPS

Quick-Chilled Cumin-Scented Fresh Tomato and Corn Soup

PREPARATION TIME: 10 MINUTES ● SERVES: 4

THIS SUPER-QUICK TOMATO SOUP is pureed in a blender or food processor and skips the time-consuming step of peeling the tomatoes. Because ice cubes are added to the blender, the soup emerges chilled and ready to serve. This is a great recipe when the tomatoes are ripe, but time is short.

- 4 cups cored and coarsely chopped ripe tomatoes (about 2 pounds)
- 6 ice cubes
- ¼ cup sliced scallions, white part only (reserve tops for garnish)
- ¼ cup chopped fresh basil or cilantro, plus more for garnish
- 1 teaspoon minced fresh jalapeño, or more to taste
- 1 garlic clove, chopped
- 1 teaspoon ground cumin
- 1 ear fresh sweet corn, husked and kernels cut from the cob (about ½ cup)
- ½ cup diced (¼ inch) green bell pepper
- 1 tablespoon fresh lime juice, or more to taste
- ½ teaspoon salt, or to taste
  Freshly ground black pepper, to taste
- ½ ripe avocado, peeled, seeded, cut into very thin wedges for garnish (optional)
- 2 tablespoons thinly sliced scallion tops

1. Combine the tomatoes, ice cubes, white part of scallions, basil or cilantro, jalapeño and garlic in a blender or food processor. Process until the mixture is pureed.

2. Sprinkle the cumin into a small skillet and heat, stirring, over low heat, just until fragrant, about 45 seconds. Add to the tomato mixture. Transfer to a bowl. Stir in the corn, green bell pepper, lime juice, salt and pepper. Taste and correct the seasonings; add more jalapeño, lime juice, salt and/or pepper.

3. Ladle into bowls and top each with 1 or 2 slices of avocado, if using. Sprinkle with the scallion tops and basil or cilantro and serve.

Chilled Avocado Soup with Tomato Salsa

PREPARATION TIME: 15 MINUTES ❁ CHILLING TIME: 1 TO 2 HOURS ❁ SERVES: 4; MAKES ABOUT 6 CUPS

I HAVE A PASSION FOR AVOCADOS, although I try to save these rather high-fat fruits for special occasions. In this soup, I temper my guilt by using low-fat milk and yogurt to add creaminess with a minimum of extra fat and calories.

2   ripe avocados, halved, peeled, pits removed
2   cups packed, rinsed, trimmed fresh spinach, steamed for 2 minutes and squeezed dry
½   cup packed fresh watercress leaves
¼   cup chopped scallions
¼   teaspoon finely chopped garlic
3   tablespoons fresh lime juice
2   cups low-fat milk
½   cup low-fat plain yogurt
1   cup unsalted homemade or sodium-reduced canned chicken broth, or more as needed
    Salt, to taste

SALSA

½   cup diced cored plum tomato
1   tablespoon diced red onion
1   teaspoon extra-virgin olive oil
1   teaspoon fresh lime juice
    Pinch salt

Chopped fresh cilantro, to taste (optional)

1. Dice half an avocado into ¼-inch pieces and reserve for the salsa. Cut the remaining avocados into ½-inch chunks and place in a food processor.

PLAN AHEAD:

Allow 1 to 2 hours for this soup to chill.

2. Add the cooked spinach, watercress, scallions, garlic and lime juice; process until smooth. With the motor running, gradually add the milk; process until smooth. Transfer to a bowl and stir in the yogurt until blended. Stir in the chicken broth until the soup is of the desired consistency. Season with salt. Refrigerate until cold, 1 to 2 hours.

3. Meanwhile, Make the Salsa: In a small bowl, combine the reserved diced avocado, the tomato, red onion, oil, lime juice and salt. Stir to blend. Top each serving of the soup with a spoonful of salsa. Garnish with the cilantro, if desired.

Curried Carrot Soup

PREPARATION TIME: 15 MINUTES ● COOKING TIME: 25 MINUTES

OPTIONAL CHILLING TIME: 2 TO 3 HOURS ● SERVES: 4

THIS SOUP CAN BE SERVED either hot or cold. For the chilled version, try substituting plain yogurt or buttermilk for some or all of the milk. Yogurt and buttermilk both have a tangy taste that will help balance the sweetness of the carrots.

1   tablespoon extra-virgin olive oil
½   cup chopped onion
1   teaspoon curry powder
½   teaspoon ground cumin
2   cups unsalted homemade or
      reduced-sodium canned
      chicken broth
4   cups sliced peeled carrots
      (about 1 pound)
1   cup diced peeled russet potatoes
2   cups low-fat or whole milk, or as
      needed (or use yogurt or
      buttermilk)
      Salt and freshly ground black
      pepper
2   tablespoons thinly sliced
      scallion tops
1   fresh jalapeño, cut into paper-thin
      crosswise slices (optional)

1. Heat the oil in a large, wide saucepan; add the onion and cook, stirring, until tender, about 5 minutes. Add the curry and cumin and stir until blended. Add the broth, carrots and potatoes. Cover and cook over low heat until the carrots are very tender, about 20 minutes.

> **PLAN AHEAD:**
> If you want to serve this soup cold, allow 2 to 3 hours to chill it.

2. Cool the carrot mixture slightly and puree in a food processor, working in batches if necessary, until the mixture is very smooth. Return the mixture to the saucepan and add milk to thin the soup to the desired consistency.

3. Season with salt and pepper to taste. Serve hot or cold, garnished with the sliced scallion tops and the jalapeño, if you like a little spice.

Chilled Curried Tomato Soup with Cilantro Cream

PREPARATION TIME: 10 MINUTES ● COOKING TIME: ABOUT 20 MINUTES

CHILLING TIME: 1 TO 2 HOURS ● SERVES: 4; MAKES ABOUT 5 CUPS

FOR THIS SOUP, I prefer strained tomatoes available in aseptic packages under the label Pomi. They have a lighter, fresher taste than canned tomato puree. Make this thick, creamy soup with either whole or low-fat yogurt and milk. The cilantro topping is made "creamy" with yogurt and just a tiny amount of optional heavy cream.

2	tablespoons extra-virgin olive oil
1	cup finely chopped onion
2	garlic cloves, finely chopped or crushed through a press
4	teaspoons curry powder, or to taste
1	box (35 ounces) Pomi strained tomatoes
2	cups plain yogurt, at room temperature, stirred until smooth
¼-½	cup milk (optional), or as needed to thin the soup
	Salt and freshly ground black pepper, to taste

CILANTRO CREAM

½	cup packed fresh cilantro leaves
½	cup plain whole-milk yogurt
2	tablespoons heavy cream (optional)

1. Combine the oil and onion in a large saucepan. Cook, stirring, over low heat until the onion is golden and soft, about 5 minutes. Add the garlic and the curry powder; cook, stirring, for 1 minute.

2. Stir in the tomatoes; cover and cook over low heat for 15 minutes, or until the flavors blend; cool slightly. For an extra-smooth soup, press through a strainer or process in a food processor until smooth. Transfer to a bowl. Gradually whisk the yogurt into the soup. Refrigerate until well chilled before serving. The soup will thicken upon standing. Before serving, thin to the desired consistency with milk. Correct the seasonings.

> **PLAN AHEAD:**
> Allow 1 to 2 hours for this soup to chill.

3. Make the Cilantro Cream: Combine the cilantro, yogurt and heavy cream, if using, in a food processor. Process until smooth. Refrigerate until ready to serve.

4. To serve, ladle into bowls and swirl a spoonful of the cilantro cream into each serving.

Cold Curried Spinach Soup with Yogurt Swirl

PREPARATION TIME: 20 MINUTES ● COOKING TIME: 25 MINUTES

CHILLING TIME: ABOUT 3 HOURS ● SERVES: 4

THIS IS A LOVELY GREEN SOUP, wonderful for entertaining on a warm summer night. Garnish with a spoonful of chopped raw tomato, a chiffonade (paper-thin slivers) of fresh spinach or simply a swirl of stirred yogurt.

½   cup chopped onion
2   teaspoons extra-virgin olive oil
2   teaspoons curry powder
½   teaspoon ground cumin
1   garlic clove, crushed through a press
1   teaspoon grated peeled fresh ginger
1   cup unsalted homemade or reduced-
      sodium canned
      chicken broth
1   cup cubed (½ inch) peeled potato
2   packages (10 ounces each) fresh
      spinach, rinsed, stems trimmed
      (about 8 cups packed)
1   cup low-fat milk, or more as needed
      to thin the soup
1   teaspoon salt, or to taste
⅛   teaspoon cayenne (ground red
      pepper), or to taste
1   tablespoon fresh lime juice

TOMATO RELISH

½   cup diced seeded tomato
1   scallion, trimmed and finely
      chopped
1   tablespoon chopped fresh cilantro
1   garlic clove, minced
      Pinch salt

½   cup low-fat plain yogurt, stirred
      until smooth

1. Combine the onion and oil in a large, wide saucepan. Cook, stirring, over low heat until the onion is soft, about 5 minutes. Add the curry, cumin, garlic and ginger; stir to blend. Add the broth and potato; heat to boiling. Cook, covered, over medium heat until the potatoes are very tender, about 10 minutes. Stir in the spinach. Cover and cook over medium heat until the spinach is wilted and tender, about 10 minutes. Cool slightly.

PLAN AHEAD:

Allow 3 hours for this soup to chill.

● SOUPS ●

47

2. Transfer the spinach mixture to the bowl of a food processor. Puree the spinach; add 1 cup milk and puree until smooth. Transfer to a large bowl; add the salt and cayenne. Refrigerate until well chilled, about 3 hours, or less if chilled in the freezer.

3. Before serving, add additional milk to thin the soup to the desired consistency. Taste and correct the seasonings. Stir in the lime juice.

4. Make the Tomato Relish: In a small bowl, combine the tomato, scallion, cilantro, garlic and salt.

5. To serve, ladle the soup into 4 large soup bowls. Swirl the yogurt into the center of each, dividing evenly. Sprinkle the tomato relish on top of each bowl.

Chilled Fresh Corn and
Buttermilk Chowder with Shrimp

PREPARATION TIME: 30 MINUTES ❁ CHILLING TIME: ABOUT 2 HOURS ❁ SERVES: 4 TO 6

THIS TANGY SOUP is served cold and garnished with slivers of fresh basil. To make it a heartier main dish, serve with cold cooked shrimp or substitute chunks of steamed or broiled boneless, skinless salmon steak. (See photograph, page 33.)

6   ears fresh sweet corn, husked
2½ cups buttermilk
2   crisp cucumbers, peeled and seeded
2   medium-sized cooked and peeled
        potatoes
½   cup diced (⅛ inch) red onion
2   tablespoons finely chopped fresh
        basil, plus 4 large leaves, rolled
        tight and thinly sliced, for garnish
     Salt and freshly ground black
        pepper, to taste
½   pound cooked, shelled and deveined
        shrimp or ½ pound cooked
        salmon steak, skin and bones
        discarded, cut into ½-inch
        chunks (optional)
¼   cup seeded and diced (¼ inch)
        tomato, for garnish (optional)

1. One at a time, stand the ears of corn on end, and using a small paring knife, cut off the kernels. Reserve 1 cup of the kernels for later. Place the remaining kernels in the bowl of a food processor; you should have about 3 cups.

> **PLAN AHEAD:**
> Allow 2 hours for this soup to chill.

2. Add 1 cup of the buttermilk to the corn in the food processor and puree. Place a food mill or a large strainer over a bowl and add the buttermilk-corn mixture; press through the food mill until all of the pulp and juices are extracted from the kernels and the remaining kernel skins are dry. Discard the kernel skins.

3. Coarsely chop 1 of the cucumbers and carefully dice the remaining cucumber into ¼-inch pieces; reserve separately. Cube 1 of the potatoes and carefully dice the remaining potato into ¼-inch pieces; reserve separately.

4. Rinse and dry the food processor bowl; add the remaining 1½ cups buttermilk, the coarsely chopped cucumber and the cubed potato. Puree until smooth; transfer to the buttermilk-corn mixture.

5. Add the reserved 1 cup corn kernels, the diced cucumber and potato, the red onion and the chopped basil to the soup. Add salt and pepper to taste. Add the cooked shrimp or salmon, if using, and refrigerate until very cold, about 2 hours.

6. To serve, ladle into bowls and garnish each with about 1 tablespoon diced tomato, if using, and thinly sliced fresh basil leaves.

Broccoli and Orzo Soup with Egg Threads

PREPARATION TIME: 15 MINUTES ● COOKING TIME: 20 MINUTES ● SERVES: 4 TO 6

ORZO, A TINY RICE-SHAPED PASTA, and broccoli cook quickly in broth to create a light, nourishing soup that can be prepared in about 30 minutes. Substitute rice or other small pasta shapes, such as pastina, stelline or even alphabets, for the orzo, if you like. Making egg threads is something my grandmother used to do; when I began cooking for myself, I asked her to teach me.

8	cups unsalted homemade or reduced-sodium canned chicken broth
4	cups chopped fresh broccoli (about 1 bunch), including peeled stems
1	carrot, peeled and diced
½	cup orzo or other tiny pasta
½	cup water
2	large eggs
¼	cup grated Parmigiano-Reggiano Salt and freshly ground black pepper

1. In a large saucepan, heat the broth to a boil. Add the broccoli, carrot and orzo. Cook over medium heat, stirring occasionally, until the pasta and vegetables are very tender, about 15 minutes.

2. In a measuring cup or small bowl, beat the water and eggs until frothy. Heat the soup to a full boil; gradually add the egg mixture, stirring the soup constantly so that the egg forms threads as it cooks. Stir in the cheese.

3. Taste the soup, add salt and pepper to taste and serve.

Roasted Tomato and Fresh Corn Soup

PREPARATION TIME: 20 MINUTES ✹ COOKING TIME: 1 HOUR 5 MINUTES

OPTIONAL CHILLING TIME: 2 TO 3 HOURS ✹ SERVES: 4; MAKES ABOUT 5 CUPS

THIS IS MY FAVORITE summer soup. Juicy red tomatoes are roasted to concentrate their already rich taste, and raw corn kernels add sweetness and crunch. Threads of finely slivered fresh basil are used as a garnish. Serve chilled, or if the weather dictates, heat steaming hot.

2 pounds ripe plum tomatoes, halved lengthwise

1 large sweet onion, cut into thin wedges

4 garlic cloves, bruised with the side of a knife

¼ cup extra-virgin olive oil
Salt and freshly ground black pepper, to taste

2 cups unsalted homemade or reduced-sodium canned chicken broth

1-1½ cups fresh sweet corn kernels, cut from the cobs

2 tablespoons finely slivered fresh basil leaves

1 teaspoon fresh lime juice, or to taste (optional)

1. Preheat the oven to 350 degrees F. Combine the tomatoes, onion, garlic and oil in a large (14-x-10-inch, or larger) roasting pan or on a baking sheet with sides. Season with salt and pepper. Roast for 30 minutes. Using a spatula, turn the vegetables. Roast for 25 minutes more, or until lightly browned. Transfer the vegetables to a bowl. Add about ½ cup of the broth to the pan, and scrape up the browned bits with a spatula. Transfer to the bowl.

> **PLAN AHEAD:**
> If you want to serve this soup cold, allow 2 to 3 hours for it to chill.

2. Set a food mill over a large, wide saucepan and puree the vegetable mixture and the remaining 1½ cups broth, working in batches, though the food mill.

3. Heat the pureed-vegetable mixture to simmering. Season with salt and pepper. Add the corn and cook for 1 to 2 minutes. Stir in the basil.

4. Serve the soup hot, or refrigerate for 2 to 3 hours and serve chilled. Taste and correct the seasonings before serving the chilled soup. If the tomatoes are not acidic enough, add a little fresh lime juice to heighten the flavor.

HOW TO PEEL TOMATOES QUICKLY

WHEN I HAVE ONLY A FEW TOMATOES TO PEEL, I often spear them (one at a time) on a large roasting fork with a heatproof handle and hold them over the gas flame on my stove-top burner, turning until the skin blisters and begins to peel back. Then I dip them into a bowl of cold water and quickly rub off the skins. This technique can be used only when you have a gas stove, not an electric one. In that case, I use the following tried-and-true method:

Place the tomatoes (as many as will fit comfortably) in a saucepan of boiling water, and cook until the skin peels back when the tomato is pierced with the point of a knife, 1 to 3 minutes, depending on the ripeness of the tomato. Dip the tomatoes into a bowl of cold water until cool enough to handle, then quickly peel off the skins.

Broccoli and Ditalini Soup
with Hot Pepper Oil

PREPARATION TIME: 10 MINUTES ● COOKING TIME: 15 MINUTES ● SERVES: 4

THIS THICK SOUP MAKES a delicious and comforting supper on a cold winter night. If you prefer a thinner soup, add a little more chicken broth. Serve with a bowl of coarsely chopped Pecorino Romano, and stir some into each bowl at the table. This soup is also delicious and just a little heartier when strips of boneless chicken breast are simmered in the broth along with the pasta.

4 cups unsalted homemade or reduced-sodium canned chicken broth, fat skimmed from the top

2 cups water

¾ cup ditalini or small elbow macaroni

2 cups coarsely chopped broccoli florets and tender stems

¼ cup coarsely shredded peeled carrot
Salt, to taste

1 tablespoon extra-virgin olive oil

¼ teaspoon hot red pepper flakes, or to taste
About ½ cup coarsely chopped Pecorino Romano, or to taste

1. In a large saucepan, heat the broth and water to boiling. Stir in the pasta and cook, stirring, over high heat until the pasta is al dente, or firm to the bite, about 5 minutes. Stir in the broccoli and carrot. Cook, stirring, until the vegetables are tender, about 8 minutes. Season with salt.

2. Meanwhile, combine the oil and red pepper flakes in a small skillet. Cook, stirring, over low heat, until the oil turns orange, about 2 minutes. Remove from the heat.

3. To serve, ladle the soup into bowls and stir ½ teaspoon of the hot pepper oil into each serving. Add the cheese to each serving.

Pureed Carrot, Potato and Ginger Soup

PREPARATION TIME: 15 MINUTES ✽ COOKING TIME: 20 MINUTES

COOLING TIME: 10 MINUTES ✽ SERVES: 4

MY ASSOCIATION WITH CARROTS has always been positive. When I was a little girl, my mother told me that they would make my eyes big and beautiful. I believed her. Today, carrots are a staple in my kitchen. They are a great snack and incredibly versatile, whether I am thinking about soup, stew or oven-roasting. But my eyes aren't big, and I am horribly nearsighted—so much for Mom's admonitions.

1   pound carrots, peeled, trimmed,
     cut into ½-inch lengths
2   medium potatoes (about ½ pound
     total), peeled, cut into ½-inch
     dice
1   medium onion (about ¼ pound),
     chopped
1   garlic clove, crushed through a press
3-4 cups unsalted homemade or
     reduced-sodium canned
     chicken broth
2   teaspoons ground ginger
2   teaspoons grated peeled fresh ginger
     Salt, to taste
1   teaspoon fresh lemon juice,
     or to taste
½   cup low-fat plain yogurt

1. In a large saucepan, combine the carrots, potatoes, onion, garlic, chicken broth and ground ginger. Bring to a simmer over medium heat. Cover and cook until the carrots and potatoes are very tender, about 20 minutes. Set aside, covered, for about 10 minutes to cool slightly.

2. With a slotted spoon, transfer all the solids to the bowl of a food processor. Puree until as smooth as possible. With the machine running, gradually add the hot broth to the puree. Return the soup to the saucepan and bring to a simmer. Add the fresh ginger and season with salt and lemon juice.

3. To serve, ladle the soup into bowls and top each with a swirl of yogurt.

Winter Vegetable Soup

PREPARATION TIME: 15 MINUTES ● COOKING TIME: 60 TO 65 MINUTES ● SERVES: 8

THIS SOUP COMBINES all my favorite fall farmstand vegetables: butternut squash, potatoes, leeks and cauliflower. If you don't have leeks, substitute 1 large sweet onion. The ground cumin adds interest to this rich soup.

> **PLAN AHEAD:**
>
> This soup calls for roasted and peeled red peppers as an optional garnish.

2 tablespoons unsalted butter or extra-virgin olive oil

2 large leeks, trimmed, washed thoroughly, chopped

2-3 teaspoons ground cumin

3 cups unsalted homemade or reduced-sodium canned chicken broth

1 cup water

2 cups cubed (½ inch) peeled potatoes

2 cups cubed (½ inch) peeled butternut (or acorn) squash

2 cups small cauliflower florets

1 cup milk, or as needed to thin the soup

Salt and freshly ground black pepper

½ cup diced Mom's Roasted and Peeled Red Peppers, for garnish (optional; see page 276)

1. Combine the butter or oil and the leeks in a large, wide saucepan. Cook, stirring, over medium-low heat until the leeks are very tender, about 10 minutes. Add the cumin, and cook for 1 minute. Add the broth, water and potatoes, heat to boiling, cover and cook over low heat until the vegetables are very tender, about 20 minutes. Cool slightly.

2. Puree the cooked vegetables in a food processor and return to the saucepan. Add the squash, cover and cook until almost tender, about 20 minutes. Add the cauliflower and cook for 10 minutes, or until vegetables are perfectly tender. Stir in the milk. Do not boil, or the soup will curdle. Season to taste with salt and pepper.

3. To serve, ladle into bowls and garnish each with the diced roasted pepper, if using.

White Bean, Spinach and Italian Sausage Soup

PREPARATION TIME: 10 MINUTES ❀ COOKING TIME: 15 MINUTES ❀ SERVES: 6 TO 8

THIS SOUP IS QUICK AND EASY for supper when you have a couple of cans of white kidney beans and some chicken broth in the pantry.

¼	pound (4 links) Italian sweet or hot pork or turkey sausage, casings removed
½	cup chopped onion
1	garlic clove, finely chopped
1	tablespoon extra-virgin olive oil
3½-4	cups canned (2 cans, 15 or 19 ounces each) or cooked dried cannellini (white kidney) beans
3	cups unsalted homemade or reduced-sodium canned chicken broth
1	cup chopped fresh or drained canned tomatoes
1	package (10 ounces) fresh spinach, rinsed, trimmed, torn
	Grated Parmigiano-Reggiano

1. Crumble the sausage into a nonstick skillet and cook, stirring, until browned, about 5 minutes. Transfer to a strainer and drain the fat; reserve the sausage.

2. Combine the onion, garlic and oil in a large, wide saucepan. Cook, stirring, over low heat until the onion is soft, about 5 minutes. Stir in the beans, broth, tomatoes and reserved sausage. Heat, stirring, until very hot. Add the spinach. Cover and cook until the greens are wilted and tender, about 5 minutes.

3. To serve, ladle into bowls and sprinkle each with some cheese.

Potato and Garlic Soup with Prosciutto

PREPARATION TIME: 15 MINUTES ● COOKING TIME: 40 MINUTES ● SERVES: 4

THIS SOUP IS DELICIOUS with prosciutto or other flavorful slivered ham. I have even made a version with cooked Italian sweet sausage crumbled on top.

4   cups unsalted homemade or reduced-sodium canned chicken broth, fat skimmed from surface
2   pounds all-purpose potatoes, peeled and cubed
6   garlic cloves, peeled and left whole
1   bay leaf
1   tablespoon extra-virgin olive oil
½   cup chopped onion
2   tablespoons slivered prosciutto or cured ham
    Salt and freshly ground black pepper
2   tablespoons finely chopped fresh Italian (flat-leaf) parsley
1   roasted, peeled, seeded red bell pepper, cut into thin strips, or Roasted Red Pepper Puree (page 277) or Basil and Garlic Puree (opposite page)

1. In a large saucepan, heat the broth, potatoes, garlic and bay leaf to boiling. Cover and cook over medium-low heat until the potatoes are very tender, about 25 minutes. Cool slightly. Remove the bay leaf.

2. Set a food mill or large strainer over a bowl; force the potatoes and garlic through the food mill or press through the strainer with a wooden spoon. Add the broth and stir to blend.

3. Wipe the saucepan dry and add the oil and onion. Cook, stirring, over medium heat until the onion is golden, about 10 minutes. Add the prosciutto or ham; sauté for 1 minute. Add the pureed potato mixture. Heat, stirring occasionally. Season to taste with salt and pepper. Keep warm over low heat.

4. To serve, ladle the soup into broad soup plates. Garnish each with a sprinkling of chopped parsley and a few slivers of roasted red pepper or a spoonful of puree.

Basil and Garlic Puree

PREPARATION TIME: 10 MINUTES ⚬ COOKING TIME: 2 TO 3 MINUTES ⚬ MAKES: ABOUT ½ CUP

THIS IS A DELICIOUS GARNISH for soup. I especially like it stirred into Potato and Garlic Soup with Prosciutto (opposite page) or Roasted Tomato and Fresh Corn Soup (page 52).

2   tablespoons slivered almonds
2   cups loosely packed fresh basil leaves
2   garlic cloves, chopped
½   teaspoon salt
⅓   cup extra-virgin olive oil

1. Toast the almonds in a small nonstick skillet over low heat until golden, 2 to 3 minutes.

2. Combine the almonds, basil, garlic and salt in a food processor and chop fine. With the motor running, slowly add the oil until the mixture is pureed. Scrape into a small bowl and reserve until ready to serve. If the mixture separates, stir to combine before serving.

OLD-FASHIONED CONVENIENCE

IN TODAY'S WORLD OF HIGH-TECH FOOD PROCESSORS, a food mill might seem redundant or, at the very least, old-fashioned. The fact is, I was using a food mill long before the food processor existed, and although I love my food processor for all kinds of things, I couldn't cook without my food mill. I use it to puree canned tomatoes when I make tomato sauce, to make applesauce and to make soups. I find it essential when I want a very fine puree, rather than a mixture that is finely chopped or pulverized (for that, the food processor is best).

A food mill is no harder to wash than a food processor (it goes in the dishwasher) and is easily stored by hanging from a pot rack or in the pot cabinet. I have both a Foley food mill with a single strainer and an imported brand (with two different sizes of interchangeable strainers). To be honest, the Foley food mill is the one I use most often.

Pureed Roasted Squash Soup with Shiitake Mushrooms

PREPARATION TIME: 20 MINUTES ❋ COOKING TIME: 55 TO 60 MINUTES ❋ SERVES: 4 TO 6

I ADORE ROASTED ACORN or butternut squash. Often, I buy several and roast them, cut sides down, on a large sheet pan. I might eat half a squash for lunch, save some for dinner and make a soup for later in the week. The squash becomes deep, sweet and intense when prepared this way, and I don't have to go through the pesky business of cutting it up and peeling it.

2-3   acorn or small butternut squash, about 4 pounds total

3   tablespoons unsalted butter or extra-virgin olive oil

½   cup finely chopped onion

1   garlic clove, crushed through a press

2   cups unsalted homemade or reduced-sodium canned chicken broth

1   cup half-and-half, or more as needed

1   teaspoon fresh lemon juice

1   teaspoon grated peeled fresh ginger
    Salt and cayenne (ground red pepper), to taste

SAUTÉED MUSHROOM GARNISH

1   tablespoon unsalted butter or extra-virgin olive oil

3½   ounces shiitake mushrooms, stems discarded, cut into thin strips

1   tablespoon minced red bell pepper

1   tablespoon finely chopped fresh parsley

1   garlic clove, crushed through a press
    Salt and freshly ground black pepper, to taste

1. Preheat the oven to 350 degrees F. Halve the squash lengthwise and scoop out the seeds. Using 2 tablespoons of the butter or oil, lightly coat a sheet pan; arrange the squash cut side down. Cover with a large sheet of foil and bake for 30 minutes. Uncover and turn the squash over. Bake until tender when pierced with a fork, 15 to 20 minutes more (for most squash, it's best to test before removing from the oven). Cool. Scoop the cooked squash from the skins and set aside. Discard the skins.

2. Heat the remaining 1 tablespoon butter or oil in a large, heavy saucepan over low heat. Add the onion and cook, stirring, until golden, about 8 minutes. Add the garlic; cook for 1 minute. Stir in the cooked squash and broth; remove from the heat.

3. Puree the squash mixture in a food processor, working in batches, if necessary. Return the mixture to the saucepan.

4. Stir in the half-and-half until the soup is the consistency you like, and add the lemon juice and ginger. Heat, stirring, until hot. Do not boil. Season with the salt and cayenne.

5. Meanwhile, Make the Garnish: Heat the butter or oil in a nonstick skillet. Add the mushrooms and the red pepper slivers and cook over medium heat, stirring, until golden, about 5 minutes. Add the parsley, garlic, salt and pepper; cook for 1 minute.

6. To serve, ladle the soup into bowls and garnish with the sautéed mushrooms.

Black Bean Soup with Roasted Peppers and Tomatoes

PREPARATION TIME: 20 MINUTES ● COOKING TIME: 1 HOUR ● SERVES: 6 TO 8

ALTHOUGH ROASTING the tomatoes and peppers takes time, the depth of flavor that they add more than justifies the technique. Served with a green salad and warmed bread (it is great with corn muffins), this soup makes a soul-satisfying meal.

1	pound (about 8 large) ripe plum tomatoes, halved lengthwise
4	red bell peppers, quartered, seeds and stems removed
1	large sweet onion, halved, cut into thin wedges
2	garlic cloves, coarsely chopped
1	long, thin carrot, trimmed, peeled, halved lengthwise
2	tablespoons extra-virgin olive oil
½	teaspoon dried oregano
	Salt and freshly ground black pepper
1	can (13¾ ounces) reduced-sodium chicken or vegetable broth
3½	cups drained canned (2 cans, 15 ounces each) or cooked dried black beans
½	cup low-fat or nonfat plain yogurt or 1 ounce softened fresh domestic goat cheese

1. Preheat the oven to 350 degrees F. Combine the tomatoes, red peppers, onion, garlic, carrot, oil, oregano, salt and black pepper in a 14-x-10-inch baking pan; toss to coat with the oil. Roast for 30 minutes. Using a spatula, turn and stir the vegetables; roast until the edges are browned, about 25 minutes more. Remove the carrot to a side dish; dice and reserve for later.

2. Transfer the other roasted vegetables to a large bowl. Add half of the broth to the baking pan and scrape up any browned bits from the bottom of the pan. Transfer to the bowl along with the remaining broth.

3. Reserve 1 cup of the black beans for later. Add the remaining black beans to the bowl. Puree the tomato-bean mixture, working in batches, if necessary, in a food processor or through a food mill. Transfer to a saucepan.

4. Add the reserved diced carrot and the reserved 1 cup black beans. Add salt and pepper to taste. Reheat. Ladle into bowls and serve with a tablespoon of yogurt or softened fresh goat cheese stirred into each serving.

Clear-Broth Clam Chowder

PREPARATION TIME: 20 MINUTES ● COOKING TIME: 30 MINUTES ● SERVES: 4

I FIRST TASTED A CLEAR-BROTH clam chowder like this one at Aldo's, a small restaurant, bakery and café on the north fork of Long Island, in a sleepy town called Greenport. It is clam-essence perfection.

24	small cherrystone clams, shucked and juice reserved (2-3 cups)
1½	cups diced (¼ inch) peeled waxy potatoes
1	cup diced (¼ inch) trimmed celery
1	cup diced (¼ inch) onion
½	cup diced (¼ inch) carrots
¼	cup extra-virgin olive oil
2	garlic cloves, finely minced
1	bay leaf
	Pinch dried thyme
2	plum tomatoes, cored, seeded, cut into ¼-inch dice
¼	cup finely chopped fresh Italian (flat-leaf) parsley
	Salt and freshly ground black pepper, to taste

1. Trim the dark (black) sac from the belly of the shucked clams by snipping off with scissors; discard. Cut the clams into small (¼ inch) pieces and reserve.

2. In a large, wide soup pot, combine the potatoes, celery, onion, carrots, oil, garlic, bay leaf and thyme. Stir to blend. Cover and cook over medium-low heat until the vegetables are very soft but not browned, about 12 minutes.

3. Add enough water to the reserved clam juice to equal 4 cups. Add to the vegetables, along with the tomatoes and parsley. Cover and cook for 5 minutes, or until boiling. Season with salt and pepper. Reduce the heat to low and stir in the clams. Cover and cook over very low heat (do not boil) until the clams are tender, about 10 minutes. Correct the seasonings.

4. Ladle into bowls and serve.

Seafood Soup with Saffron-Tomato Broth

PREPARATION TIME: 20 MINUTES ● COOKING TIME: 20 TO 25 MINUTES ● SERVES: 4

DON'T PASS THIS RECIPE BY if you think saffron is exotic or too expensive. You can leave it out, if you like. This is one of the fastest soups I can make. Vary the seafood with your appetite, budget and what is available in the market that day. I usually like to serve 2 large shrimp, 6 or more clams and/or mussels and a nice chunk of solid fish (about 3 or 4 ounces) per person. With the crostini and the broth, this makes a whole meal.

5-6   threads of saffron

½   cup hot tap water

24   mussels and/or 12 littleneck, Manila Bay, mahogany or other clams, washed and scrubbed

2   tablespoons extra-virgin olive oil

1   medium onion, halved lengthwise, cut into thin lengthwise slices

1   garlic clove, bruised with the side of a knife

1   strip (½ x 2 inches) orange zest

1   sprig fresh basil (optional)

1   cup dry white wine

2   cans (14½ ounces each) Italian-style plum tomatoes with juice

4   jumbo shrimp or 8 large shrimp, peeled and deveined

1   firm white fish steak (cod, halibut, shark), about ¾ pound, cut into 1-inch chunks

4-8   Crostini (page 24)

1. Combine the saffron and the hot water in a measuring cup; cover and let stand until ready to use.

2. Rinse the mussels and/or clams in two changes of cold water; drain. Pull the beards off the mussels. Refrigerate while completing steps 3 and 4.

3. In a large, wide saucepan or deep skillet with a tight-fitting lid, heat the oil over low heat. Add the onion and garlic and sauté, stirring occasionally, over medium-low heat, about 5 minutes, or until the onion is tender. Add the orange zest and basil, if using.

4. Add the wine, and heat over high heat to a hard boil; boil for 1 minute. Add the tomatoes; heat to boiling, stirring and breaking them up with the side of the spoon. Add the saffron threads and the soaking liquid. Simmer over low heat, uncovered, for 10 minutes.

5. Add the mussels and/or clams to the boiling broth. Place the shrimp and the fish on top. Cover and cook over medium-high heat until the mussels and/or clams are open and the seafood is cooked through, 3 to 5 minutes.

6. To serve, place 1 or 2 pieces of crostini in the bottom of each of 4 shallow soup plates. Add the seafood, dividing evenly. Divide the broth among the soup plates and serve.

SAFFRON

SAFFRON, THE ORANGE-COLORED STIGMA OF THE CROCUS FLOWER, is best known for the color and aroma it imparts to the paella of Spain and the risotto alla Milanese of northern Italy. The harvesting and processing are so labor-intensive that it is reputed to be the most expensive spice in the world. Fortunately, a few threads of saffron go a long way. I use a pinch, which to my eye means 5 or 6 threads.

SANDWICHES

Pandorato

PREPARATION TIME: 5 MINUTES ❀ COOKING TIME: 6 TO 10 MINUTES ❀ SERVES: 4

THIS IS THE ULTIMATE grilled cheese sandwich: mozzarella cheese and a paper-thin slice of prosciutto between slices of country bread dipped in egg and lightly fried in a mixture of olive oil and butter.

The sandwich is perfect with a bowl of Roasted Tomato and Fresh Corn Soup (page 52) or Broccoli and Ditalini Soup with Hot Pepper Oil (page 54). When basil is at its peak, tuck a whole leaf between the cheese and the bread. Another nice addition is a whole sun-dried tomato half that has been marinated in oil. If you like, omit the prosciutto and make a plain melted cheese sandwich, which I think is pure heaven.

1. Place the mozzarella slices and prosciutto, if using, between the bread slices to make 4 sandwiches. Whisk the eggs and milk together in a shallow soup bowl. Dip the sandwiches in the egg mixture to coat.

2. Heat the oil, butter and garlic in a medium skillet until the garlic begins to sizzle and turns golden; discard the garlic. Add the sandwiches and cook over medium-low heat until the bread is golden and the cheese melts, about 3 minutes per side.

3. Cut in half and serve immediately.

8	slices mozzarella (or 4 plain and 4 smoked)
4	paper-thin slices prosciutto (optional)
8	slices Italian bread, each ½ inch thick
2	large eggs
½	cup milk
2	tablespoons extra-virgin olive oil
2	tablespoons unsalted butter
1	garlic clove, bruised with the side of a knife

Dagwood Bumstead Italiano

PREPARATION TIME: 15 MINUTES *(if roasted peppers are already prepared, 35 to 40 if they are not)*

SOAKING TIME: 20 MINUTES ❋ COOKING TIME: 12 TO 15 MINUTES ❋ SERVES: 4

THE DAGWOOD BUMSTEAD is named for the cartoon character well known for his habit of raiding the refrigerator and constructing a sandwich bigger than his mouth. Friend and colleague Maria Cianci created a version similar to this when I was test-kitchen director at *Cuisine* magazine.

Begin by marinating flattened chicken or turkey cutlets in a heady mixture of crushed garlic, thyme, oregano and olive oil. I use the same marinade for the zucchini slices. I cook both the cutlets and the zucchini on my stovetop griddle, but a non-stick skillet will work as well. The roasted red peppers and reconstituted sun-dried tomatoes add color and flavor. The bread—of the utmost importance—is available at the deli department of most supermarkets. It comes presliced and has a soft, but sturdy crumb and crust.

> **PLAN AHEAD:**
>
> This recipe uses roasted red peppers.

8 halves sun-dried tomatoes (not oil-packed)

2 medium zucchini, washed and trimmed

2 tablespoons extra-virgin olive oil

1 garlic clove, crushed through a press

1 teaspoon fresh thyme leaves, stripped from the stems, or ¼ teaspoon dried

1 teaspoon fresh oregano leaves, stripped from the stems, or ¼ teaspoon dried

Salt and freshly ground black pepper

4 chicken or turkey cutlets (about ¾ pound)

12 slices Italian-style loaf, with or without seeds

8 whole fresh basil leaves (optional)

4 halves Mom's Roasted and Peeled Red Peppers (page 276) or Easy Oven-Roasted Red Bell Peppers (page 278)

1. Place the sun-dried tomatoes in a small bowl, cover with boiling water and let stand for 20 minutes, or until softened. Drain; pat dry with paper towels. Reserve.

2. Cut the zucchini into 16 diagonal slices, ¼ inch thick. Place in a medium bowl. Add 1 tablespoon of the oil, half of the garlic, ½ teaspoon each of the fresh thyme and oregano or a pinch each dried, a pinch of salt and a grinding of pepper; toss to coat. Reserve.

3. On a large plate, combine the remaining 1 tablespoon of oil, remaining half of the garlic and remaining ½ teaspoon each fresh thyme and oregano or a pinch each dried. Add the cutlets, turn to coat, and season with salt and a grinding of pepper. Let stand until ready to cook.

4. Heat a large nonstick griddle or skillet over high heat until hot enough to evaporate a drop of water upon contact. Add the zucchini and cook for 3 to 4 minutes per side, or until lightly browned; transfer to a side dish. Sprinkle with salt. Add the cutlets; cook for 3 to 4 minutes per side, or until lightly browned. Transfer to a side dish; sprinkle with salt.

5. Place 4 slices of bread on a work surface. Arrange the cutlets on the bread, dividing evenly. Top each with 2 leaves of basil, if using, and 2 sun-dried tomato halves. Top with a slice of bread.

6. Arrange a single layer (about 4) slices of zucchini on the second slice of bread. Top with a layer of roasted peppers, cut to fit properly, if necessary. Top with the remaining bread slices.

7. Press down firmly on the sandwich; secure the corners of each sandwich with wooden picks. Cut the sandwiches in half and serve.

Spinach, Sautéed Mushroom and Shaved Parmigiano Sandwich

PREPARATION TIME: 15 MINUTES ● COOKING TIME: 10 MINUTES ● SERVES: 2

BREAD IS EXTREMELY IMPORTANT when making a sandwich, but especially for this one. Select a round loaf with a chewy crust. Often, these are called "country-style." I like sourdough the best, but a multigrain or even plain white is terrific. Preheat the broiler (or use a toaster oven), and once all the filling ingredients are prepared, toast the bread and assemble the sandwiches. Toast is always best when it is warm and supple, so be sure to save that step for last.

The large flat-leaf (as opposed to the curly-leaf) spinach is the best type for this sandwich. I put in Portobello mushrooms that are sold sliced and packaged in the produce section of my supermarket. If they are not available, substitute thick slices of large white button mushrooms. Shave wide curls of Parmigiano-Reggiano from a wedge of cheese with a cheese server or a heavy-duty vegetable peeler.

4 tablespoons extra-virgin olive oil
1 package (about 7 ounces) sliced Portobello mushrooms
2 tablespoons finely chopped fresh Italian (flat-leaf) parsley
1 teaspoon fresh thyme leaves, stripped from the stems
2 garlic cloves, crushed through a press
    Salt and freshly ground black pepper
4 cups packed fresh spinach leaves (about three-fourths of a 10-ounce bag), rinsed, stems trimmed
4 slices from a round or oval loaf of peasant or sourdough bread
    Wedge Parmigiano-Reggiano
4 halves sun-dried tomatoes (packed in oil), drained and cut into thin slivers (optional)

1. Heat 3 tablespoons of the oil in a large non-stick skillet. Add the mushrooms and cook, turning as they begin to brown, about 5 minutes. Add the parsley, thyme and 1 garlic clove; sprinkle with salt and pepper to taste. Cook, stirring, for 1 minute. Transfer to a side dish.

2. Add the remaining 1 tablespoon oil to the skillet and the remaining garlic clove. Heat until the garlic begins to sizzle, about 2 minutes. Add the spinach all at once, and carefully turn with tongs until coated with oil. Cover and cook over medium-low heat for 1 minute. Uncover and remove from the heat immediately. The spinach should be just barely wilted. Do not overcook.

3. Toast the bread. Place 2 slices on each plate. Arrange the spinach in an even layer on one slice of toast. Top with 2 or 3 large shavings of cheese. Spoon the mushrooms onto the second slice. Drizzle with any juices left in the dish. Top with a few slivers of sun-dried tomatoes, if using.

4. To serve the sandwich, flop the toast spread with the spinach and cheese over onto the mushroom layer. Carefully cut with a serrated knife and serve at once.

Pan-Grilled Smoked Turkey, Fontina, Bacon and Avocado Sandwich

PREPARATION TIME: 10 MINUTES ❋ COOKING TIME: 15 MINUTES ❋ SERVES: 4

THE TASTE AND TEXTURE of each ingredient in this sandwich play off each other as they meld into one perfect mouthful. The subtle, smoky flavor of the turkey, the crisp texture of the cooked bacon, the soft creaminess of the fontina cheese and the avocado and the acid tang of the tomato come together between two slices of bread. (See photograph, page 37.)

8   slices lean smoked bacon
8   thick (½ inch) slices crusty, round,
        peasant-style Italian bread
6   ounces thinly sliced smoked turkey
6   ounces Italian fontina cheese,
        cut into thin slices
1   ripe avocado, peeled, pit removed,
        cut into ½-inch-thick wedges
1   large tomato, cored and cut into
        8 thin slices
    Extra-virgin olive oil, for grilling

1. Cook the bacon, turning, until crisp, about 5 minutes. Drain on paper towels; set aside. Wipe out the skillet.

2. Lay 4 slices of the bread on a work surface. Dividing the sandwich ingredients evenly, arrange them on the bread in this order: turkey, fontina, bacon, avocado and tomato. Top with the remaining 4 bread slices.

3. Heat 2 large nonstick skillets or a griddle over medium heat until hot enough to evaporate a drop of water upon contact. Drizzle with a thin film of oil. Arrange the sandwiches in the skillet(s); reduce the heat to medium-low. Weight the sandwiches with a heat-resistant plate or a flat lid placed directly on top of the sandwiches. (A weight used to keep bacon from curling while cooking also works.) Cook until the bread is golden on one side. Carefully turn the sandwiches and cook until golden and the cheese is melted, about 5 minutes per side.

4. Cut in half and serve immediately.

Tomato, Basil and Mayonnaise on a
Toasted English Muffin

PREPARATION TIME: 5 MINUTES ❋ COOKING TIME: 5 MINUTES ❋ SERVES: 1

THE MINUTE VINE-RIPENED tomatoes arrive at my local farmstands, I rush home and make this sandwich for lunch.

1   English muffin, split, or 2 slices
     chewy, slightly sour bread
1   tablespoon mayonnaise
2-3 thin slices ripe tomato
     Pinch salt
1   large fresh basil leaf

1. Toast the muffin or the bread.

2. While the muffin or toast is still warm, spread it with mayonnaise. Layer the tomato on one muffin half or piece of toast. Sprinkle with salt. Add the basil leaf. Top with the remaining muffin half or piece of toast. Serve immediately.

Warm Egg Salad on Whole Wheat Toast

PREPARATION TIME: 10 MINUTES ❖ COOKING TIME: 15 MINUTES ❖ SERVES: 2

EGGS WERE MEANT TO BE EATEN warm. If you need to watch your cholesterol intake, leave out two of the egg yolks.

4	large eggs
2	tablespoons finely chopped onion
2	tablespoons finely chopped celery
1	tablespoon thinly slivered fresh basil
½	teaspoon Dijon-style mustard
	Salt and freshly ground black pepper, to taste
¼	cup mayonnaise or yogurt or half mayonnaise and half yogurt
4	slices whole-wheat or multigrain bread
2	large soft lettuce leaves

1. Place the eggs in a small saucepan; cover with water. Heat to boiling; cover and remove from the heat. Let stand for 15 minutes. Rinse under cold water and carefully crack the shells.

2. Peel the eggs and cut them into chunks; do not mash. Combine the eggs with the onion, celery, basil, mustard, salt and pepper. Add the mayonnaise and/or yogurt mixture and gently fold together.

3. Toast the bread. Place 2 slices on a cutting board. Top each with a lettuce leaf. Spoon the egg salad on top, dividing evenly. Top with the remaining 2 slices of toast, cut in half and serve.

Mashed Avocado, Bacon, Lettuce and Tomato on Sourdough Toast

PREPARATION TIME: 15 MINUTES ❀ COOKING TIME: 10 MINUTES ❀ SERVES: 4

THIS IS MY VERSION OF A BLT, with a few twists and turns—I add mashed avocado and cilantro. If you aren't a cilantro fan, leave it out or substitute basil. Sliced smoked turkey is a very good stand-in for bacon. Most important, use sturdy slices of a chewy, slightly sour bread.

1 ripe avocado, halved, peeled, pitted
1 tablespoon fresh lime juice
1 tablespoon minced fresh cilantro or basil (optional)
  Salt, to taste
8 slices sourdough bread
8 thin slices ripe tomato
12 slices bacon, cooked until crisp and drained
4 large soft lettuce leaves
2 tablespoons (approximately) mayonnaise

1. Combine the avocado, lime juice, cilantro or basil, if using, and salt in a bowl. Mash with a fork until blended. The mixture can be slightly lumpy.

2. Toast 4 slices of the bread and line up on a cutting board. Spread each slice with a layer of the avocado, distributing evenly. Top each sandwich with 2 slices of tomato. Top the tomato with the bacon and top the bacon with the lettuce.

3. Meanwhile, toast the remaining 4 slices of bread. Spread each slice with a thin layer of mayonnaise. Place the top portion of each sandwich over the lettuce layer. Cut the sandwiches in half and serve at once.

Sausage, Pepper and Egg Sandwiches

PREPARATION TIME: 15 MINUTES * COOKING TIME: 25 MINUTES * SERVES: 4

THIS WAS MOM'S VERSION of road food. As I write this, I can still see her frying the peppers in her battered skillet. Nearby, rolls are lined up on the counter waiting for the soft, warm eggs that had been scrambled with the fried peppers and little bits of crumbled sweet Italian sausage. Along with these sweet thoughts comes the memory of waxed paper—slightly steamed and a wee bit soggy—for this was a sandwich reserved for travel. Whenever Mom packed something to eat, whether for a picnic outing or for taking the train back to college after a weekend at home, it was always this.

3	tablespoons extra-virgin olive oil
1	garlic clove, bruised with the side of a knife
1	pound long, pale green Italian peppers (also called cubanelle or frying peppers), halved lengthwise, cored, seeded
2	large onions, peeled and sliced (about 2 cups)
¾	pound Italian sweet sausage, removed from casings
6	large eggs
4	tablespoons cold water
	Salt and freshly ground black pepper, to taste

4 round, hard (Kaiser) rolls

1. Heat the oil and garlic over low heat in a large, heavy skillet. When the garlic sizzles and begins to brown, about 2 minutes, remove it from the oil and discard. Add the peppers and onions to the skillet. Reduce the heat to medium. Cover and cook the vegetables until limp, about 10 minutes. Uncover and turn the heat to medium-high. Cook the vegetables until browned, stirring often, about 5 minutes. Using tongs, remove the vegetables to a side dish.

2. Add the sausage to the skillet and cook, stirring, over medium heat until browned and crumbled, about 5 minutes. Remove with a slotted spoon to another side plate.

3. Remove and discard all but a thin coating of oil from the skillet. Return the vegetables and sausage to the skillet. Reheat. Whisk the eggs, water, salt and pepper until foamy. Add to the hot skillet, and when the eggs begin to set, stir carefully with a big spoon until set, about 4 minutes. Remove the skillet from the heat.

4. Open the rolls, and spoon the egg mixture onto the bottom half, distributing evenly. Cover with the tops and serve, or wrap in waxed paper for later.

GREAT SANDWICH SPREADS

OLIVADA *(page 25)*

Spread Olivada on Dagwood Bumstead Italiano (page 68); Spinach, Sautéed Mushroom and Shaved Parmigiano Sandwich (page 70); Sliced Pork Loin Sandwich with Fennel, Garlic and Roasted Red Pepper (page 80); or Grilled Marinated Lamb with Cucumber-Yogurt Sauce in Pita (page 89).

ROASTED GARLIC PUREE *(page 27)*

Spread Roasted Garlic Puree on Dagwood Bumstead Italiano (page 68); Spinach, Sautéed Mushroom and Shaved Parmigiano Sandwich (page 70); Sausage, Pepper and Egg Sandwiches (page 76); Sliced Pork Loin Sandwich with Fennel, Garlic and Roasted Red Pepper (page 80); Grilled Marinated Lamb with Cucumber-Yogurt Sauce in Pita (page 89).

ROASTED RED PEPPER PUREE *(page 277)*

Spread Roasted Red Pepper Puree on Dagwood Bumstead Italiano (page 68); Warm Egg Salad on Whole Wheat Toast (page 74); Sausage, Pepper and Egg Sandwiches (page 76); Sliced Pork Loin Sandwich with Fennel, Garlic and Roasted Red Pepper (page 80); Grilled Marinated Lamb with Cucumber-Yogurt Sauce in Pita (page 89).

Crisp-Fried Soft-Shell Crab in a Pita Pocket with Spicy Tahini

PREPARATION TIME: 15 MINUTES ❋ COOKING TIME: 15 MINUTES ❋ SERVES: 4

THE SECRET TO A PERFECTLY CRISP soft-shell crab is cracker meal and deep-frying. In fact, if you simply want a meal of fried soft-shell crabs, use the formula below and skip the sandwich part of the recipe. We love these for Saturday lunch. This recipe makes 4 sandwiches for 4 people with average appetites.

SPICY TAHINI SAUCE

1 cup low-fat plain yogurt
3 tablespoons tahini
2 teaspoons fresh lemon juice
1 garlic clove, crushed through a press
Dash hot pepper sauce
   (Tabasco is good)
Salt

CRABS

½ cup all-purpose flour
½ teaspoon salt
Freshly ground black pepper,
   to taste
1 large egg
¼ cup milk
1 cup cracker meal
4 soft-shell crabs, cleaned
   (see page 154)

Vegetable oil
4 fresh pita breads
4 leaves curly red-leaf lettuce,
   rinsed and dried

1. Make the Spicy Tahini Sauce: Combine the yogurt, tahini, lemon juice, garlic and hot pepper sauce in a small bowl. Whisk to blend. Season to taste with salt. Refrigerate until ready to use.

2. Make the Crabs: Place the flour, salt and pepper on a large sheet of waxed paper and stir with a fork to combine. Beat the egg and milk in a shallow soup bowl. Place the cracker meal on a sheet of waxed paper. Dredge the crabs, one at a time, in the flour; shake off the excess. Dip into the egg wash; let the excess drip back into the bowl. Carefully roll the crabs in the cracker meal, coating them thoroughly.

3. Just before serving, heat about 2 inches of oil in a wide pot large enough to hold 2 crabs side by side. When a piece of bread crust sizzles and turns golden when dropped into the oil, the oil is hot enough.

4. Fry the prepared crabs in the hot oil, 2 at a time, turning, until crisp and golden brown, about 3 minutes per side. Let drain on a wire rack set over paper towels.

5. To serve, cut a ½-inch strip off one edge of the pita bread; slip your fingertips into the bread to form a pocket. Tuck a lettuce leaf and a whole fried crab into the pocket. Top with a spoonful of tahini sauce. Serve at once.

FRIED SOFT-SHELL CRABS FOR DINNER

These can be served without the tahini sauce as a main course, allotting 2 crabs per person. You can also add 2 tablespoons sesame seeds to the cracker mixture.

Sliced Pork Loin Sandwich with Fennel, Garlic and Roasted Red Pepper

PREPARATION TIME: 5 MINUTES ❋ COOKING TIME: 5 MINUTES ❋ SERVES: 1

THIS IS A GREAT SANDWICH for when you have leftover roast pork. Layer thin slices of the meat on bread that has been spread with roasted garlic. To save time, you could use either Easy Oven-Roasted Red Bell Peppers (page 278) or a thin layer of Roasted Red Pepper Puree (page 277) instead of the peppers listed below. The arugula adds a fresh peppery taste.

2 slices round or oval peasant or sourdough bread

1 tablespoon Roasted Garlic Puree (page 27)

3-4 thin slices Pork Loin with Fennel and Garlic (page 135)

Arugula leaves or mixed salad greens

2-3 pieces Mom's Roasted and Peeled Red Peppers (page 276)

1. Toast the bread, if desired.

2. Spread one side of the bread with the garlic puree. Cover with a layer of pork, arugula leaves or salad greens and red peppers, in that order. Top with the remaining slice of bread. Cut in half and serve.

PLAN AHEAD:

This recipe uses garlic puree, leftover roast pork and roasted red peppers.

Herb-Marinated Chicken, Shiitake Mushrooms and Roasted Potatoes Vinaigrette *(page 202)*

Polenta Toasts *(page 190)* with Broccoli Rabe with Olive Oil and Garlic *(page 249)*

Cabbage Salad with Lemon and Olive Oil *(page 216)* with Spicy Marinated Shrimp *(page 160)*

Mussels in White Wine with Fresh Tomato Salsa *(page 162)*

Marie's Pasta Fagiola *(page 182)*

Favorite Meat Loaf *(page 136)*

Oven-Roasted Halibut with Herb Citrus Vinaigrette *(page 142)*

Peach and Blueberry Crisp with Toasted Almonds *(page 340)*

Grilled Marinated Lamb with Cucumber-Yogurt Sauce in Pita

PREPARATION TIME: 20 MINUTES • COOKING TIME: 10 MINUTES • SERVES: 4

LEFTOVER BROILED or grilled lamb makes a fine sandwich. This favorite recipe is borrowed from friend and colleague Babs Chernetz. The thin slices of lamb are tucked into a pocket of warm pita bread. A tangy "salad" of crisp cucumber, yogurt, scallion and fresh herbs is spooned on top.

There are two kinds of pita available. One is a large, smooth disk that has a pocket in the center, perfect for a sandwich filling. The other type is large, with a rough texture and a chewy consistency; you put your sandwich filling on the surface of the bread, roll it up (tortilla-style) and eat it. It is equally delicious but not as neat.

PLAN AHEAD:

This recipe uses grilled or broiled leg of lamb.

4   pita breads

12   thin slices Grilled or Broiled Leg of Lamb with Garlic and Rosemary Crust (page 129)

4-8   thin slices tomato

CUCUMBER-YOGURT SAUCE

1   medium cucumber, peeled, halved lengthwise, seeded, or ½ seedless cucumber, thinly sliced (about 1 cup)

1   cup low-fat plain yogurt

1   scallion, trimmed and cut into thin diagonal slices

1   tablespoon snipped fresh dill

1   tablespoon snipped fresh mint (optional)

1   tablespoon fresh lime juice
     Salt and freshly ground black pepper

1. Preheat the oven to 350 degrees F. Wrap the pita in foil, and heat until warmed, about 10 minutes.

2. Make the Cucumber-Yogurt Sauce: Combine the cucumber, yogurt, scallion, dill, mint (if using), lime juice and salt and pepper in a small bowl. Taste; correct the seasonings. Set aside.

3. To assemble the sandwiches, cut a thin strip from the edge of each pita and carefully open to form a pocket. Slide 3 slices of lamb and 1 or 2 slices of tomato into each pocket. Spoon in some of the cucumber-yogurt sauce. Serve at once.

VARIATION

Grilled Marinated Lamb with Roasted Eggplant, Grilled Zucchini and Olivada: Spread Olivada (page 25) on thick slices from a round loaf of sourdough bread. Top with thin slices of grilled or broiled leg of lamb, Herb-Marinated Baked Eggplant Slices (page 261) and grilled zucchini (see steps 2 and 4 of Dagwood Bumstead Italiano, page 68).

PASTA

FAST

Pasta Primavera, Asian Style **96**

Farfalle with Fresh Tomatoes and Basil **97**

Farfalle with Zucchini, Yellow Squash and Mint **98**

Cavatelli with Spinach and Tomatoes **99**

Pasta with Arugula, Olives and Fresh Tomatoes **101**

Pasta with Toasted Walnut and Parmigiano-Reggiano Butter Sauce **102**

Penne with Asparagus, Smoked Salmon and Dill **103**

Penne Rigate with Asparagus, Prosciutto and Mushrooms **104**

Penne with White Beans, Tomatoes and Basil **105**

Pasta with Smoked Mozzarella, Browned Red Peppers and Shiitake Mushrooms **107**

Linguine with Fresh Clams **108**

Linguine with Spicy Tomato Sauce and Mussels **109**

Ceci e Pasta **110**

Orecchiette with Broccoli Rabe, White Beans and Garlic-and-Red-Pepper Oil **111**

WHEN YOU HAVE MORE TIME

Penne with Roasted Vegetables **106**

Pasta Perfect

I WAS RAISED ON FRESH, HOMEMADE pasta, and I know how silky, sweet and wonderful it should be. Because I have been spoiled, I cannot eat commercial fresh pasta, which is often rubbery, dense and bland, unless it is from an Italian specialty shop where it is made daily.

So now I prefer to use dried pasta—for its convenience, taste and variety. But all brands are not created equal. If your pasta cooks soggy, crumbles as it cooks or is bland and tasteless, change brands.

COOKING PASTA

The best guide to perfect pasta is to taste it. Stir the pasta into a large pot of boiling, salted water and don't leave it unattended. Stir occasionally but gently to keep the pasta from sticking to the bottom of the pot. Make sure the heat is on high so the water comes back to a boil quickly.

After 5 minutes, begin tasting. Use a slotted spoon and keep a small plate handy. Taste one piece at a time. Thin, tubular pasta shapes like penne and elbows cook more quickly because the boiling water reaches the inside as well as the surface. Thicker, more solid shapes like radiatore and orecchiette take a little longer. Although my recipes give cooking times, it is the description of "firm to the bite," or "al dente," that should be your guide.

DRAINING PASTA

Drain the pasta by pouring it into a large colander set in the sink. Do not rinse the pasta; you will wash away all the flavor. And do not allow the pasta to sit in the colander, which makes it sticky and gummy. Protecting your hands with oven mitts, shake the colander once or twice, then immediately pour the drained pasta back into the cooking pot. Add the sauce or vegetables, stir and serve. Or pour the cooked pasta into a serving bowl, top with the sauce or vegetables, stir and serve. When I was growing up, we had to be seated at the table as the pasta was drained. My grandmother always said, "The pasta won't wait," and she was right.

SAUCING THE PASTA

The freshest and fastest pasta dishes use fresh vegetables. Use your eye and creativity when cutting the vegetables. The object is to match the pasta shape to the shape of the vegetables so that you can easily have a little of each in every forkful.

For penne, penne rigate, ziti or other tubular pasta shapes:

Asparagus: Cut into 1½-inch length.
Carrots: Cut into short sticks about 1½ inches long and ¼ inch thick.
Onions: Cut into ¼-inch-thick wedges.

Broccoli: Leave about ¾ inch of the stem on the florets, and halve or quarter lengthwise.

Mushrooms: Halve the mushrooms lengthwise through the caps and stems, place cut side down and cut the halves into thick lengthwise slices.

Red Bell Peppers: Cut into ¼-to-½-inch strips, and then halve crosswise.

Tomatoes: Core and cut into thin wedges.

For radiatore, shells, orecchiette or other short, chunky pasta shapes:

Carrots: Cut into thin rounds or coins.

Onions: Cut into chunks or large dice.

Broccoli: Cut into small bushy florets; trim the stems, and cut into thin disk shapes.

Mushrooms: Quarter through the stems.

Red Bell Peppers and Tomatoes: Cut into ½-to-1-inch chunks.

For linguine, spaghetti and other long, thin shapes:

Cut all vegetables into long, thin strands to match the pasta, or finely chop so that the vegetables can be easily tangled up in the long strands of pasta and become incorporated into every forkful.

ADDING CHEESE TO PASTA

Parmigiano-Reggiano: This partially skimmed cow's milk cheese from the city of Parma in northern Italy is my favorite. Buy the best. With just a spoonful of the real thing, you will get more flavor and taste than if you used twice as much of a lesser-quality cheese. Select a wedge, making sure the words "Parmigiano-Reggiano" are stamped all along the pale yellow rind. Grate it yourself as you need it, since pre-grated cheese loses its flavor. I prefer the hand-held Mouli grater to all others.

Pecorino Romano: This tangy sheep's milk cheese comes from southern Italy. The flavor is sharper and more salty than Parmigiano-Reggiano, but it has a nice nutty edge. If you like a sharp cheese, try it with the pasta dishes made spicy with hot red pepper flakes.

Three Pasta Recipes

WHILE THE WATER IS BOILING, survey the fresh vegetable drawer in search of inspiration for a quick sauce. Assuming you have extra-virgin olive oil, garlic and Parmigiano-Reggiano on hand, here are some possibilities. All of these toppings will work on 12 to 16 ounces of penne, shells, rotelle or radiatore, and all serve 4. Cook the pasta in plenty of boiling, salted water until al dente, or firm to the bite, 8 to 12 minutes, depending on the brand.

Broccoli and Pepper

Serve over penne, shells or rotelle.

1	bunch broccoli
1	red bell pepper, cut into strips
½	yellow bell pepper, cut into strips
¼	cup extra-virgin olive oil
1	garlic clove, crushed through a press
	Salt and freshly ground black pepper
	Grated Parmigiano-Reggiano

CUT THE TENDER STEMS and florets of the broccoli into ½-inch pieces. Boil them along with the pasta. Meanwhile, cook the red and yellow peppers in the oil with the garlic until softened; season to taste with salt and pepper.

Drain the pasta and broccoli, reserving ¼ cup of the cooking water. Toss the pasta with the peppers and garlic. Moisten the pasta with the reserved cooking water. Add freshly grated cheese to taste and serve.

Mushroom and Sun-Dried Tomatoes

Serve over radiatore or shells.

10-14	ounces white button mushrooms, quartered
½	large sweet onion, cut into thin wedges
¼	cup extra-virgin olive oil
1	garlic clove, crushed through a press
	Salt and freshly ground black pepper
4	halves sun-dried tomatoes, packed in olive oil, thinly sliced
	Grated Parmigiano-Reggiano

IN A LARGE SAUCEPAN over medium heat, cook the mushrooms and onion in the oil until browned, 8 to 10 minutes. Add the garlic and salt and pepper to taste.

Drain the pasta, reserving ¼ cup of the cooking water. Toss the pasta with the mushroom mixture, the reserved cooking water and the sun-dried tomatoes. Serve with freshly grated cheese to taste.

Carrots and Parsley

Serve over shells or radiatore.

1	pound carrots, peeled
½	large sweet onion, cut into thin wedges
¼	teaspoon hot red pepper flakes
¼	cup extra-virgin olive oil
½	cup chopped fresh Italian (flat-leaf) parsley
1	garlic clove, crushed through a press
	Grated Parmigiano-Reggiano

SLICE THE CARROTS VERY THIN with a food processor. In a large saucepan over medium heat, cook the carrots, onion and red pepper flakes in the oil until tender, about 10 minutes. Add the parsley and garlic.

Drain the pasta, reserving ½ cup of the cooking water. Toss the pasta with the carrot mixture, adding the reserved cooking water to moisten it. Add cheese to taste.

Pasta Primavera, Asian Style

PREPARATION TIME: 25 MINUTES ● COOKING TIME: 7 TO 10 MINUTES ● SERVES: 4

IN THIS RECIPE, PASTA PRIMAVERA, or pasta with spring vegetables, takes on a decidedly Asian flavor with the addition of ingredients like fresh ginger, rice vinegar, sesame oil and sesame seeds.

It takes more time to prepare the ingredients for this dish than it does to cook it, but once the measuring and cutting are out of the way, just a few minutes are needed to cook the pasta and vegetables. (See photograph, page 36.)

16   ounces thin spaghetti
 2   medium carrots, trimmed, peeled, cut into 2-x-⅛-inch julienne
 ¼   pound fresh Chinese snow peas, stems trimmed, strings pulled, halved diagonally lengthwise

DRESSING

 ½   cup vegetable oil
 1   tablespoon dark sesame oil
 3   tablespoons rice vinegar
 1   tablespoon fresh lime juice
 1   teaspoon grated peeled fresh ginger
 1   garlic clove, crushed through a press
 ¼   teaspoon chili-flavored sesame oil or pinch hot red pepper flakes
      Pinch salt

10-12   ounces cooked, peeled and deveined small shrimp, coarsely chopped
 2   scallions, trimmed, cut into 2-x-⅛-inch julienne
 2   slices cooked ham, cut into 2-x-⅛-inch julienne
 2   slices smoked turkey, cut into 2-x-⅛-inch julienne
 1   tablespoon sesame seeds, toasted in a dry skillet for 20 seconds

1. Cook the pasta in plenty of boiling, salted water, stirring occasionally, for 5 to 6 minutes. Add the carrots and snow peas; cook for 2 to 3 minutes, or until tender and the spaghetti is al dente, or firm to the bite. Drain.

2. Make the Dressing: Whisk the vegetable oil, sesame oil, rice vinegar, lime juice, ginger, garlic, chili oil or red pepper flakes and salt in a large bowl. Add the pasta and half of the shrimp; toss to blend. Taste and add more salt and sesame oil, if needed. Transfer to a large, deep platter.

3. Sprinkle the top of the noodles with the remaining shrimp, scallions, ham, turkey and sesame seeds. Serve at room temperature.

Farfalle with Fresh Tomatoes and Basil

PREPARATION TIME: 10 MINUTES ✽ COOKING TIME: 10 TO 12 MINUTES ✽ SERVES: 4

THIS DISH IS TRADITIONALLY made with ditalini or other small pasta shapes that match the size of the chopped sauce. But I like the look and feel of butterfly-shaped pasta, and it holds the sauce nicely. The classic summer sauce, a mixture of fresh chopped tomatoes, basil, olive oil and garlic, is tossed with the hot pasta and served warm or at room temperature.

I often add any of the following to this dish: diced cucumber, fresh raw corn kernels, minced green pepper or red onion. A few finely chopped pitted brine-cured black olives are also nice.

16   ounces farfalle (butterfly-shaped
       pasta; also called bow ties)
1½   pounds ripe tomatoes, cored and
       diced (about 4 cups)
¼   cup extra-virgin olive oil
¼   cup coarsely chopped fresh basil
       leaves
1   small garlic clove, crushed through
       a press
½   teaspoon salt, or to taste
       Grated Parmigiano-Reggiano
       (optional)

1. Cook the pasta in plenty of boiling, salted water, stirring occasionally, until al dente, or firm to the bite, 10 to 12 minutes.

2. Meanwhile, combine the tomatoes, oil, basil, garlic and salt in a large bowl. Set aside.

3. Drain the cooked pasta; add it immediately to the tomato mixture. Toss to blend. Sprinkle to taste with cheese, if using, and serve.

Farfalle with Zucchini, Yellow Squash and Mint

PREPARATION TIME: 15 MINUTES ● COOKING TIME: 10 TO 12 MINUTES ● SERVES: 4

THE MONOCHROMATIC COLORS of this dish add to its lightness and gracefulness. Serve as a first or main course. Because both zucchini and squash are high in water content, they cook quickly. To keep them from getting soggy, it is important to undercook them slightly. The hot pasta and the addition of some of the boiling pasta liquid will finish the vegetables just enough so they will still be bright and pretty. Use a light dusting of robustly flavored Parmigiano-Reggiano or Pecorino Romano for a blast of flavor with a minimum of fat and calories.

12 ounces farfalle (butterfly-shaped pasta; also called bow ties)
1   tablespoon extra-virgin olive oil or unsalted butter
1   scallion, trimmed, thinly sliced
½   garlic clove, finely chopped
2   small zucchini, scrubbed, trimmed, very thinly sliced
1   small yellow squash, scrubbed, trimmed, very thinly sliced
¼   cup chopped fresh basil leaves
1   tablespoon minced fresh mint leaves
1   tablespoon grated Parmigiano-Reggiano or Pecorino Romano, plus more for topping

1. Cook the pasta in plenty of boiling, salted water, stirring occasionally, until al dente, or firm to the bite, 10 to 12 minutes. Before draining, ladle out ½ cup of the boiling cooking water and reserve.

2. Meanwhile, heat the oil in a large skillet over medium heat. Add the scallion and garlic; cook, stirring, for 2 minutes. Add the zucchini and yellow squash and cook, stirring, over medium-low heat just until wilted, about 3 minutes.

3. Toss the pasta with the zucchini mixture and stir in the basil, mint, reserved cooking water and 1 tablespoon of the cheese. Spoon onto plates, and serve with a light sprinkling of cheese over each serving.

Cavatelli with Spinach and Tomatoes

PREPARATION TIME: 15 MINUTES ❋ COOKING TIME: 10 TO 20 MINUTES ❋ SERVES: 4

ONE OF MY MOTHER'S SPECIALTIES is homemade cavatelli. Tender little "lumps" of soft dough, Mom's cavatelli are made of flour, water and ricotta. She used to make them completely by hand, but now she uses a small hand-cranked cavatelli machine. In goes the dough, and as she turns the handle, out pop the little twisted blobs. Mom always serves her cavatelli with a rich meat-based red sauce. I make mine with spinach and tomatoes, using Mom's homemade cavatelli, or the frozen cavatelli found in many Italian specialty stores. Imported dried cavatelli are also available, and although they lack the density of the fresh, they are quite good.

1   bag or bunch (10-16 ounces) fresh
      spinach, washed, stems trimmed
¼   cup extra-virgin olive oil
½   teaspoon hot red pepper flakes,
      or to taste
1   tablespoon thinly sliced fresh garlic
2-3   ripe tomatoes, cored and cut into
      thin wedges
½   teaspoon salt, or to taste
¼   cup packed, torn fresh basil leaves
16   ounces fresh, dried or frozen
      cavatelli

¼   cup grated Pecorino Romano,
      or to taste

1. Steam the spinach in a vegetable steamer set over boiling water, covered, just until wilted, about 2 minutes. Remove from the heat and set aside.

2. Combine the oil, red pepper flakes and garlic in a large, wide saucepan or deep skillet and cook, stirring, over low heat until the garlic is softened and golden (do not brown), about 5 minutes. Remove from the heat. Stir in the tomatoes, salt, basil and spinach. Set aside.

3. Cook the cavatelli in plenty of boiling, salted water, stirring occasionally, until al dente, or firm to the bite, 5 to 15 minutes, depending on whether the cavatelli are fresh, dried or frozen. Drain and add to the tomato mixture. Add the cheese and toss. Serve at once, with more cheese at the table.

OLIVE OIL

I RELY ALMOST EXCLUSIVELY ON OLIVE OIL in my cooking, keeping two or three bottles on hand for different uses, depending on the season. For summer cooking, when tomatoes are ripe and juicy, I invest in a bottle of fine extra-virgin Italian or Spanish olive oil for drizzling on crostini, salads, grilled vegetables, fish and chicken and pasta. For my all-purpose cooking oil, I use any of the moderately priced extra-virgin olive oils readily available in most supermarkets. These are usually blends of olive oil of varying quality (and acidity). While they don't have the subtlety and flavor of the more expensive varieties, they are a good value at less than $10 per liter.

Students often ask me to recommend a specific brand. This is difficult, as I am always experimenting with new ones. What I do recommend is to buy oil, especially the more expensive ones, in a small bottle and try it before investing more money in a larger quantity.

Never cook with the finest, most expensive oil. Instead, use it as the Italians do—as a condiment on salads, stirred into a dish after it is cooked or drizzled over toasted bread or a finished dish, much as you would add salt and pepper.

Pasta with Arugula, Olives and Fresh Tomatoes

PREPARATION TIME: 10 MINUTES   ✺   COOKING TIME: 15 TO 20 MINUTES   ✺   SERVES: 4

THIS IS ONE OF THOSE RECIPES that was born of necessity. I had run out of time and energy, so on my way home from work, I made a quick stop at the store and picked up some plum tomatoes and a bunch of arugula. In a short time, dinner was on the table.

2   tablespoons extra-virgin olive oil

12   fresh plum tomatoes, trimmed and cut into thin wedges (3-4 cups)

1   garlic clove, crushed through a press
     Salt and freshly ground black pepper

1   pound orecchiette, shells or other round, plump pasta

2   bunches arugula, washed and long stems trimmed

¼   cup chopped fresh basil (optional)

1   tablespoon coarsely chopped pitted brine-cured black olives (Kalamata)

1. Heat the oil in a large skillet. Add the plum tomatoes and garlic. Cook, stirring, over low heat, until the tomatoes are softened and heated through, about 5 minutes. Sprinkle with salt and pepper to taste and set aside.

2. Cook the pasta in a large pot of boiling, salted water, stirring occasionally, until the pasta is al dente, or firm to the bite, 8 to 12 minutes, depending on the shape. Ladle out ½ cup of the cooking water and reserve.

3. Drain the pasta and add to the skillet with the tomatoes. Add the arugula, basil (if using), olives and reserved cooking water. Heat over medium heat, stirring, for about 2 minutes, or until the arugula is wilted. Serve immediately.

Pasta with Toasted Walnut and Parmigiano-Reggiano Butter Sauce

PREPARATION TIME: 10 MINUTES ✺ COOKING TIME: 3 TO 8 MINUTES ✺ SERVES: 4

THIS SAUCE IS ESPECIALLY GOOD on fresh pasta noodles. But it also goes well with delicate dried pasta shapes like farfalle or fettuccine.

16   ounces fresh fettuccine or 12 ounces imported dried fettuccine or other flat pasta

½   cup finely chopped walnuts

¼   cup unsalted butter, cut into small pieces

¼   cup grated Parmigiano-Reggiano

1. Cook the pasta in plenty of boiling, salted water, stirring occasionally, until al dente, or firm to the bite, about 3 minutes for fresh fettuccine or 8 minutes for dried.

2. Meanwhile, heat the walnuts in a large skillet over low heat, stirring, until fragrant, about 3 minutes. Add the butter and stir until melted.

3. Drain the pasta, leaving plenty of moisture still clinging to the surface of the noodles. Transfer to a platter. Pour half of the walnut butter on top; toss. Add the remaining walnut butter and a generous layer of grated cheese, and serve at once.

Penne with Asparagus, Smoked Salmon and Dill

PREPARATION TIME: 20 MINUTES ● COOKING TIME: 18 TO 20 MINUTES ● SERVES: 4

PENNE IS A FAVORITE SHAPE because it matches the natural contour of so many vegetables. Smoked salmon is too expensive to buy very often, but I like to treat myself to the small vacuum-sealed packages that contain just the right amount of salmon for pasta or for tiny canapés for 4 people (see page 21).

2	tablespoons unsalted butter
2	tablespoons extra-virgin olive oil
½	red onion, cut into thin lengthwise slices
1	bunch asparagus, rinsed, trimmed, diagonally cut into 1-to-1½-inch lengths
2-3	slices (about 3 ounces) smoked salmon, cut into 1½-x-¼ -inch strips
	Freshly ground black pepper
16	ounces penne or other tubular pasta
2	tablespoons snipped fresh dill

1. Heat the butter and oil in a large skillet. Add the onion and cook, stirring, over low heat until tender, about 5 minutes. Do not brown. Add the asparagus and stir-fry until crisp-tender, about 5 minutes. Remove from the heat.

2. Add the salmon to the skillet and stir to blend. Sprinkle with pepper to taste.

3. Cook the pasta in plenty of boiling, salted water, stirring occasionally, until al dente, or firm to the bite, 8 to 10 minutes. Drain. Return the pasta to the pot. Add the asparagus mixture and the dill. Toss to blend.

4. Spoon into a large serving bowl and serve at once.

Penne Rigate with Asparagus, Prosciutto and Mushrooms

PREPARATION TIME: 10 MINUTES ● COOKING TIME: ABOUT 25 MINUTES ● SERVES: 4

PENNE RIGATE are quills, with ridges. The ridges hold the flavor of the garlic oil close to the pasta and add a little sturdiness.

Cut the asparagus into lengths that match the penne. A small fistful of freshly grated Parmigiano-Reggiano, sprinkled on just before serving, is the crowning glory to this simple dish.

3	tablespoons extra-virgin olive oil
2	cups sliced white button mushrooms
1	garlic clove, slivered
	Salt and freshly ground black pepper, to taste
1-2	slices prosciutto, fat trimmed, cut into thin slivers
16	ounces penne rigate
1	bunch (about 1 pound) asparagus, trimmed, cut into 1-to-1½-inch diagonal pieces
½	cup shredded mozzarella (optional)
¼	cup grated Parmigiano-Reggiano
2	tablespoons slivered fresh basil leaves

1. Heat the oil in a large, deep skillet until hot; add the mushrooms and cook, stirring, over medium heat until golden and tender, about 10 minutes. Add the garlic, salt and pepper; cook for 2 minutes. Add the prosciutto; stir to blend. Remove from the heat.

2. Cook the penne in plenty of boiling, salted water until al dente, or firm to the bite, about 8 minutes. Add the asparagus and cook until tender, 2 to 3 minutes more. Drain.

3. Add the penne and asparagus to the skillet and stir to coat with the mushroom mixture. Add the mozzarella, if using, and the cheese. Sprinkle with the basil. Serve at once.

Penne with White Beans, Tomatoes and Basil

PREPARATION TIME: 10 MINUTES ● COOKING TIME: 10 TO 12 MINUTES ● SERVES: 4

THIS IS A HEARTY DISH, one I enjoy making in late summer or early fall, when the air is cool but the tomatoes and basil are still with us.

¼ cup extra-virgin olive oil

1 garlic clove, minced or crushed through a press

2-3 cups rinsed canned or cooked dried cannellini (white kidney) beans

2 large ripe tomatoes, cored and cut into thin wedges (about 4 cups)

½ cup lightly packed torn fresh basil leaves

Salt and freshly ground black pepper, to taste

1 pound pasta (penne, medium shells or rotelle)

Grated Parmigiano-Reggiano

1. Heat the oil and garlic in a skillet over low heat until the garlic begins to sizzle and turn golden, about 2 minutes. Add the beans, tomatoes, basil, salt and pepper.

2. Cook the pasta in plenty of boiling, salted water, stirring occasionally, until the pasta is al dente, or firm to the bite, 8 to 10 minutes. Ladle out ⅓ cup cooking water and reserve. Drain the pasta.

3. Combine the pasta, bean mixture and the reserved cooking water. Toss. Sprinkle to taste with the cheese, and serve.

Penne with Roasted Vegetables

PREPARATION TIME: 20 MINUTES ✸ COOKING TIME: 50 TO 60 MINUTES ✸ SERVES: 4

THIS RECIPE WAS ONE OF THOSE wonderful accidents of cooking. Falling in love with the fresh baby zucchini, yellow squash, shiny and taut purple eggplants and bright red bell peppers at our local farmstand, I bought too many. My husband helped me cook them on the grill. We ate a few for dinner, and the next day, I tossed them with pasta. To grill the vegetables instead of oven-roasting them, halve or quarter them and toss with just enough olive oil (adding crushed garlic and salt and pepper to taste) to coat them. (See photograph, page 38.)

Note: If fresh thyme isn't available, finely chop ¼ teaspoon dried thyme with the parsley.

1   small eggplant, stem trimmed, halved, cut into 1-inch chunks

1   medium red or sweet onion, cut into ½-inch chunks

1   small zucchini, scrubbed, trimmed, cut into ½-inch-thick slices

1   medium carrot, trimmed, peeled, cut into thin diagonal slices

1   *each* red and green bell pepper, stems and seeds removed, quartered, cut into 1-inch pieces

3   garlic cloves, bruised with the side of a knife, peeled, chopped

⅓   cup extra-virgin olive oil

     Salt and freshly ground black pepper, to taste

2   tablespoons chopped fresh Italian (flat-leaf) parsley

1   teaspoon fresh thyme leaves, stripped from the stems

16 ounces penne or other tubular pasta Grated Parmigiano-Reggiano

1. Preheat the oven to 450 degrees F. Select a large (11-x-14-inch) baking pan, preferably with a nonstick coating. Add the vegetables and garlic; drizzle with the oil. Sprinkle with salt and pepper. Toss to blend.

2. Bake for 20 minutes. Turn the vegetables so that they brown evenly. Bake for 20 to 25 minutes longer, or until the vegetables are tender and the edges are browned or slightly charred. Sprinkle with the fresh herbs.

3. Cook the pasta in plenty of boiling, salted water, stirring occasionally, until al dente, or firm to the bite, 10 to 12 minutes. Ladle out about ¼ cup of the cooking water and reserve. Drain the pasta.

4. Toss the pasta with the roasted vegetables and the reserved cooking water. Sprinkle on the cheese and serve.

✸ PASTA ✸

Pasta with Smoked Mozzarella, Browned Red Peppers and Shiitake Mushrooms

PREPARATION TIME: 15 MINUTES • COOKING TIME: 20 MINUTES • SERVES: 4

THIS PASTA DISH MAKES FREQUENT appearances at our table. The smoked mozzarella adds an especially wonderful quality, setting off the earthiness of the mushrooms. If smoked mozzarella is not available, use regular mozzarella.

¼ cup extra-virgin olive oil

2 red bell peppers, quartered, stems and seeds discarded, cut into ½-inch-wide diagonals

1 box (3½ ounces) shiitake mushrooms, stems discarded, cut into ½-inch strips

1 garlic clove, crushed through a press

2 tablespoons coarsely chopped fresh Italian (flat-leaf) parsley
Salt and freshly ground black pepper

16 ounces penne, rotelle or shell-shaped pasta

1 cup diced or coarsely shredded smoked mozzarella or regular whole- or skim-milk mozzarella

1. Heat the oil in a large nonstick skillet, add the red bell peppers and cook, stirring, over medium-high heat until the peppers begin to brown, about 5 minutes. Add the mushrooms and cook, stirring, until lightly browned, about 5 minutes. Add the garlic, parsley and salt and pepper to taste; cook, stirring, for 2 minutes. Keep warm over low heat.

2. Meanwhile, cook the pasta in plenty of boiling, salted water, stirring occasionally, until al dente, or firm to the bite, 8 to 10 minutes.

3. Drain the pasta. Add to the skillet with the vegetables. Add the mozzarella and stir to blend. Serve at once.

Linguine with Fresh Clams

PREPARATION TIME: 15 MINUTES ● COOKING TIME: 15 TO 20 MINUTES ● SERVES: 4

LITTLENECK OR THE EVEN SMALLER Manila Bay or mahogany clams all work in this dish, but my favorite are the smallest littleneck clams available. In this rendition, the clams are left in their shells in true Italian style.

¼	cup extra-virgin olive oil
½	cup thin vertical slivers of sweet onion
3	garlic cloves, finely chopped Pinch hot red pepper flakes (optional)
1	leafy celery top
1	bay leaf
1	strip (½ x 2 inches) orange zest
1	fresh basil sprig
2	cups dry white wine (I like Sauvignon Blanc)
1	large tomato, cored and cut into ½-inch chunks
4	dozen littleneck or other small fresh clams, rinsed and scrubbed
16	ounces linguine
¼	cup lightly packed chopped fresh Italian (flat-leaf) parsley

1. Combine the oil, onion, garlic and red pepper flakes, if using, in a large, deep skillet or wide pot with a tight-fitting lid. Cook, stirring, over low heat until the onion is limp and tender, about 5 minutes. Stir in the celery top, bay leaf, orange zest and basil. Add the wine and heat to boiling. Boil, uncovered, for 5 minutes.

2. Add the tomato and the clams. Cover and cook just until the clams open, about 4 minutes. Do not overcook. Discard any unopened clams. Transfer the clams to a side dish and cover with foil. Remove the celery, bay leaf, orange zest and basil from the broth. Keep the broth warm over very low heat.

3. Meanwhile, cook the pasta in plenty of boiling, salted water, stirring occasionally, until al dente, or firm to the bite, 8 to 10 minutes. Drain. Transfer to the pot with the clam broth; stir to blend.

4. Transfer the pasta to a large, deep platter. Place the clams and parsley on top and toss once to combine with the pasta. Serve at once.

Linguine with Spicy Tomato Sauce and Mussels

PREPARATION TIME: **20 MINUTES** ● COOKING TIME: **25 MINUTES** ● SERVES: **4**

LEAVE THE MUSSELS in their shells for this spirited rendition. The shells make a striking contrast to the red sauce, and you'll have one less task to do when cooking. Don't shy away from the anchovy; it adds a pleasantly salty bite, not a fishy taste.

1 cup dry white wine

1 sprig each fresh basil and parsley

2 garlic cloves

2 pounds mussels, scrubbed, debearded, rinsed thoroughly

1 tablespoon extra-virgin olive oil

1 can (14 ounces) plum tomatoes with juices

1 flat anchovy fillet, rinsed, patted dry, minced

1 strip (½ x 2 inches) orange zest

16 ounces dried linguine

1 tablespoon small capers, rinsed and dried

¼ cup packed combined chopped fresh Italian (flat-leaf) parsley and basil

Salt and freshly ground black pepper

1. In a large, wide skillet or saucepan with a tight-fitting lid, heat the wine, basil and parsley sprigs and 1 clove of the garlic, bruised with the side of a knife, to boiling. Boil, uncovered, over medium-high heat for 3 minutes. Add the mussels, cover and cook until they open, about 5 minutes. Discard any unopened mussels. Lift the mussels from the broth with tongs or a slotted spoon and place on a platter; cover with foil.

2. Place a fine sieve over a bowl and strain the broth. Reserve the broth; discard the solids.

3. Wipe out the skillet or saucepan. Add the oil and the remaining garlic clove, crushed through a press. Heat over low heat just until the garlic begins to sizzle. Add the reserved broth, tomatoes, anchovy and orange zest. Heat to boiling, breaking up the tomatoes with the side of a spoon. Lower the heat and cook the sauce at a low boil until it has reduced and thickened slightly, about 15 minutes.

4. Meanwhile, cook the pasta in plenty of boiling, salted water, stirring occasionally, until al dente, or firm to the bite, 8 to 10 minutes. Drain.

5. Add the mussels, capers, fresh herbs and salt and pepper to taste to the sauce; reheat gently. Add the pasta and stir to combine.

6. Transfer to a large platter and serve at once.

Ceci e Pasta

PREPARATION TIME: 10 MINUTES ❋ COOKING TIME: 30 MINUTES ❋ SERVES: 4 (GENEROUSLY)

CECI E PASTA WAS A FAVORITE Friday night dinner when I was growing up. We ate this soupy pasta dish out of shallow soup plates with large spoons.

I'm sure at the time that my mother wasn't fully aware of the term "complementary proteins," referring to two incomplete vegetable proteins combined in one dish to give the nutritional benefit of a complete (meat) protein. But she did know that pasta and beans make a wholesome combination. She also knew that we loved it.

My version of ceci e pasta is slightly different from the dish I grew up with. I have added canned Italian tomatoes, and I substitute small shells for the elbows my mother used.

¼	cup extra-virgin olive oil
1	medium onion, chopped
3	garlic cloves, thinly sliced
½	carrot, chopped
1	can (28 ounces) Italian plum tomatoes with juice
1	can (17 ounces) chick-peas (ceci or garbanzo beans), rinsed and drained
16	ounces medium shells

Salt, to taste
¼ cup chopped fresh Italian (flat-leaf) parsley
Grated Parmigiano-Reggiano

1. Combine the oil, onion, garlic and carrot in a large skillet. Cook over low heat, stirring, until the onion is tender, about 10 minutes. Do not brown. Add the tomatoes and chick-peas; simmer over low heat for about 20 minutes.

2. Meanwhile, cook the pasta in plenty of boiling, salted water, stirring occasionally, until al dente, or firm to the bite, 5 to 8 minutes. Ladle out about 1 cup of the cooking water; reserve.

3. Drain the pasta and immediately add it to the skillet with the tomato and chick-peas. Stir to blend; add the reserved cooking water as needed for extra moisture. The mixture should be very juicy. Season with salt.

4. To serve, ladle into soup plates; sprinkle with the parsley and cheese to taste. Pass extra cheese at the table to sprinkle on each serving.

Orecchiette with Broccoli Rabe, White Beans and Garlic-and-Red-Pepper Oil

PREPARATION TIME: 10 MINUTES ❀ COOKING TIME: ABOUT 15 MINUTES ❀ SERVES: 4

BROCCOLI CAN BE USED instead of broccoli rabe in this dish, but add it during the last half of the pasta-cooking time. The rabe adds a more interesting flavor, however. Serve this with an assertively flavored Pecorino Romano cheese.

16	ounces orecchiette or other shell-shaped dried pasta
1	pound broccoli rabe, rinsed, ends trimmed, stems cut into 1-inch lengths
⅓	cup extra-virgin olive oil
2	garlic cloves, finely chopped
¼	teaspoon hot red pepper flakes, or to taste
1½	cups canned or cooked dried cannellini (white kidney) beans
	Salt and freshly ground black pepper
	Grated Pecorino Romano

1. Cook the pasta and broccoli rabe in plenty of boiling, salted water, stirring occasionally, until the pasta is al dente, or firm to the bite, and the broccoli rabe is tender, 13 to 15 minutes. Ladle out ½ cup of the cooking water and reserve.

2. Meanwhile, heat the oil, garlic and red pepper flakes in a large skillet over low heat, stirring occasionally, until the garlic sizzles. Add the beans and stir to blend. Add salt and pepper to taste.

3. Drain the pasta and add to the skillet, along with the reserved cooking water. Spoon into a serving bowl and sprinkle to taste with the cheese. Pass extra cheese at the table for sprinkling on each serving.

POULTRY AND OTHER MEATS

FAST

Famous Lemon and Basil Chicken 113

Chicken with Broccoli Rabe and Bacon 114

Sautéed Chicken with Prosciutto and Orange Gremolata 116

Provençal Chicken with Green Olives and Dried Currants 118

Honey-Glazed Orange and Rosemary Chicken 120

Butterflied Cornish Hens in Rosemary and Lemon 121

Chicken and Shiitake Mushrooms in Tomato Sauce 124

Two-Cheese Turkey Burgers 126

Soy and Ginger Turkey Burgers 127

Broiled Lamb Marinated in Tangerine, Soy and Ginger 128

Rosemary-Garlic Broiled Lamb Hash 130

Pork Cutlets with Onions and Bell Pepper Vinaigrette 132

Pork Tenderloin Marinated in Soy and Orange 134

WHEN YOU HAVE MORE TIME

Chicken Breasts Oven-Roasted with Bell Peppers 115

Stir-Fried Chicken, Green Beans and Walnuts 122

Grilled or Broiled Leg of Lamb with Garlic and Rosemary Crust 129

Lamb with Lentils and Caramelized Onions 131

Pork Loin with Fennel and Garlic 135

Favorite Meat Loaf 136

Veal Stew with Green Peppers and Potatoes 137

Famous Lemon and Basil Chicken

PREPARATION TIME: 10 MINUTES ❊ BAKING TIME: 35 TO 50 MINUTES ❊ SERVES: 4

I CALL THIS DISH "FAMOUS" because I show my students how to prepare it every summer and spring. I also make it at home all the time. It is especially good cold or at room temperature, so double the recipe and use the leftovers the next day. (This is a great way to cook chicken for salad.)

4   chicken breast halves with skin
       and bones (8-10 ounces each),
       fat trimmed, or 1 whole chicken
       (about 2 pounds), cut up
     Salt and freshly ground black
       pepper, to taste
4   large basil leaves
4   garlic cloves, bruised with the
       side of a knife
4   thin lemon slices
1   tablespoon extra-virgin olive oil

1. Preheat the oven to 400 degrees F. Place the chicken in a baking dish; sprinkle both sides with salt and pepper; arrange skin side up.

2. Loosen the skin from each chicken breast and slip a basil leaf between the skin and the meat. Add the garlic to the baking dish. Place a slice of lemon on top of each piece of chicken. Drizzle with the oil.

3. Bake, basting occasionally with the pan juices and turning the chicken and the baking dish occasionally so the chicken browns evenly, 35 to 40 minutes. If using a whole chicken, the baking time will be about 50 minutes.

4. To serve, place a browned lemon slice and garlic clove on top of each portion of chicken.

Chicken with Broccoli Rabe and Bacon

PREPARATION TIME: 15 MINUTES ● COOKING TIME: 35 MINUTES ● SERVES: 4

BROCCOLI RABE IS ONE of my favorite foods, so when Tom Meyer of Clyde's Restaurant Group in Washington, D.C., described a favorite dish of broccoli rabe cooked with pan-fried chicken, I couldn't wait to try it. This is a loose interpretation of his hearty dish. Expedite the preparation of this skillet dinner by blanching the broccoli rabe on one burner of the stove while you cook the bacon on another. This is delicious served with boiled cubed potatoes that are rough-mashed with a fork and then used to help sop up the good juices.

2   slices bacon
4   chicken breast halves, with skin and
      bones (8-10 ounces each), excess
      skin and fat trimmed
    Salt and freshly ground pepper,
      to taste
1   bunch (about 1¼ pounds) broccoli
      rabe, rinsed, thick stems trimmed,
      cut into 1-inch lengths
2   tablespoons extra-virgin olive oil
1   medium onion, halved lengthwise,
      cut into thin lengthwise slices
1   garlic clove, thinly sliced
½   teaspoon hot red pepper flakes

1. Cook the bacon in a large nonstick skillet until crisp, about 5 minutes; drain on paper towels, and set aside. Discard all but about 1 teaspoon of the bacon fat. Add the chicken breasts to the skillet and cook over medium heat, turning occasionally, until golden and cooked through, about 15 minutes. Sprinkle with salt and pepper.

2. Meanwhile, cook the broccoli rabe in a large pot of boiling, salted water until tender, about 5 minutes. Drain well. Place the chicken on a plate, and set aside. Add the oil to the skillet. Add the onion and cook over medium heat, stirring, until golden, about 5 minutes. Add the garlic and red pepper flakes and cook until the garlic is golden, about 2 minutes. Add the drained broccoli rabe and cook, stirring, until coated with the oil.

3. Place the chicken on top of the broccoli rabe and add any juices that have accumulated on the plate. Cover and heat through, about 2 minutes.

4. To serve, transfer to a deep platter. Cut the bacon into ½-inch pieces and sprinkle over the top. Serve at once.

Chicken Breasts Oven-Roasted
with Bell Peppers

PREPARATION TIME: 15 MINUTES ❋ COOKING TIME: 45 TO 50 MINUTES ❋ SERVES: 4

BELL PEPPERS ROASTED in a very hot oven until they are blackened around the edges have a wonderful caramelized flavor. This recipe calls for red bell peppers, but a combination of red, green and yellow can also be used.

2   large red bell peppers, halved, seeds, stem and ribs removed, cut into ½-inch strips

4   garlic cloves, lightly bruised with the side of a knife

1   teaspoon extra-virgin olive oil

4   boneless, skinless chicken breast halves (6-8 ounces each)

1   teaspoon fresh rosemary or thyme leaves or ½ teaspoon dried

Salt and freshly ground black pepper, to taste

Orange Gremolata (optional; page 116)

1. Preheat the oven to 400 degrees F. Place the peppers and garlic in a 13-x-9-inch baking dish or roasting pan. Drizzle with the oil and toss to coat. Bake for 25 minutes, stirring once or twice, until the peppers begin to brown.

2. Meanwhile, rinse the chicken and pat dry. Season with the rosemary or thyme, salt and a grinding of pepper. Remove the baking dish from the oven; stir the peppers and garlic; add the chicken and spoon some of the peppers on top.

3. Continue to roast, turning the chicken once or twice, until the chicken is cooked through and the peppers are browned and tender, 20 to 25 minutes. Season with salt and pepper, or add a little gremolata, if desired, and serve.

Sautéed Chicken with Prosciutto and Orange Gremolata

PREPARATION TIME: 15 MINUTES ❋ COOKING TIME: 15 TO 25 MINUTES ❋ SERVES: 4

THIS DISH CAN BE PREPARED either on the stovetop or oven-roasted. The prosciutto is optional, but it gives a nice salty edge to the mellow flavor of the chicken. Serve with Mom's Roasted and Peeled Red Peppers (page 276) or Easy Oven-Roasted Red Bell Peppers (page 278).

4	boneless, skinless chicken breast halves (6-8 ounces each; *not* pounded cutlets), fat trimmed
1	teaspoon fresh thyme, stripped from the stems, or ½ teaspoon dried, plus sprigs for optional garnish
	Freshly ground black pepper, to taste
1	tablespoon extra-virgin olive oil
2	tablespoons minced trimmed prosciutto or other cured ham
⅔	cup dry white wine
	Salt

ORANGE GREMOLATA

¼	cup packed fresh Italian (flat-leaf) parsley leaves and tender stems
1	garlic clove, trimmed and chopped
1	strip (½ x 2 inches) orange zest, coarsely chopped

1. Arrange the chicken on a plate and sprinkle with the 1 teaspoon fresh thyme or ½ teaspoon dried and pepper.

2. Heat the oil in a large, heavy nonstick skillet. Add the chicken and prosciutto or ham; cook over medium heat until lightly browned on both sides, about 5 minutes per side. Using tongs, remove to a side dish.

3. Add the wine to the skillet and boil over high heat, stirring with a wooden spoon, until the wine is reduced by more than one-half, to a glaze, about 5 minutes. Return the chicken, prosciutto and any juices on the plate to the skillet and cook over medium heat until the chicken is cooked through, 5 to 10 minutes.

4. Meanwhile, Make the Gremolata: Finely chop the parsley, garlic and orange zest together.

5. To serve, arrange the chicken on a platter. Spoon the gremolata on top. Drizzle with the pan juices. Season to taste with salt and pepper. Garnish with the thyme sprigs, if using.

ABOUT GREMOLATA

GREMOLATA IS A FINELY CHOPPED MIXTURE of parsley, garlic and lemon zest that is traditionally sprinkled over osso buco, a classic veal shank stew of northern Italy. I like the fresh flavors that gremolata adds to a dish. Lemon zest is classic, but I sometimes use orange zest instead. And I occasionally add small amounts of fresh thyme or rosemary to the mixture. Sprinkle gremolata over roasted vegetables, broiled fish and chicken, bean dishes and thick soups.

Provençal Chicken with Green Olives and Dried Currants

PREPARATION TIME: 15 MINUTES ❋ COOKING TIME: 45 MINUTES ❋ SERVES: 4

THE FLAVORS IN THIS DISH, especially the olives and herbs, are reminiscent of the cooking of Provence. Use the cracked green olives (they are usually Spanish) if you can find them, because they are easier to pit. Serve with Simple Pilaf (page 165).

1   whole chicken breast, split, and 2 legs, thighs and drumsticks, separated (about 2½ pounds total), skin and fat removed

¼   cup all-purpose flour

½   teaspoon salt

¾   teaspoon fresh thyme, stripped from the stems, or ½ teaspoon dried

¾   teaspoon fresh rosemary, snipped, or ½ teaspoon dried

2   tablespoons extra-virgin olive oil

1   large onion, cut into thin wedges

1   garlic clove, finely chopped

1   cup reduced-sodium canned chicken broth, fat skimmed

12   large green olives, rinsed, drained, crushed with the side of a knife, pitted

2   tablespoons dried currants
Freshly ground black pepper, to taste
Fresh thyme and/or rosemary sprigs, for garnish (optional)

1. Place the chicken in a plastic bag with the flour, salt and half of the thyme and rosemary; shake to coat with the flour mixture. Heat 1 tablespoon of the oil in a large nonstick skillet. Add the chicken pieces, a few at a time, and cook over medium heat, turning, until evenly browned, about 20 minutes. Drain on paper towels and set aside.

2. Add the onion and the remaining 1 tablespoon oil to the skillet and cook, stirring, until golden, about 8 minutes. Add the garlic and remaining thyme and rosemary; cook for 1 minute. Add the broth and heat to boiling. Return the chicken pieces and any juices on the plate to the skillet; top with the olives and currants. Cover and cook until the chicken is cooked through, about 15 minutes.

3. Season the chicken with pepper. Garnish with fresh herbs, if using, and serve.

USING FRESH HERBS

Fresh herbs have become a staple in my kitchen. I buy them and keep each bunch refrigerated in a glass or other container half filled with water, like a bouquet of flowers, and covered with an inverted plastic bag. As I need them, I snip off sprigs with kitchen scissors and rinse them.

Parsley (both Italian—the flat-leaf variety—and curly-leaf), cilantro and fresh dill will keep a least a week and sometimes longer. Be sure to change the water every few days.

Fresh thyme, rosemary and sage are fairly hardy and will keep more than 1 week. I store them the same way, and because the stems tend to be shorter than those of parsley, I keep them in a separate container. (The shelf on my refrigerator door is a favorite storage spot.)

Basil is a special case. Out-of-season, or hothouse, basil is fragile and expensive. I store it as I do the parsley and other herbs and use it within 2 days. I tear up the leaves and add them to seafood stew, soup, tomato sauce, pasta sauce and even mixed green salad. Locally grown basil is hardier than hothouse and will keep for about 1 week.

If you find yourself out of fresh herbs, the two dried herbs I depend on most are thyme and rosemary. (Dried dill, parsley and basil have little taste.) I rehydrate thyme and rosemary by chopping them along with fresh parsley, which gives the dried herbs a livelier taste.

Honey-Glazed Orange and Rosemary Chicken

PREPARATION TIME: 10 MINUTES ❧ OPTIONAL MARINATING TIME: 30 MINUTES TO 2 HOURS

BAKING TIME: 50 MINUTES ❧ SERVES: 4

ORANGE AND ROSEMARY seem to have an affinity for the taste and fragrance of honey. To make clean-up a little easier, line the baking pan with foil or use a pan with a nonstick coating. Use all chicken breasts or a mixture of parts, if preferred, in place of the whole cut-up chicken.

PLAN AHEAD:

To heighten the flavor, marinate the chicken for 30 minutes or up to 2 hours.

2 seedless oranges
½ cup honey
2 teaspoons dried rosemary
1 large chicken (2½-3 pounds), cut into 8 serving pieces
8 garlic cloves, peeled and left whole
½ teaspoon salt
Freshly ground black pepper

1. Using a vegetable peeler, cut 2 strips of orange zest from 1 orange; cut into thin slivers and set aside. Halve the orange and squeeze the juice into a bowl large enough to hold the chicken; add the honey and rosemary and stir to blend. Cut the remaining orange in half lengthwise and then into thick half-moon slices.

2. Add the chicken, orange slices and garlic to the orange juice mixture; sprinkle with salt and pepper to taste, and toss to blend. (The chicken can be marinated for 30 minutes at room temperature or for up to 2 hours, covered and refrigerated.)

3. Preheat the oven to 400 degrees F. Line a large baking pan with foil. Arrange the chicken and all the marinade ingredients in the baking pan.

4. Bake for 50 minutes, or until the chicken is golden, turning it and basting it with the marinade every 10 to 15 minutes while it is cooking. Serve immediately.

Butterflied Cornish Hens in Rosemary and Lemon

PREPARATION TIME: 15 MINUTES ◈ OPTIONAL MARINATING TIME: 30 MINUTES TO 2 HOURS
ROASTING TIME: 45 MINUTES ◈ SERVES: 4

I SERVE CORNISH HENS more frequently now that I know how easy it is to butterfly them and how quickly they cook. They can be oven-roasted, broiled or grilled and will be ready in approximately 45 minutes.

4   small (about 1½ pounds each)
      Cornish hens
      Salt and freshly ground black
      pepper, to taste
1   sprig fresh rosemary, leaves stripped
      from the stem, plus extra sprigs
      for optional garnish, or 2
      teaspoons dried
1   lemon
4   garlic cloves, bruised with the
      side of a knife
2   tablespoons extra-virgin olive oil

1. Rinse the hens with cold water and pat dry. Using kitchen shears, cut along either side of the backbone to remove it. Trim off the excess fat and skin. Spread the hens on a work surface, skin side up, and flatten by pressing down on breastbones. Arrange the hens, skin side down, on a foil-lined baking sheet with sides.

2. Sprinkle the hens with salt and pepper. Spread the fresh or dried rosemary leaves over the hens. Cut 4 thin slices from the lemon and place on the hens. Squeeze the juice from the lemon over the hens. Place the rosemary stems on the hens. Add the garlic and drizzle with the oil.

> **PLAN AHEAD:**
>
> For increased flavor, marinate the Cornish hens for 30 minutes or up to 2 hours.

3. Marinate for 30 minutes to 2 hours, if time allows. Preheat the oven to 400 degrees F.

4. Roast the hens for 25 minutes. Remove from the oven and using a spatula, carefully turn the hens over. Baste with the pan juices. Return to the oven and roast until golden and cooked through, about 20 minutes more.

5. Transfer the hens to a serving platter and garnish with the browned garlic, lemon slices and fresh sprigs of rosemary, if using.

Stir-Fried Chicken, Green Beans and Walnuts

PREPARATION TIME: 20 MINUTES ❋ MARINATING TIME: 30 MINUTES TO 4 HOURS

COOKING TIME: 20 MINUTES ❋ SERVES: 4

IT TAKES TIME TO ASSEMBLE, measure and prepare these ingredients, but once they are lined up on your counter, the cooking takes just minutes. The hoisin sauce and Asian sesame oil in this recipe are widely available in many supermarkets. Both have a fairly long shelf life if kept tightly covered and refrigerated. Serve this dish with rice.

MARINADE

1   tablespoon soy sauce
2   teaspoons cornstarch
1   teaspoon vegetable oil
1   teaspoon honey
1   small garlic clove, crushed
      through a press
2   boneless, skinless chicken breasts
      (6-8 ounces each), trimmed, cut
      into long strips about ½ inch wide
      and ½ inch thick

SAUCE

1   tablespoon cider vinegar
2   teaspoons honey
2   teaspoons soy sauce
1½   teaspoons hoisin sauce
½   teaspoon dark sesame oil

1   cup long-grain white rice
2   cups water, plus 1 tablespoon
¼   cup broken walnut pieces
3   teaspoons peanut or other
      vegetable oil
1   teaspoon minced peeled fresh ginger
½   teaspoon minced garlic
6   ounces green beans, stem ends
      trimmed, cut into 1-inch-long
      diagonal pieces
    Thinly sliced tops of 1 scallion,
      for garnish

1. Marinate the Chicken: In a pie plate or medium bowl, whisk together the soy sauce, cornstarch, oil, honey and garlic. Add the chicken strips, cover and refrigerate for at least 30 minutes (the mixture can be marinated for up to 4 hours, if more convenient).

2. Make the Sauce: In a small bowl, whisk the vinegar, honey, soy sauce, hoisin sauce and sesame oil; cover and set aside until ready to use.

3. Cook the rice in 2 cups boiling, salted water in a covered saucepan until tender, about 15 minutes. Keep warm.

4. Meanwhile, heat a wok or a large, heavy skillet over medium-high heat until hot enough to evaporate a drop of water upon contact. Add the walnuts to the dry skillet and quickly stir just until fragrant, about 20 seconds. Scrape the nuts out of the skillet onto a side dish; reserve.

5. Add 1 teaspoon of the oil to the hot skillet, sprinkle in the ginger and garlic and stir-fry for 10 seconds. Add the green beans; stir-fry just to coat with the oil. Sprinkle with the remaining 1 tablespoon water; cover and steam until crisp-tender, about 3 minutes. Scrape the beans out of the skillet onto a side dish.

PLAN AHEAD:

Allow at least 30 minutes to marinate the chicken. While it marinates, prepare the remaining ingredients.

6. Wipe out the skillet with a paper towel. Reheat over medium-high heat until hot enough to evaporate a drop of water upon contact; add the remaining 2 teaspoons oil. When the oil is very hot, add the chicken gradually in three or four additions. Stir-fry until the chicken is lightly browned, about 5 minutes. Add the green beans and the sauce. Stir-fry over high heat until the sauce thickens and coats the chicken and green beans. Stir in the reserved walnuts.

7. Serve over the hot rice. Sprinkle with scallion.

Chicken and Shiitake Mushrooms in Tomato Sauce

PREPARATION TIME: 5 MINUTES

COOKING TIME: 25 TO 30 MINUTES (INCLUDING COOKING OF PASTA, RICE OR ORZO) ● SERVES: 4

SERVE THIS CHICKEN SAUTÉ and flavorful tomato sauce over spinach pasta, rice, plain cooked orzo (small rice-shaped pasta) or Parmesan Orzo (page 167).

1 tablespoon extra-virgin olive oil

4 chicken breast halves, with bone (8-10 ounces each), or 4 boneless, skinless chicken breast halves (6-8 ounces each)

1 package (3½ ounces) shiitake mushrooms, stems discarded, caps sliced (¼ inch thick), or 4 ounces large white button mushrooms, sliced through the stems (¼ inch thick)

1 small garlic clove, crushed through a press

Salt and freshly ground black pepper, to taste

½ cup dry white wine

1 can (14½ ounces) Italian-style plum tomatoes with juice
  a pinch of dried oregano or thyme or 1 teaspoon minced fresh

2 tablespoons chopped fresh parsley

1. Heat the oil in a large skillet; add the chicken and mushrooms. Cook over medium-low heat until golden, about 6 minutes per side for bone-in chicken breasts and 3 minutes per side for boneless chicken breasts. Add the garlic, salt and pepper; stir until blended.

2. Transfer the chicken and mushrooms to a side dish. Add the wine to the skillet. Increase the heat to high and boil the wine, scraping up any browned pieces from the bottom of the skillet, until reduced to a thin film.

3. Add the tomatoes and heat to boiling, breaking the whole tomatoes into pieces with the side of a wooden spoon or spatula. Return the chicken, mushrooms and any juices to the skillet. Add the dried oregano or thyme, if using (add fresh later). Heat to a gentle simmer, stirring to combine the ingredients.

4. Cover and cook over medium-low heat until the chicken is cooked through, about 15 minutes for bone-in breasts and 8 minutes for boneless. Add the parsley and fresh oregano or thyme, if using.

5. Transfer the chicken to a serving platter. Boil the tomato sauce over high heat, stirring occasionally, until slightly thickened, about 3 minutes. Add salt and pepper to taste.

6. Spoon the tomato sauce over the chicken and serve immediately.

Two-Cheese Turkey Burgers

PREPARATION TIME: 5 MINUTES ❀ COOKING TIME: 10 MINUTES ❀ SERVES: 4

GROUND TURKEY MAKES A JUICY burger when it isn't overcooked. Don't press down on the burger while it fries, because you will squeeze out all the juices. Cook the burgers slowly over medium heat so they don't dry out as they brown. The Parmesan cheese and sun-dried tomatoes add a welcome sparkle. To cut sun-dried tomatoes quickly, snip them into small pieces with kitchen scissors.

1¼	pounds ground turkey
¼	cup sun-dried tomato bits or cut-up sun-dried tomato halves
¼	cup cold water
2	tablespoons grated Parmigiano-Reggiano
2	tablespoons snipped fresh basil or parsley (optional)
4	thin slices part-skim mozzarella
4	rolls, split and toasted
	Lettuce leaves, sliced tomato and sliced onion (optional)

1. Place the turkey, sun-dried tomatoes, water, grated cheese and basil or parsley, if using, in a large bowl. Gently mix with a fork or your fingertips until blended; do not overmix. Shape the mixture into 4 patties about ½ inch thick.

2. Heat a large nonstick skillet over medium-high heat until hot enough to evaporate a drop of water upon contact. Add the patties and cook over high heat until browned, about 3 minutes. Carefully turn the patties, reduce the heat to medium and cook for 6 to 8 minutes, or until cooked through. Top each patty with a slice of mozzarella; cover and cook until melted, about 1 minute.

3. Place each patty on a roll, and serve with lettuce, tomato and onion, if desired.

Soy and Ginger Turkey Burgers

PREPARATION TIME: 10 MINUTES ● COOKING TIME: 10 TO 12 MINUTES ● SERVES: 4

TURKEY HAS SUCH A MILD FLAVOR that it welcomes—and needs—assertive flavors like soy sauce and ginger to give it a little personality. Serve with Cabbage Salad with Sesame Oil and Rice Vinegar (page 217).

1¼ pounds ground turkey
1 tablespoon reduced-sodium
    soy sauce
1 teaspoon grated peeled fresh ginger
1 garlic clove, crushed through a press
4 sesame buns (optional)

1. Combine the turkey, soy sauce, ginger and garlic in a large bowl; blend the ingredients lightly with your fingers or a large fork.

2. Rinse your hands with cold water and form the meat into 4 patties about ½ inch thick.

3. Heat a large nonstick skillet over medium-high heat until hot enough to evaporate a drop of water upon contact. Add the turkey patties and cook until browned on one side, about 3 minutes. Carefully turn the patties, reduce the heat to medium and cook until cooked through but still juicy, 7 to 9 minutes.

4. Serve on sesame buns, if using.

Broiled Lamb Marinated in Tangerine, Soy and Ginger

PREPARATION TIME: 15 MINUTES ❋ MARINATING TIME: 30 MINUTES

COOKING TIME: 10 TO 16 MINUTES ❋ SERVES: 4, WITH LEFTOVERS

LAMB STEAKS, cut from the sirloin end of a leg, are now featured in many supermarket meat sections. I like to marinate and broil this cut much as I would a boned and butterflied leg of lamb. If lamb steaks are not available, use this marinade on the boned and butterflied sirloin portion of the leg. You can substitute orange for the tangerine. Remove the zest (orange part) from the tangerine with a vegetable peeler and then finely chop with a knife. This is delicious with Couscous with Confetti Vegetables (page 225).

2 tablespoons reduced-sodium
    soy sauce

2 teaspoons finely chopped peeled
    fresh ginger

2 teaspoons finely chopped garlic

2 teaspoons finely chopped
    tangerine zest

¼ teaspoon hot red pepper flakes,
    or more to taste

2-3 lamb steaks, ¾ inch thick
    (about 2 pounds), or 1 sirloin end
    leg of lamb, boned, butterflied,
    trimmed (about 2 pounds)

1. Combine the soy sauce, ginger, garlic, tangerine zest and red pepper flakes on a platter. Add the lamb and turn to coat with the marinade. Cover and marinate for about 30 minutes at room temperature or refrigerate and marinate longer, if preferred.

PLAN AHEAD:

Allow at least 30 minutes for the lamb to marinate.

2. Preheat the broiler. Arrange the lamb on a broiler pan (for easy clean-up, cover the broiling rack with foil, but make slits so the juices can drain off). For medium-rare, broil the lamb about 3 inches from the heat source for 5 to 8 minutes per side, depending on the thickness of the meat.

3. Let stand for 5 minutes before cutting into thin diagonal slices and serving.

Grilled or Broiled Leg of Lamb with Garlic and Rosemary Crust

PREPARATION TIME: **10 MINUTES** ❋ STANDING TIME: AT LEAST 30 MINUTES

COOKING TIME: **20 TO 30 MINUTES** ❋ SERVES: 8 OR MORE

WHENEVER I HAVE TO FEED a crowd, I make broiled or grilled lamb. Thinly sliced and arranged on a platter garnished with rosemary sprigs, it looks superb. Don't hesitate to cook the whole leg, because the leftovers make a great hash (see page 130) or sandwich (see page 89).

8	garlic cloves, crushed through a press
2	tablespoons fresh rosemary leaves or 1 tablespoon dried
1	teaspoon salt, preferably coarse or kosher
½	teaspoon freshly ground black pepper
1	boned and butterflied leg of lamb (about 4 pounds boned), trimmed of excess fat

1. In a small bowl, combine the garlic, rosemary, salt and pepper. Using a fork, stir the mixture into a paste.

2. Place the lamb, smooth side down, on a large platter or in a shallow baking dish. Using your fingers or a small, flexible spatula, rub half of the paste into the flesh, covering it as evenly as possible. Turn the lamb over and spread the remaining paste on the outside part.

3. Let marinate for at least 30 minutes at room temperature or refrigerate for 2 hours or longer. Remove from the refrigerator and let stand at room temperature for 30 minutes before cooking.

4. Preheat the grill or broiler. Cook the lamb, turning occasionally, until the outside is browned and crusty and the inside is medium-rare, 20 to 30 minutes total, depending on the intensity of the heat and the thickness of the meat. Let stand for 10 minutes before cutting into thin diagonal slices and serving.

PLAN AHEAD:

For best flavor, marinate the lamb for the full 30 minutes. If you marinate overnight in the refrigerator, allow 30 minutes for it to return to room temperature before cooking. It should cool for 10 minutes before it is sliced.

Rosemary-Garlic Broiled Lamb Hash

PREPARATION TIME: 15 MINUTES ● COOKING TIME: ABOUT 20 MINUTES ● SERVES: 4

BEFORE BECOMING A CONVERT, I thought all hash came in a can. But a good friend and excellent chef, Christopher Styler, changed my mind. Chris's hash starts out with golden-fried cubes of potatoes, chopped onion, a little red bell pepper, juicy chunks of meat and a sprinkling of fresh herbs. Suddenly, leftover lamb becomes a great dinner—with very little effort.

> **PLAN AHEAD:**
>
> This recipe calls for cooked lamb.

3   tablespoons extra-virgin olive oil

4   large potatoes, preferably red-skinned, unpeeled, cut into ½-inch dice (about 4 cups)

1   small onion, chopped

½   red bell pepper, cut into ½-inch dice

1   garlic clove, crushed through a press
    Salt and freshly ground black pepper, to taste

2   cups diced (½ inch) cooked lamb

1   tablespoon chopped fresh parsley

1   teaspoon snipped fresh rosemary or fresh thyme leaves, stripped from the stems, or to taste

1. Heat the oil in a large nonstick skillet until very hot. Add the potatoes all at once and fry over medium-high heat, stirring and turning frequently, until evenly crisp and golden, about 10 minutes.

2. Add the onion and red pepper; sauté, stirring, until golden, about 5 minutes. Add the garlic, salt and pepper; sauté for 1 minute. Add the lamb and herbs, and sauté, stirring, for a few more minutes, just until the meat is heated through. Serve at once.

Lamb with Lentils and Caramelized Onions

PREPARATION TIME: 15 MINUTES ● COOKING TIME: ABOUT 1 HOUR ● SERVES: 4

I LIKE THIS SIMPLE STEW made with dark green French lentils. They hold their shape a little better than brown lentils and have a distinct flavor that complements the fragrance and taste of the rosemary. Leave the vegetables chunky, like the lamb, and make sure the meat is cut into small cubes so it cooks in 1 hour or less.

1 pound lamb shoulder, well trimmed, cut into ½-inch cubes

2 tablespoons extra-virgin olive oil

2 small carrots, trimmed, cut into ½-inch lengths

2 garlic cloves, 1 finely chopped, 1 left whole

½ teaspoon fresh rosemary leaves, snipped from the stems, or a pinch of dried

½ teaspoon fresh thyme, stripped from the stems, or a pinch of dried
Salt and freshly ground black pepper, to taste

1 can (16 ounces) Italian plum tomatoes with juice

1½ cups green or brown lentils, rinsed and picked over

1 bay leaf

1 celery top

8 ounces (about 12) small white onions, peeled

1 cup frozen green peas, thawed

1. In a large nonstick skillet over medium heat, brown the lamb in 1 tablespoon of the oil. Add the carrots, chopped garlic, rosemary, thyme, salt and pepper. Cook, stirring, for 5 minutes. Add the tomatoes, breaking them up with the side of a spoon. Cover and cook over low heat until the meat is tender, 45 to 55 minutes.

2. Meanwhile, cook the lentils in plenty of boiling, unsalted water with the remaining whole garlic, bay leaf and celery top until tender, about 20 minutes. Drain. Discard the seasonings.

3. In a separate skillet, brown the onions in the remaining 1 tablespoon oil over high heat. Reduce the heat, cover and cook until tender, about 5 minutes. Season with salt and pepper.

4. Add the onions, lentils and peas to the lamb. Stir to blend; heat through. Taste and correct the seasonings and serve.

Pork Cutlets with Onions and Bell Pepper Vinaigrette

PREPARATION TIME: 10 MINUTES ❋ COOKING TIME: ABOUT 20 MINUTES ❋ SERVES: 4

I LIKE TO SERVE THIS FAST-COOKING pork cutlet dish with boiled potatoes, crisp oven-roasted potato slices or rough-mashed potatoes.

8-10 well-trimmed thinly sliced boneless pork cutlets (about 1½ pounds)

½ teaspoon dried thyme
Salt and freshly ground black pepper, to taste

1 tablespoon extra-virgin olive oil, or more as needed

1 large sweet onion, cut into thin wedges

1 large green bell pepper, seeds and stem removed, cut into ½-inch strips

1 large red bell pepper, seeds and stem removed, cut into ½-inch strips

1 garlic clove, crushed through a press

1 tablespoon red wine vinegar, or more to taste

1. Sprinkle the pork with the thyme, salt and pepper. Brush a large nonstick skillet with a thin film of oil. Heat over medium heat. Add the pork and brown lightly, about 2 minutes per side. Remove to a side dish.

2. Add 1 tablespoon oil, the onion and the peppers to the skillet. Cook, stirring, over medium-low heat until the vegetables are tender and the edges begin to brown, about 10 minutes. Add the garlic and toss to blend, about 1 minute. Season with salt and pepper.

3. Return the pork and any meat juices to the skillet, add the vinegar and heat to boiling. Serve hot.

PORK: FAST AND LEAN

THANKS TO SELECTIVE BREEDING and a more wholesome diet, pork is about 30 percent leaner today than it was a decade ago. Long, slow cooking is no longer required for pork to be palatable; in fact, just the opposite is true. If you want juicy, tender pork, cook it for a shorter length of time.

Many newer cuts cook especially quickly. For instance, a boned and tied **pork loin roast**— a long, well-trimmed loin that has had the tenderloin (the long, slender strip of meat under the loin) removed—will cook in an hour or less. When the loin is tied, it is about 3 inches wide and can be 8 inches or more long, and it usually weighs approximately 2 pounds. The small tenderloins, now sold separately, also cook in a flash in a hot skillet.

Pork cutlets, actually ½-inch-thick slices cut from the boneless pork loin, cook very quickly and provide constant inspiration for new flavor combinations. Neat and well trimmed, they are often sold five slices per package. One package is more than enough for 2 servings, and two packages are perfect for 4 or 5 servings. Pork cutlets cook quickly in a nonstick skillet, making them an ideal choice for a fast meal.

Pork Tenderloin Marinated in Soy and Orange

PREPARATION TIME: 10 MINUTES ● MARINATING TIME: AT LEAST 30 MINUTES

COOKING TIME: LESS THAN 15 MINUTES ● STANDING TIME: 5 MINUTES ● SERVES: 4

THIS IS DELICIOUS SERVED WARM with brown rice and stir-fried asparagus or with Sesame Brown Rice Salad with Peanuts (page 223) or cold and sliced in a salad or a sandwich. Leftovers are great in stir-fried rice.

MARINADE

1   tablespoon soy sauce
1   tablespoon honey
1   garlic clove, crushed through a press
2   teaspoons grated orange zest
¼   teaspoon hot red pepper flakes

2   pork tenderloins (pork fillet), about 7 ounces each

1. Combine the soy sauce, honey, garlic, orange zest and pepper flakes in a pie plate. Add the pork tenderloins and turn to coat. Marinate, turning occasionally, for 30 minutes, or cover and marinate in the refrigerator for longer.

2. Heat a large nonstick skillet over medium-high heat until hot enough to evaporate a drop of water upon contact. Lift the pork from the marinade and place in the hot skillet. Cover and cook for 7 minutes, adjusting the heat to maintain a steady sizzle, or until very well browned but not charred. Turn and cook, covered, for 7 minutes more. Remove from the skillet.

> **PLAN AHEAD:**
>
> Allow at least 30 minutes for the pork to marinate.

3. Let rest for 5 minutes before cutting into thin diagonal slices and serving.

Pork Loin with Fennel and Garlic

PREPARATION TIME: **10 MINUTES** ❧ ROASTING TIME: **1 HOUR 10 MINUTES**

STANDING TIME: **10 MINUTES** ❧ SERVES: **4 WITH LEFTOVERS, OR 8**

THIS IS A GREAT DISH if you need to cook ahead, feed a crowd or plan for leftovers. I like to serve it at room temperature on a buffet table, as the thin slices are easy to eat. Vary the seasoning with your preference or mood. This roast is excellent rubbed with rosemary or thyme, lemon zest, black pepper and garlic—or a little of each. Leftovers are great in sandwiches (see page 80).

2   teaspoons fennel seeds

2   garlic cloves, crushed through
        a press

½   teaspoon salt, preferably coarse
        or kosher

¼   teaspoon freshly ground black
        pepper

1   boneless pork loin end roast,
        very well trimmed and tied
        (about 1¼ pounds)

1. Preheat the oven to 400 degrees F.

2. Place the fennel seeds on a cutting board and break them by cutting once or twice with a large, heavy knife. Or if you have a mortar and pestle, give them a couple grinds to lightly crush and release the aroma. Combine the fennel, garlic, salt and pepper and stir to blend.

> ### PLAN AHEAD:
> Allow about 1 hour for the pork to roast and 10 minutes for it to stand before slicing.

3. Rub the fennel seed mixture over the entire surface of the pork.

4. Place the pork in a 13-x-9-inch baking dish. Roast for 30 minutes. Remove the pan from the oven and using large tongs or two spatulas, carefully turn the roast over. Return to the oven and continue roasting until well browned, about 30 minutes.

5. Remove roast from the oven, and let stand for about 10 minutes. Carefully remove the string and cut meat into thin (⅛-inch) slices; arrange the overlapping slices on a platter. Spoon any pan juices over the meat and serve.

Favorite Meat Loaf

PREPARATION TIME: 15 MINUTES ✽ COOKING TIME: 50 MINUTES TO 1½ HOURS

STANDING TIME: 15 MINUTES ✽ SERVES: 8

I CAN MIX ALL THE INGREDIENTS for a meat loaf and bake it while I tend to other chores around the house. We love meat loaf sandwiches or just sliced cold meat loaf served with pickles (like pâté) the next day. (See photograph, page 86.)

1 cup milk (use low-fat or skim milk, if preferred)

½ cup plain fine dry bread crumbs

1 large egg, lightly beaten

½ cup chopped onion

1 tablespoon extra-virgin olive oil

1 garlic clove, crushed through a press

1 teaspoon curry powder

½ teaspoon ground ginger

1½ pounds meat loaf mixture
   (usually 1 pound beef and
   ¼ pound *each* pork and veal)

1 cup coarsely shredded carrots

1 teaspoon Dijon-style mustard,
   plus 1 tablespoon for topping

1 teaspoon anchovy paste (optional)

½ teaspoon salt
   Freshly ground black pepper

1. Preheat the oven to 350 degrees F. In a large bowl, combine the milk, bread crumbs and egg; set aside while preparing the other ingredients.

2. In a small skillet, combine the onion and oil and cook, stirring, until golden, about 5 minutes. Stir in the garlic until blended. Add the curry and ginger; stir to blend. Remove from the heat.

3. Add the onion mixture to the bowl with the bread crumbs. Add the meat, carrots, 1 teaspoon of the mustard, anchovy paste (if using), salt and pepper. Mix thoroughly with your hands until blended.

PLAN AHEAD:

The meat loaf takes 1 to 1½ hours to cook and should stand for at least 15 minutes before it is sliced.

4. Transfer to a 9-x-5-inch loaf pan or a shallow 9-inch baking dish. Smooth the top with a spatula. Spread the remaining 1 tablespoon of mustard over the surface of the meat loaf.

5. Bake until the juices run clear when the meat loaf is pierced with a skewer. The loaf pan will take 1 hour 30 minutes; the baking dish, 45 to 50 minutes.

6. Let stand for at least 15 minutes to allow the meat loaf to reabsorb the juices before slicing and serving.

Veal Stew with Green Peppers and Potatoes

PREPARATION TIME: **10 MINUTES** ● COOKING TIME: **1 HOUR 5 MINUTES** ● SERVES: **4**

ALTHOUGH VEAL IS CONSIDERED by some cooks to be a mild meat, I find that it gives a full, rich flavor to a stew. My mother made a stew like this when I was a child, and when I was away at college, I made the same one for my apartment-mates. The recipe has evolved over the years. Now I prepare it with less veal and fewer green peppers, and I have added potatoes. To perk up the seasoning, I put in snipped fresh rosemary and a twist of fresh orange zest. Fresh rosemary has a strong pine aroma and should be used with a light hand.

To shorten the cooking time substantially, use veal cut from the leg instead of stewing veal, and cut the well-trimmed meat into small pieces (smaller than ½-inch).

½ cup chopped onion
¼ cup chopped celery
¼ cup diced peeled carrot
1 garlic clove, finely chopped
1 tablespoon extra-virgin olive oil
¾ pound well-trimmed veal shoulder
   or leg, cut into 1-inch cubes
   Salt and freshly ground black
      pepper, to taste

1 can (14½ ounces) Italian plum
   tomatoes with juice
1 strip (½ x 2 inches) orange zest
½ teaspoon snipped fresh rosemary
   or 1 teaspoon dried
1 pound (about 4 medium) red-
   skinned potatoes, peeled and
   cut into 1-inch cubes
1 green bell pepper, stemmed,
   seeded, cut into 1-inch pieces

1. In a large nonstick skillet, combine the onion, celery, carrot, garlic and oil. Cook, stirring, over low heat until the vegetables are tender, about 10 minutes.

2. Stir in the veal; season with salt and pepper. Add the tomatoes, orange zest and rosemary. Cover and cook over medium-low heat, stirring occasionally, until the veal is tender, about 45 minutes.

3. Add the potatoes and the green pepper. Cover and cook until the potatoes are tender, about 10 minutes. Taste and correct the seasonings, then serve.

SEAFOOD

FAST

Fish

Skillet-Browned Tuna Steaks with Ginger, Garlic and Soy Glaze 139

Soy-and-Ginger-Glazed Salmon Steaks 140

Oven-Roasted Salmon Steaks with Braised Leeks and Dill 141

Oven-Roasted Halibut with Herb Citrus Vinaigrette 142

Foil-Poached Salmon Fillets with Warm Tomato Salad 148

Baked Fish Fillets with Herb and Citrus Topping 150

Tomato-and-Herb-Topped Fish Fillets Roasted with Potatoes 151

Rosemary Roasted Potatoes with Cod and Asparagus 152

Cod with Roasted Tomato Sauce and Black Olives 153

Shellfish

Pan-Seared Scallops with Pesto and Salsa 155

Baked Scallops with Bacon, Sautéed Apples and Cider Sauce 156

Grilled Sea Scallop Brochettes, Greek Style 158

Shrimp with Tomatoes, Spinach and Basil 159

Spicy Marinated Shrimp 160

Mussels in Tomato-Herb Broth 161

Mussels in White Wine with Fresh Tomato Salsa 162

WHEN YOU HAVE MORE TIME

Grilled Cumin-Marinated Swordfish 144

Swordfish Marinated in Lemon, Rosemary and Garlic 145

Mako Shark with Provençal Marinade 146

Skillet-Browned Tuna Steaks with Ginger, Garlic and Soy Glaze

PREPARATION TIME: 10 MINUTES ● COOKING TIME: 4 MINUTES

STANDING TIME: 5 MINUTES ● SERVES: 4

A PERFECTLY COOKED TUNA STEAK is pink in the center, moist and juicy. Although broiled tuna is excellent, often an oven broiler just isn't hot enough to brown the surface of the steak and still keep the center from overcooking. This recipe gives precise directions for skillet-cooked tuna and produces a perfectly cooked steak every time. If your tuna steaks are less than ¾ inch thick, reduce the cooking time by 1 minute; if they are thicker than ¾ inch, increase the time by 1 minute. In keeping with the Oriental theme, serve the tuna steaks with stir-fried vegetables seasoned with a little sesame oil and sprinkled with toasted sesame seeds.

1 large garlic clove, crushed through a press

1 teaspoon grated peeled fresh ginger

4 tuna steaks, ¾ inch thick (about ½ pound each)

2 teaspoons vegetable oil

2 tablespoons reduced-sodium soy sauce

Fresh lime wedges, for garnish

Sprigs of fresh cilantro, for garnish (optional)

1. Rub a portion of the garlic and ginger on both sides of the tuna steaks. Brush a large nonstick skillet with the oil and heat over medium-high heat until hot enough to evaporate a drop of water on contact.

2. Add the tuna steaks and cook over high heat for 1 minute. Using a spatula, turn the steaks over and cook for 1 minute more. Pour the soy sauce over the top of the steaks and cook over high heat, tipping the skillet to spread the soy sauce evenly, for 1 minute. Quickly turn the steaks over and cook for 1 minute more. The tuna should be pink in the center. It will continue to cook while standing. Transfer to a platter and drizzle with any of the thickened soy sauce left in the skillet.

3. Let stand for 5 minutes before serving. Garnish with lime wedges and cilantro sprigs, if using.

Soy-and-Ginger-Glazed Salmon Steaks

PREPARATION TIME: **10** MINUTES ● MARINATING TIME: **15** MINUTES TO **1** HOUR

COOKING TIME: **12** TO **16** MINUTES ● SERVES: **4**

THIS MARINADE OF SOY SAUCE, fresh ginger, garlic and sesame oil is intensely flavored and can season foods—from salmon steaks to chicken breasts and even lamb chops—in a short time. "Grate" the ginger using the fine-shred side of a grater rather than the perforated side. These fine shreds are not as moist and clumpy and are therefore easier to distribute over the food.

PLAN AHEAD:

For increased flavor, marinate the salmon steaks for 1 hour or more.

1. Combine the soy sauce, ginger, garlic and sesame oil in a pie plate or on a platter. Add the salmon and turn to coat with the soy mixture. Marinate at room temperature for at least 15 minutes, turning frequently and rubbing with the marinade, or cover and marinate in the refrigerator for 1 hour or more, turning occasionally.

2. Preheat the grill or broiler. Place the broiler rack about 4 inches from the heat source.

3. Grill or broil the salmon, basting with any marinade left in the dish, turning the salmon to brown both sides until the center looks opaque when tested with the tip of a knife, 6 to 8 minutes per side depending on the intensity of the heat.

4. Garnish with the lime wedges, if using, and serve.

2 tablespoons soy sauce

2 teaspoons grated peeled fresh ginger

1 garlic clove, crushed through a press

1 teaspoon dark sesame oil

2-4 salmon steaks, about ¾ inch thick (about ½ pound each)

Lime wedges, for garnish (optional)

Oven-Roasted Salmon Steaks with Braised Leeks and Dill

PREPARATION TIME: 15 MINUTES ● COOKING TIME: 30 TO 35 MINUTES
STANDING TIME: 5 MINUTES ● SERVES: 4

LEEKS ARE IN SEASON twice a year: April through July and September through November. Although they are in the onion family, their delicate, sweet taste is not at all oniony. This pretty salmon and leek dish bakes in the oven in under 30 minutes. Halibut, shark or cod steaks can also be used. Serve with a side dish of aromatic rice, such as American basmati.

3 medium leeks (½ pound each), roots and green tops trimmed, washed thoroughly, cut into thin (¼ inch) slices (about 4 cups)

2 tablespoons water

1 tablespoon extra-virgin olive oil

2 teaspoons snipped fresh dill or parsley

1 teaspoon finely shredded or grated lemon zest

4 salmon steaks, ½-¾ inch thick (about ½ pound each)
Salt and freshly ground black pepper, to taste

2 tablespoons fresh lemon juice

4 lemon wedges, for garnish
Sprigs of fresh dill, for garnish (optional)

1. Preheat the oven to 425 degrees F. Place the leeks, water, oil, dill or parsley and lemon zest in a 13-x-9-inch shallow baking dish; stir to combine. Cover tightly with foil.

2. Bake for 20 minutes, stirring once halfway through the cooking. Remove the baking dish from the oven. Push the leeks aside and arrange the salmon steaks in the baking dish. Spoon the leeks on top of the salmon, dividing evenly. Add salt, pepper and lemon juice.

3. Return to the oven and bake, uncovered, until the salmon looks opaque along the center bone when checked with the tip of a knife, 10 to 12 minutes.

4. Remove from the oven and let stand for 5 minutes. Garnish with lemon wedges and dill, if using, and serve.

Oven-Roasted Halibut with Herb Citrus Vinaigrette

PREPARATION TIME: 15 MINUTES ✸ COOKING TIME: 10 TO 12 MINUTES ✸ SERVES: 4

THIS RECIPE DEMONSTRATES the quick, foolproof method of roasting thick cuts of fish in a very hot oven (450-degree) for 10 minutes per inch. Then the fish is "dressed" with a piquant mixture of lemon juice, fresh herbs, grated lemon and orange zest and bits of sun-dried tomato. For a change, add a few capers and vary the fresh herbs to taste. This preparation can also be used for salmon, cod or swordfish. (See photograph, page 87.)

4   pieces halibut steak or thick
      portion of fillet, ¾ inch thick
      (about 6 ounces each)
      Salt and freshly ground black
      pepper, to taste

HERB CITRUS VINAIGRETTE

¼   cup extra-virgin olive oil
3   tablespoons fresh lemon juice
2   tablespoons ice water
½   teaspoon grated lemon zest
½   teaspoon grated orange zest
1   small garlic clove, crushed through
      a press
1   tablespoon minced sun-dried
      tomato (packed in oil or dry and
      reconstituted in boiling water
      for 5 minutes)
1   tablespoon chopped fresh basil
1   tablespoon chopped fresh Italian
      (flat-leaf) parsley
1   tablespoon chopped fresh dill
1   teaspoon fresh thyme leaves,
      stripped from the stems
      Salt and freshly ground black
      pepper, to taste

4   very thin slices of lemon, for garnish
      (optional)
      Herb sprigs, for garnish (optional)

1. Preheat the oven to 450 degrees F. Arrange the fish in a large baking pan. Sprinkle with salt and pepper. Bake just until the center turns from translucent to opaque, 10 to 12 minutes.

2. Meanwhile, Make the Herb Citrus Vinaigrette: Whisk together the oil, lemon juice, water, lemon and orange zests and garlic. Stir in the sun-dried tomato, basil, parsley, dill and thyme; add salt and pepper.

3. Transfer the fish to a platter or individual serving plates and spoon the vinaigrette on top. Serve hot, warm or at room temperature, garnished with lemon slices and herb sprigs, if using.

FAST MARINADES

MARINADES ADD MOISTURE, JUICINESS AND FLAVOR TO FISH. The optimum marinating time is about 1 hour, but if you find yourself rushed, adjust it to fit your schedule.

Grilled Cumin-Marinated Swordfish

PREPARATION TIME: 10 MINUTES ❋ MARINATING TIME: 30 MINUTES OR LONGER

COOKING TIME: 10 TO 12 MINUTES ❋ SERVES: 4

SWORDFISH IS A RICH FISH, making it particularly suitable for the robust flavors of ground cumin and fresh herbs. I like to serve it with Yellow Confetti Rice Salad (page 224) or Couscous with Confetti Vegetables (page 225) and small purple eggplants that I halve lengthwise, brush with olive oil and grill with the fish.

> **PLAN AHEAD:**
>
> Allow at least 30 minutes for the fish to marinate.

5   tablespoons fresh lime juice (from 2 limes)

3   tablespoons extra-virgin olive oil

1   teaspoon ground cumin

1   garlic clove, crushed through a press

¼   red or sweet yellow onion, cut into thin vertical slices

¼   cup coarsely chopped fresh cilantro or basil, plus sprigs for optional garnish

1   tablespoon fresh oregano leaves or ½ teaspoon dried, plus sprigs for optional garnish

1   teaspoon fresh thyme leaves, stripped from the stems, or

¼   teaspoon dried, plus sprigs for optional garnish

½   teaspoon salt

     Freshly ground black pepper,

4   swordfish steaks, about ¾ inch thick (about ½ pound each), or other fish

     Lime wedges, for garnish

1. Combine the lime juice, oil, cumin, garlic, onion, cilantro or basil, oregano, thyme, salt and pepper in a pie plate or other deep platter; stir to blend. Add the fish to the marinade; turn to coat. Cover and marinate for 30 minutes or longer in the refrigerator.

2. Preheat the grill or broiler. Grill or broil the fish steaks about 3 inches from the heat source until lightly browned on one side, 5 to 7 minutes, depending on the intensity of the heat. Turn and grill or broil on the other side for 5 minutes. Check for doneness by cutting into the thickest part of the fish with the tip of a knife. The fish is done when it changes color from translucent to opaque.

3. Arrange the fish on a platter. Garnish with the lime wedges and sprigs of cilantro or basil, oregano and thyme, if using.

Swordfish Marinated in Lemon, Rosemary and Garlic

PREPARATION TIME: 5 MINUTES ❋ MARINATING TIME: 1 HOUR OR MORE
COOKING TIME: 10 TO 16 MINUTES ❋ SERVES: 4

SIMPLE YET SHARP FLAVORS like citrus, capers, garlic and fresh herbs cut through and complement the richness of swordfish. This combination of lemon, rosemary and capers is one of my favorites.

4   strips (½ x 3 inches) lemon zest
      (removed with a vegetable peeler)
2   tablespoons extra-virgin olive oil
1   tablespoon snipped fresh rosemary
      leaves or 1 teaspoon dried
1   garlic clove, crushed through a press
4   swordfish steaks, ¾ inch thick
      (about ½ pound each)
      Salt and freshly ground black
      pepper, to taste
1   tablespoon capers, rinsed and
      drained
      Lemon wedges, for garnish

1. Combine the lemon zest, oil, rosemary and garlic on a large, shallow platter or a tray large enough to hold the swordfish steaks in a single layer. Add the swordfish, sprinkle with salt and pepper and turn to coat with the marinade.

Cover and marinate in the refrigerator for 1 to 2 hours.

2. Brush the grill or broiler pan with a thin film of oil. Just before serving time, preheat the grill or broiler.

> ### PLAN AHEAD:
> Allow 1 to 2 hours for the swordfish to marinate.

3. Transfer the swordfish to the grill or broiler pan; reserve the marinade left on the platter. If broiling, adjust the oven rack so that the tops of the swordfish are about 3 inches from the heat source. Grill or broil the swordfish until lightly browned, 5 to 8 minutes, depending on the intensity of the heat. Using a spatula, carefully turn each steak. Spoon any marinade and pieces of lemon zest and rosemary onto the tops of the steaks. Broil until lightly browned and the center of the fish is opaque when tested with the tip of a knife, about 5 to 8 minutes.

4. Serve garnished with the capers and lemon wedges.

Mako Shark with Provençal Marinade

PREPARATION TIME: **10 MINUTES** ● MARINATING TIME: **1 HOUR OR MORE**

COOKING TIME: **10 TO 16 MINUTES** ● SERVES: **6**

SEAFOOD, THYME, ROSEMARY and basil, oranges, olives and their oil and garlic unite forces in this grilled dish. I assemble the fish and seasonings early in the day and forget about dinner until the fire is ready. Shark is often an economical choice for a crowd of people, but I have also used this marinade on salmon, halibut and swordfish. The fish can be grilled, broiled or baked.

PLAN AHEAD:

Allow 1 hour or longer for the fish to marinate.

3 tablespoons extra-virgin olive oil

2 strips (½ x 2 inches) orange zest, cut into thin lengthwise strips

2 garlic cloves, crushed through a press

1 tablespoon fresh thyme leaves, stripped from the stems, plus sprigs for garnish

1 teaspoon fresh rosemary leaves, snipped small, plus sprigs for garnish

Salt and freshly ground black pepper, to taste

6 mako shark or other fish steaks (6-8 ounces each)

1 firm, ripe tomato, cored and diced

10 Kalamata or other brine-cured black olives, pits removed, coarsely chopped

4 large basil leaves, stacked, rolled tightly from the stem ends, cut into thin strips

2 thick (¼ inch) orange slices, halved

1. Combine 2 tablespoons of the oil, orange zest, garlic, thyme, rosemary, salt and pepper in a large dish; stir to blend. Arrange the fish in a single layer on the dish, and turn to coat with the marinade. Cover and refrigerate for 1 hour or longer before cooking.

2. Preheat the grill or broiler or preheat the oven to 450 degrees F.

3. Lift the fish from the marinade (save the marinade) and grill or broil 3 inches from the heat source until lightly browned on one side, 5 to 8 minutes. Turn the fish and spoon a little marinade on top of each steak. Grill or broil until the center looks opaque when checked with the tip of a knife, 5 to 8 minutes, depending on the intensity of the heat. (To bake, place the fish on a large nonstick baking sheet with sides and arrange the steaks so they do not touch. Spoon some of the seasonings in the marinade onto the fish. Bake for 10 to 12 minutes, or until the center of the fish looks opaque when checked with the tip of a small knife.)

4. Meanwhile, combine the tomato, remaining 1 tablespoon oil, olives and basil in a small bowl. Arrange the cooked fish on a serving platter and sprinkle with the tomato mixture. Garnish the platter with the orange slices.

Foil-Poached Salmon Fillets with Warm Tomato Salad

PREPARATION TIME: 15 MINUTES ❁ COOKING TIME: 11 TO 15 MINUTES ❁ SERVES: 4

EN PAPILLOTE is a French culinary term for foods cooked in a paper package, usually parchment paper. Here, I simplify the technique by using a strip of aluminum foil, since parchment is often available only in specialty stores.

Traditionally, a folded piece of parchment is cut into a half-heart shape that, when unfolded, resembles a butterfly (*papillon* in French). The food is sealed in the package with tight double folds. As it cooks, the package puffs as it fills with steam, making for a dramatic presentation.

This is an excellent technique for those on a low-fat diet. Prepare it in the summer, when tomatoes and basil are at their best. Cook the packages directly on a hot grill, just as you would plain fish steaks or meats.

You can vary the fresh herbs used on top of the fish, depending on what is available. Fresh basil, thyme, cilantro, dill and whatever else is in the garden or at the market will be equally tasty. For variety, substitute firm white fish fillets (flounder or sole) for the salmon.

2 medium tomatoes, cored and cut into thin wedges (about 2 cups)

2 tablespoons thin lengthwise slices red onion

2 tablespoons extra-virgin olive oil

2 tablespoons julienned fresh basil

1 tablespoon *each* chopped fresh dill and mint

1 garlic clove, crushed through a press
Salt and freshly ground black pepper, to taste

4 boneless, skinless salmon fillets (6 ounces each)

1. Preheat the grill, or if you prefer to bake the fish, preheat the oven to 450 degrees F. Combine the tomatoes, onion, oil, basil, dill, mint, garlic, salt and pepper in a bowl; toss to blend.

2. Cut 4 large pieces of foil. Place 1 salmon fillet in the center of each. Sprinkle with salt and pepper. Top with the tomato mixture, dividing evenly. Fold up the edges of the foil to make 4 individually sealed packages, double-folding all the edges so the juices cannot escape.

3. Place the foil packets, folded side up, on a preheated grill. Grill until the fish is cooked through and the tomato salad is warm, about 12 minutes, depending on the intensity of the heat. Or place the foil packets on a baking sheet in the oven for 12 minutes. (Thinner fillets will take 11 to 12 minutes; thicker fillets will take 13 to 15 minutes.)

4. Open the packets, and using a spatula, transfer the fillets to individual serving plates. Spoon the juices in the foil over the fish and serve.

Baked Fish Fillets with Herb and Citrus Topping

PREPARATION TIME: 10 MINUTES ❋ COOKING TIME: 10 MINUTES ❋ SERVES: 4

WHEN I WANT A LIGHT, quick meal, I usually have fish. For this recipe, I like flounder, cod, orange roughy or turbot, to name just a few. A 6-ounce portion is a fairly modest serving; increase the number of fillets to match the appetite of the diners. Sometimes, I take culinary license and add fresh basil or mint to the finely chopped seasonings.

- 4   firm white fish fillets
       (about 6 ounces each)
- 1   tablespoon extra-virgin olive oil
       Salt and freshly ground black
          pepper, to taste
- ¼   cup packed fresh Italian (flat-leaf)
          parsley leaves
- 1   garlic clove, chopped
- 1   tablespoon chopped lemon zest
          (or orange zest, if preferred)

1. Preheat the oven to 450 degrees F. Arrange the fish in a large baking dish. Drizzle with the oil; sprinkle with salt and pepper.

2. Finely chop the parsley, garlic and lemon (or orange) zest together in a food processor or with a chef's knife. Sprinkle evenly over the fish.

3. Bake until the fish has turned from translucent to opaque in the center when tested with the tip of a knife, about 10 minutes. Serve at once.

Tomato-and-Herb-Topped Fish Fillets Roasted with Potatoes

PREPARATION TIME: 15 MINUTES ❁ COOKING TIME: 45 MINUTES ❁ SERVES: 4

USE ANY FIRM-FLESHED BONELESS, skinless fish fillet for this dish. Varieties like cod, orange roughy or even flounder work well. Any potato type is fine here, but to save peeling time, use red-skinned new potatoes or thin-skinned russets.

Serve this fish with a green salad on the side and a dish of fruit for dessert, and you'll have a simple, satisfying meal.

1½ pounds large red-skinned new potatoes or thin-skinned russet potatoes, cut into ¼-inch-thick slices (about 4 cups)

2 tablespoons extra-virgin olive oil Salt and freshly ground black pepper, to taste

½ cup diced firm, ripe tomatoes

1 tablespoon snipped fresh Italian (flat-leaf) parsley

1 tablespoon chopped pitted Kalamata or other brine-cured black olives

1 teaspoon rinsed dried small capers

1 teaspoon finely chopped garlic

4 firm white fish fillets (cod, tilefish, orange roughy or flounder), about 6 ounces each

1. Preheat the oven to 400 degrees F. In a large bowl, combine the potato slices, oil and salt and pepper. Toss to blend. Spread on a nonstick baking sheet with sides. Roast until the potatoes are browned on one side, about 35 minutes.

2. Meanwhile, in a small bowl, combine the tomatoes, parsley, olives, capers and garlic. When the potatoes are browned, remove the pan from the oven and carefully turn the potatoes over; increase the oven temperature to 450 degrees. Place the fish fillets on top of the potatoes. Sprinkle lightly with pepper. Top each fish fillet with some of the tomato mixture, dividing evenly.

3. Roast the potatoes and fish until the fish is opaque in the center when checked with the tip of a knife, about 10 minutes. Use a spatula to scoop up crusty potatoes topped with a fish fillet for each serving.

Rosemary Roasted Potatoes with Cod and Asparagus

PREPARATION TIME: 15 MINUTES ❂ COOKING TIME: ABOUT 50 MINUTES ❂ SERVES: 4

CRISP OVEN-BROWNED POTATO slices are a family favorite. Here, I add thick fillets of cod and slender asparagus spears. By carefully timing the potatoes and adding the faster-cooking fish and asparagus during the last 12 to 15 minutes, the entire dish—potatoes, fish and vegetables—emerges from the oven simultaneously and perfectly cooked.

4 large all-purpose potatoes (about 1¾ pounds), peeled, cut into ¼-inch-thick slices

2 tablespoons extra-virgin olive oil

1 teaspoon snipped fresh rosemary or ½ teaspoon dried

1 garlic clove, crushed through a press

4 skinless cod fillets (or other firm white fish, such as flounder, orange roughy or sole), about 6 ounces each

1 bunch (about ¾ pound) slender asparagus spears, rinsed and trimmed

Salt and freshly ground black pepper, to taste

1. Preheat the oven to 400 degrees F. In a large bowl, combine the potato slices, 1 tablespoon of the oil and half of the rosemary. Toss to blend. Arrange in a single layer on a large jelly-roll or other baking pan. Roast until the potatoes are browned on the bottom, about 35 minutes. Remove from the oven and increase the oven temperature to 450 degrees.

2. Meanwhile, combine the remaining 1 tablespoon oil, the remaining rosemary and the garlic. Spread on the surface of the cod fillets. Arrange the fillets on top of the partially roasted potatoes and place the asparagus between the fillets. Sprinkle everything with salt and pepper.

3. Return the pan to the oven and roast until the fish looks opaque in the center when checked with the tip of a knife and the asparagus spears are crisp-tender, 12 to 15 minutes, depending on the thickness of the fish. Use a wide spatula to serve browned potatoes and a portion of fish for each person. Distribute the asparagus evenly.

Cod with Roasted Tomato Sauce and Black Olives

PREPARATION TIME: 15 MINUTES ● COOKING TIME: 35 TO 40 MINUTES ● SERVES: 4

PREPARE THIS DISH WHEN JUICY, vine-ripened tomatoes are available. It is also good with thin wedges of red bell pepper. Fresh herbs are best, but use rosemary with a light hand, for it has a very pungent taste.

3-4 large ripe tomatoes, cut into
thin wedges (3 cups)

1 large sweet onion, cut into
thin wedges

1 strip (½ x 2 inches) orange zest,
cut into thin slivers

2 tablespoons extra-virgin olive oil

1 garlic clove, crushed through a press

2 teaspoons fresh thyme leaves,
stripped from the stems,
or ½ teaspoon dried

1 teaspoon snipped fresh rosemary
leaves or ½ teaspoon dried
Salt and freshly ground black
pepper, to taste

4 firm white fish fillets (cod or
flounder), about 6 ounces each

2 tablespoons coarsely chopped pitted
Kalamata or other brine-cured
black olives

1. Preheat the oven to 400 degrees F. Combine the tomatoes, onion, orange zest, oil, garlic, thyme and rosemary in a shallow baking dish. Season with salt and pepper. Bake until the vegetables begin to brown around the edges, about 25 minutes.

2. Tuck the fish fillets into the sauce; sprinkle with salt and pepper. Spoon some tomatoes over the fish. Increase the oven temperature to 450 degrees and bake until the fish is cooked through and looks opaque in the center when checked with the tip of a knife, 10 to 12 minutes.

3. Sprinkle with the olives and serve.

SOFT-SHELL CRABS

Now that fresh food from the southern hemisphere is so common in our markets, the concept of seasonality is almost a thing of the past. But there are still a few "sacred" seasonal foods left, and one of my favorites is soft-shell crabs.

All crabs go through a natural process of shedding their hard shells in early summer. When they emerge from their discarded shells, their coverings are soft and just right for eating. In June, the first meaty and succulent soft-shell crabs of the season appear in my fish market. Then, as the prices begin a steady decline, my husband and I start planning our annual soft-shell crab feast.

I love crabs breaded with cracker meal, then fried until crisp and crunchy on the outside and moist, meaty and lush on the inside (for the recipe, see page 78).

Buy the crabs live and ask the fish merchant to clean them. Or if you are cleaning them yourself, turn them over and pull off the "apron," or loose flap, on the underside. Then flip them right side up, and lift the loose flaps on either side to remove the spongy gills. If the crabs are large, two per serving should be enough.

We always serve crabs with an assortment of salads. Yellow Confetti Rice Salad (page 224) or potato salad and Green Beans with Basil and Mint (page 241) or a cabbage salad (pages 216 or 217) make light accompaniments to this rich seafood.

Pan-Seared Scallops with Pesto and Salsa

PREPARATION TIME: 20 MINUTES ● COOKING TIME: 2 TO 4 MINUTES ● SERVES: 4

SCALLOPS COOK QUICKLY, so watch them carefully. Here, they are placed on a bed of pesto sauce and garnished with a speedily made salsa. Yellow Confetti Rice Salad (page 224) is a pretty side dish.

PESTO SAUCE

- 2 cups lightly packed fresh basil leaves
- 2 tablespoons pignoli (pine nuts) or walnuts, toasted in a skillet
- 1 garlic clove, coarsely chopped
- ½ teaspoon salt
- ⅓ cup extra-virgin olive oil

SALSA

- 1 cup chopped seeded tomato, drained
- 2 tablespoons minced sweet onion
- 1 tablespoon chopped fresh mint
- 1 teaspoon fresh lime juice
- 1 teaspoon extra-virgin olive oil
  Pinch salt

SCALLOPS

  Extra-virgin olive oil
- 12-16 large sea scallops
  Salt and freshly ground black pepper, to taste
- ¼ cup dry vermouth

1. **Make the Pesto:** Combine the basil, nuts, garlic and salt in a food processor and finely chop. With the motor running, add the oil gradually through the feed tube until the mixture forms a thick sauce. Transfer to a bowl.

2. **Make the Salsa:** Combine the tomato, onion, mint, lime juice, oil and salt. Set aside.

3. **Prepare the Scallops:** Just before serving, cook the scallops. Heat a large nonstick skillet over high heat until hot enough to evaporate a drop of water upon contact. Add a thin film of oil. Add the scallops, a few at a time. Cook until golden brown on one side, about 1 minute. Turn and cook the other side until the scallops are golden on the outside and opaque in the center, about 1 minute. Transfer to a side dish as they cook. Sprinkle with salt and pepper.

4. Add the vermouth and any accumulated juices from the dish of cooked scallops to the hot pan, and boil until reduced to about 2 tablespoons, about 2 minutes. Stir into the pesto sauce.

5. To serve, spoon a bed of pesto sauce on each plate. Arrange the scallops in a circle on top of the sauce. Top each scallop with a tiny mound of salsa, or if preferred, spoon the salsa into the center of the circle of scallops.

Baked Scallops with Bacon, Sautéed Apples and Cider Sauce

PREPARATION TIME: 15 MINUTES ❈ COOKING TIME: 15 MINUTES ❈ SERVES: 4

THE SCALLOP IS ONE OF NATURE'S most precious gifts to the world of convenience foods. Portions are already allotted, so the cook need only briefly sear the scallops and season to taste for dinner to be ready.

I first sampled a version of this dish years ago when visiting Brussels. The scallops are browned with bacon in the oven and served with sautéed apples and cider sauce. The delicate and somewhat sweet taste of the scallops and their soft texture are perfectly complemented by the tang and texture of the apples. I use Golden Delicious, because they don't need to be peeled and they hold their shape when cooked. The smoky taste of the bacon adds just the right counterpoint to the other ingredients. You will want to serve this dish from the kitchen on individual plates that have been kept warm on the back of the stove. Serve with Smothered Spinach (page 285) and Simple Pilaf (page 165).

4 thin slices bacon, quartered crosswise
12-16 large sea scallops (about 1 pound total)
2 tablespoons unsalted butter
2 large Golden Delicious apples, each cored, cut into 8 wedges
Pinch sugar
½ cup apple cider or apple juice
1 tablespoon fresh lemon juice
Salt and freshly ground black pepper, to taste

1. Preheat the oven to 450 degrees F.

2. Sauté the bacon in a large skillet over medium-low heat just until it renders its fat, about 4 minutes; do not brown. Transfer to a piece of paper towel and drain. Discard the bacon fat and wipe out the skillet.

3. Lightly butter a medium baking dish and arrange the scallops in a single layer, leaving space between them, then place the bacon on top of the scallops. (If the scallops are small, arrange in clusters of two or three, and place a piece of bacon over each cluster.)

4. Bake just until the bacon browns and the scallops are cooked, 10 to 12 minutes for large scallops and 8 to 10 minutes for small scallops.

5. Meanwhile, heat the butter in the skillet until melted. Add the apple wedges, and sprinkle with the sugar. Sauté over medium heat, stirring and turning, until the apples are golden, about 5 minutes.

6. When the scallops are cooked, remove from the oven and spoon off the juices (you will have 1 to 3 tablespoons). Add the juices to the apples, along with the cider or apple juice and lemon juice. Heat, stirring gently, over high heat until the juices boil and coat the apples, 3 to 4 minutes.

7. Place the bacon-topped scallops on each of 4 dinner plates, dividing evenly. Arrange 4 apples slices in a fan design on each plate. Spoon the skillet juices over the scallops. Season with salt and pepper and serve.

Grilled Sea Scallop Brochettes, Greek Style

PREPARATION TIME: **10** MINUTES ● COOKING TIME: **5 TO 10** MINUTES ● SERVES: **4**

IN THE FALL, I CAN USUALLY FIND large, sparkling scallops in my seafood market. They should be translucent in appearance and have a briny aroma. Scallops are quite perishable, so make sure you cook them a day or two after you purchase them. Serve with a rice salad or couscous. (See photograph, page 35.)

> **PLAN AHEAD:**
>
> If you use wooden skewers, allow 1 hour to soak them.

12-16	large sea scallops
3	tablespoons extra-virgin olive oil
1	garlic clove, crushed through a press
1	tablespoon fresh oregano leaves, stripped from the stems, chopped
	Salt and freshly ground black pepper, to taste
1	lemon, halved lengthwise, cut into ¼-inch-thick slices
4	California bay leaves, broken in half crosswise

1. If using wooden skewers, soak 4 skewers in water for about 1 hour before preparing brochettes. Combine the scallops, oil, garlic, oregano, salt and pepper in a large bowl and toss to coat. Preheat the grill.

2. Brush the grill with a thin film of oil. Thread each skewer with 3 or 4 scallops, alternating them with 3 or 4 half-slices of lemon and 2 pieces of bay leaf.

3. Grill on a hot grill just until the scallops look opaque, 5 to 10 minutes total cooking time, depending on the intensity of the heat.

4. Serve hot.

Shrimp with Tomatoes, Spinach and Basil

PREPARATION TIME: 15 MINUTES ❀ COOKING TIME: ABOUT 10 MINUTES ❀ SERVES: 4

THE PREPARATION TIME for this dish is short, but the pace is quick. First, I put some rice on to simmer on the back of the stove, then I move to the sink and quickly shell the shrimp. I rinse the spinach and trim off the stems. Next, I warm the garlic in the oil, add wine and, when it boils, stir in the shrimp and tomatoes. Within 25 minutes—albeit busy ones—dinner is ready.

Using extra-large shrimp shortens the time spent peeling and adds to the aesthetic appeal of this simple dish. Serve with Parmesan Rice (page 167).

1. Combine the oil and the garlic in a large, deep skillet with a lid. Cook over low heat just until the garlic begins to sizzle, about 1 minute. Add the wine and boil, uncovered, until reduced by half, about 3 minutes.

2. Stir in the shrimp and the tomatoes. Cook, stirring, over medium heat just until the shrimp are cooked through, about 3 minutes. Season with salt and pepper. Add the spinach and basil; stir once. Cover and cook until the spinach is wilted, about 2 minutes. Uncover; stir and serve immediately.

3 tablespoons extra-virgin olive oil

2 garlic cloves, crushed through
   a press

½ cup dry white wine

1 pound extra-large shrimp (20-24),
   shelled with tails left intact,
   deveined

⅓ cup diced, drained canned plum
   tomatoes or diced ripe tomato
   Salt and freshly ground black
   pepper, to taste

1 package (10 ounces) fresh spinach,
   rinsed, long stems trimmed

¼ cup torn fresh basil leaves

Spicy Marinated Shrimp

PREPARATION TIME: 10 MINUTES ❖ MARINATING TIME: 15 MINUTES OR MORE

COOKING TIME: 4 MINUTES ❖ SERVES: 4

SERVE THESE SIMPLY DELICIOUS shrimp with Yellow Confetti Rice Salad (page 224) or Sesame Brown Rice Salad with Peanuts (page 223) or over Cabbage Salad with Lemon and Olive Oil (page 216) as a main dish. (See photograph, page 83.)

PLAN AHEAD:

Allow at least 15 minutes, or ideally up to 2 hours, for the shrimp to marinate

1 tablespoon extra-virgin olive oil

2 garlic cloves, crushed through a press

½ teaspoon hot red pepper flakes

1 teaspoon grated peeled fresh ginger

¼ teaspoon salt

⅛ teaspoon freshly ground black pepper

1 pound jumbo shrimp (about 16), peeled, deveined

1 tablespoon finely chopped fresh parsley, basil or cilantro

Lemon or lime wedges, for garnish

1. Combine the oil, garlic, red pepper flakes, ginger, salt and pepper on a large platter. Stir to blend. Add the shrimp, turning and patting with the marinade. Cover with plastic and let stand at room temperature for 15 minutes. Or, if there is time, refrigerate for up to 2 hours.

2. Heat a large nonstick skillet over medium-high heat until hot enough to evaporate a drop of water upon contact. Add the shrimp, a few at a time, and quickly sear on both sides, about 2 minutes per side, or until cooked through.

3. Sprinkle with the chopped herb and serve, garnished with lemon or lime wedges.

Mussels in Tomato-Herb Broth

PREPARATION TIME: **10 MINUTES** ❋ COOKING TIME: **35 MINUTES** ❋ SERVES: **4**

INSPIRED BY THE FLAVORS of the classic Provençal fish stew, bouillabaisse, I like to experiment with making light but satisfying main-dish seafood soups. Mussels, which are both plentiful and inexpensive, make a wonderful soup on their own. You might want to place a Crostini (page 24) that has been spread with Roasted Garlic Puree (page 27) in the soup bowl before adding the mussels and broth. If not, serve with plenty of crusty bread to sop up the delicious juices. To save time, pull the beards from the mussels while simmering the tomato mixture.

4   pounds mussels, thoroughly washed and rinsed, beards pulled from the shells (see page 163)
¼   cup extra-virgin olive oil
1   large yellow onion, cut into thin wedges
2   garlic cloves, bruised with the side of a knife
1   strip (½ x 2 inches) orange zest
1   sprig fresh basil or fresh Italian (flat-leaf) parsley
1   sprig fresh thyme or a pinch of dried
1   cup dry white wine
2   cans (14½ ounces each) Italian plum tomatoes with juice

1. Place the mussels in a shallow pan, cover with a damp paper towel and refrigerate until ready to use.

2. In a large, wide saucepan or a deep skillet, combine the oil, onion and garlic. Cook, stirring, over low heat until the onion is tender and golden, about 10 minutes. Do not brown. Add the orange zest, basil or parsley, thyme and wine. Heat to boiling and boil, uncovered, for about 2 minutes. Add the tomatoes with their juices, cover and simmer the mixture for 15 minutes to blend the flavors.

3. Add the mussels to the simmering tomato mixture. Cover and cook over medium to medium-high heat until the mussels open, about 5 minutes. Remove the opened mussels and continue boiling any unopened mussels for 1 to 2 minutes longer. Discard any mussels that do not open.

4. To serve, divide the mussels evenly among 4 large, broad soup bowls and ladle the juice on top.

Mussels in White Wine with Fresh Tomato Salsa

PREPARATION TIME: 20 MINUTES ● COOKING TIME: 10 TO 12 MINUTES

SERVES: 2 AS A MAIN COURSE, 4 AS AN APPETIZER

PLUMP, SWEET MUSSELS served in their ebony-black shells make a striking presentation when topped with a vibrant fresh tomato salsa.

This is delicious any time of the year as a main dish with lots of crusty bread. But I have also made it ahead and served it chilled as an appetizer in the heat of summer. To do this, pull off and discard the top half of the cooked mussel shell. Arrange the mussels, still in the bottom half of their shells, on a large platter. Spoon some of the strained broth over each mussel, and top with a little of the salsa. Cover and refrigerate until well chilled, at least 2 hours. Just before serving, garnish the platter with sprigs of parsley, basil, cilantro or other herbs. Serve as a finger food or with a plate and fork. Prepared either way, the mussels are perfectly complemented by a glass of well-chilled dry white wine. (See photograph, page 84.)

4 pounds mussels, thoroughly washed and rinsed, beards pulled from the shells

TOMATO SALSA

2 cups diced (¼ inch) cored ripe tomatoes (2-3 large)

1 tablespoon chopped fresh basil

1 tablespoon chopped red onion

½ teaspoon grated orange zest

1 tablespoon extra-virgin olive oil

1 teaspoon fresh lemon juice

¼ teaspoon salt
  Coarsely ground black pepper

BROTH

2 cups dry white wine

1 sprig fresh basil or parsley

1 sprig fresh thyme, or a pinch of dried

1 bay leaf

1 strip (½ x 2 inches) orange zest

1 garlic clove, bruised with the side of a knife

½ cup thin onion slices (1 medium)
  Salt and freshly ground black pepper, to taste

1. Place the mussels in a shallow pan, cover with a damp paper towel and refrigerate until ready to cook.

2. Make the Tomato Salsa: Combine the tomatoes, basil, onion, orange zest, oil, lemon juice, salt and pepper in a small bowl. Set aside until ready to serve.

3. Make the Broth: Combine the wine, basil or parsley, thyme, bay leaf, orange zest, garlic and onion in a large, wide saucepan or a deep skillet with a tight-fitting lid. Heat to boiling and boil, uncovered, for 5 minutes. Add the mussels; cover and cook over high heat until the mussels have opened, about 5 minutes. Remove the opened mussels and continue boiling any unopened mussels for 1 to 2 minutes longer. Discard any mussels that do not open.

4. Using tongs, transfer the mussels to a large serving bowl. Strain the broth into a bowl; add salt and pepper to taste and pour over the mussels. Spoon the tomato salsa over the top. Serve hot.

HANDLING CLAMS AND MUSSELS

BUY CLAMS AND MUSSELS THAT ARE TIGHTLY CLOSED. Mussels are sometimes slightly open, but when tapped roughly with a fingertip, they should close tightly.

Do not refrigerate clams or mussels in a plastic bag. As soon as you get them home, rinse them with cold water, drain them well and arrange them in a shallow pan or on a platter; cover lightly with a dampened cloth or paper towel. Store in the coldest part of the refrigerator, and use within 48 hours.

Scrub the shellfish with a stiff brush, and rinse several times in clean, cold tap water. Do not let them sit in cold water.

The strawlike filament protruding from the mussel is called the beard. Grasp the strands between your fingers, and pull off the beard. Removing the beard is easier if you protect your fingers with a small cloth; the tip of a dishcloth can be used.

GRAINS AND BEANS

Simple Pilaf

PREPARATION TIME: 5 MINUTES ❈ COOKING TIME: 20 MINUTES

STANDING TIME: 5 MINUTES ❈ SERVES: 4

PILAF IS A WONDERFUL WAY to jazz up a pot of plain cooked rice. For a simple version, start with raw rice (a long-grain aromatic one like basmati is excellent), butter or oil, chopped onion and perhaps some garlic. Cook the onion in the butter or oil until golden, then add garlic or spices and herbs. This pilaf is topped with walnuts, but toasted pignoli (pine nuts) are also delicious. It is very easy to make and goes with just about anything. Serve with grilled shrimp, broiled lamb or roasted chicken.

2   tablespoons unsalted butter
     or extra-virgin olive oil
½   cup chopped onion
1   cup long-grain white basmati rice
1¾ cups water or reduced-sodium
     canned chicken broth
1   teaspoon salt, or as needed
¼   cup broken walnuts

1. Heat the butter or oil in a large, wide saucepan. Add the onion and sauté, stirring, over medium-low heat until golden, about 5 minutes. Add the rice and sauté, stirring, until coated with oil and heated through, about 2 minutes.

2. Stir in the water or broth and salt, if necessary. Heat to boiling over high heat. Stir once thoroughly. Cover and cook over medium-low heat until the water is absorbed and the rice is tender, about 15 minutes.

3. Let stand off the heat, covered, for 5 minutes before serving. Meanwhile, heat the walnuts in a dry skillet, stirring constantly, until fragrant, about 2 minutes. Spoon the rice into a dish, sprinkle with the walnuts and serve.

Rice Pilaf with Currants, Garlic and Toasted Walnuts

PREPARATION TIME: 5 MINUTES ● COOKING TIME: 18 MINUTES

STANDING TIME: 5 MINUTES ● SERVES: 4

BASMATI, A LONG-GRAIN RICE that cooks dry and separate, makes a terrific pilaf. It is available in some stores imported from India and Pakistan, and a new hybrid called Texmati can be found in most supermarkets.

Pilaf is a versatile dish. Onions, carrots or celery are sautéed along with garlic and spices like saffron, curry or cumin and/or dried fruits such as currants, raisins, apricots or cherries are added. If bits of cooked meat or shrimp are stirred in, the pilaf becomes a main dish rather than a side. This is a straightforward but flavorful version with garlic, dried currants and walnuts.

1	tablespoon extra-virgin olive oil
1	garlic clove, crushed through a press
1½	cups long-grain white basmati rice
2	tablespoons dried currants or raisins
2¾	cups water or half water and half reduced-sodium canned chicken broth
½	teaspoon salt
¼	cup broken walnuts

1. In a large, wide saucepan, heat the oil and garlic over low heat until the garlic begins to sizzle, about 2 minutes. Stir in the rice and currants. Heat, stirring, until the rice begins to change color, about 1 minute. Add the water and/or broth and salt. Bring to a boil, stirring once thoroughly.

2. Cook, covered, over low heat until the water is absorbed and the rice is tender, about 18 minutes. Do not stir or uncover during cooking. Let stand, uncovered, for 5 minutes.

3. Meanwhile, place the walnuts in a small nonstick skillet. Heat over medium heat, stirring, until the walnuts are toasted and fragrant, about 3 minutes. Sprinkle over the pilaf and serve.

Parmesan Rice

PREPARATION TIME: 5 MINUTES ✻ COOKING TIME: 20 MINUTES ✻ SERVES: 4

MAKE THIS RECIPE when you want the taste of risotto but don't have an extra hand for stirring. Use regular long-grain white rice or a domestically grown medium-grain or imported rice, such as Arborio. My friend Gloria Spitz gave me this recipe. A family favorite, it is affectionately called "Cheesy Rice."

2 tablespoons unsalted butter or extra-virgin olive oil

1 cup long- or medium-grain white rice

2 cups water

½ teaspoon salt

2 tablespoons grated Parmigiano-Reggiano, or more to taste

1. Heat 1 tablespoon of the butter or oil in a large, wide saucepan or a deep skillet with a tight-fitting lid. Stir in the rice to coat it with the butter or oil. Add the water and the salt. Heat to boiling; stir thoroughly. Cover and cook over low heat until all the liquid is absorbed and the rice is tender, about 15 minutes.

2. Uncover and stir the cheese and the remaining 1 tablespoon butter or oil into the rice until the mixture is creamy. Serve immediately.

VARIATION

Parmesan Orzo: Omit the butter or oil, and cook 1½ cups orzo or other small pasta shape in boiling, salted water, partially covered, stirring frequently to prevent sticking. When the water returns to a boil, uncover and boil until tender, about 15 minutes. Toss with the cheese and 1 tablespoon finely chopped fresh parsley.

Sesame Brown Rice Pilaf with Garlic and Vegetables

PREPARATION TIME: 15 MINUTES ● COOKING TIME: 55 TO 60 MINUTES ● SERVES: 4 TO 6

THIS DISH, dotted with brightly colored pieces of vegetables and laced with toasted sesame seeds and sesame oil, makes an excellent one-pot vegetarian meal. First, put the rice on to cook. While the rice is cooking, prepare the vegetables. Vary the vegetables according to what looks good in the market, but be sure you cut hard vegetables like carrots into smaller pieces (or shred them, as I do) to ensure that they all cook in the same amount of time.

1	cup chopped onion
1	tablespoon extra-virgin olive oil
1½	cups brown basmati or other long-grain brown rice
4	garlic cloves, crushed through a press
3	cups water
1	teaspoon salt
1	cup *each* broccoli florets, cut green beans and diced yellow squash
½	cup coarsely shredded carrot
⅓	cup diced (¼ inch) red bell pepper
1	tablespoon hulled sesame seeds, toasted in a dry skillet
1	teaspoon dark sesame oil, or more to taste

1. Combine the onion and oil in a large, shallow saucepan or a deep skillet with a tight-fitting lid. Cook over low heat, stirring often, until the onion is golden, about 10 minutes. Stir in the rice and cook for 1 minute. Add the garlic, and cook, stirring, for 1 minute.

2. Add the water and heat to boiling. Add the salt, stir thoroughly, cover and cook for 35 to 40 minutes, or until almost all the liquid is absorbed. Do not stir.

3. Uncover the pot and while it is still on the heat, sprinkle the broccoli, green beans, squash, carrot and red bell pepper evenly over the surface of the rice. Cover and cook for 6 to 8 minutes, or until the vegetables are crisp-tender and the rice is cooked.

4. Sprinkle with the sesame seeds and drizzle with the sesame oil. Spoon into a serving dish and serve immediately.

FASTER BROWN RICE

Do you love brown rice but rarely cook it because it takes 45 to 55 minutes compared with 15 minutes for white rice? If you plan ahead, you can cook brown rice in almost half the time it normally takes.

Place 1 cup brown rice in 3 cups water in a medium saucepan, and refrigerate overnight. The next day, cook it in the soaking water (add salt to taste). It will become tender in just 20 to 25 minutes.

Barley and Wild Rice Pilaf with Sautéed Mushrooms

PREPARATION TIME: **10** MINUTES ◈ COOKING TIME: **55 TO 65** MINUTES ◈ SERVES: **6**

WILD RICE AND BARLEY need equally long cooking times, making this combination a natural.

1 cup chopped onion

2 garlic cloves, crushed through
   a press

1 tablespoon extra-virgin olive oil

½ cup barley

½ cup wild rice

4 cups water or half water and half
   reduced-sodium canned beef
   or chicken broth

2 tablespoons diced (¼ inch)
   dried apricots
   Salt, to taste

MUSHROOMS

2 tablespoons extra-virgin olive oil

1 package (10 ounces) white button
   mushrooms, trimmed, sliced

1 package (3½ ounces) shiitake
   mushrooms, stems discarded,
   caps sliced (¼ inch thick)

¼ cup packed fresh Italian (flat-leaf)
   parsley leaves

1 teaspoon fresh thyme leaves,
   stripped from the stems, or

¼ teaspoon dried

1 garlic clove, chopped
   Salt and freshly ground black
   pepper

2 tablespoons sliced natural almonds,
   toasted (optional)

1. Combine the onion, garlic and oil in a large, wide saucepan. Cook, stirring, over low heat until the onion is tender, about 5 minutes. Add the barley, wild rice, water and/or broth, apricots and salt. Bring to a boil; stir. Cover and cook over medium-low heat until the liquid is absorbed and the grains are tender, 50 to 60 minutes. Uncover and cook off any excess liquid.

2. Meanwhile, Make the Mushrooms: Heat the oil in a large skillet. Add the mushrooms and cook, stirring, over medium-high heat until browned, about 10 minutes. Finely chop the parsley, thyme and garlic together. Add to the mushrooms; cook for 1 minute. Season to taste with salt and pepper.

3. Toss the mushrooms with the grains. Transfer to a serving dish. Top with the toasted almonds, if using.

Rice with Broccoli and Parmesan

PREPARATION TIME: 5 MINUTES ❋ COOKING TIME: 20 MINUTES ❋ SERVES: 4

BECAUSE THE RICE IS STIRRED at the end of the cooking time, it becomes soft and creamy, almost like risotto.

1	tablespoon extra-virgin olive oil
¼	cup finely chopped onion
1	cup long- or medium-grain white rice
2	cups reduced-sodium canned chicken broth or half broth and half water
½	teaspoon salt
2	cups broccoli florets
¼	cup grated Parmigiano-Reggiano, plus more for topping
2	tablespoons unsalted butter

1. Heat the oil in a large, wide saucepan or a deep skillet. Add the onion and cook, stirring, over medium heat, until tender but not browned, about 5 minutes. Stir in the rice until coated. Stir in the broth and/or water and salt. Heat to boiling. Cover and cook over medium heat until the water is absorbed and the rice is tender, about 15 minutes.

2. Meanwhile, place the broccoli in a vegetable steamer set over 1 inch of boiling water in a covered skillet or saucepan and steam until tender, 6 to 8 minutes.

3. When the rice is cooked, stir in the ¼ cup cheese and the butter. Spoon into a serving bowl and top with the broccoli. Sprinkle a little extra cheese over the broccoli.

Rice, Parmesan and Sun-Dried Tomato Pancakes

PREPARATION TIME: 15 MINUTES ❋ COOKING TIME: 25 MINUTES ❋ SERVES: 4; MAKES 12 SMALL PANCAKES

SERVE THESE SMALL PATTIES of sticky rice, sun-dried tomatoes, Parmesan and herbs as an appetizer or a side dish with beef or chicken. Be sure you use a soft high-starch medium-grain rice such as Arborio or a California or Japanese-style rice. The patties hold together even better if allowed to chill for about 15 minutes before frying.

½   cup chopped onion
1   tablespoon extra-virgin olive oil,
      plus more as needed
1   cup medium-grain rice
      (preferably California rice)
¼   cup snipped sun-dried tomatoes
1   teaspoon dried rosemary
2½ cups water or reduced-sodium
      canned chicken broth
½   teaspoon salt, or to taste
½   cup grated Parmigiano-
      Reggiano
1   large egg, slightly beaten

1. Combine the onion and oil in a large, wide saucepan or a skillet with a tight-fitting lid. Cook, stirring, over low heat until the onion is tender, about 5 minutes. Stir in the rice, sun-dried tomatoes and rosemary; stir for 1 minute.

2. Add the water or broth and salt, and heat to boiling over high heat. Stir once thoroughly. Cover and cook over low heat until the liquid is absorbed, about 15 minutes. Uncover, stir in the cheese, and let stand until lukewarm.

3. Add the egg and stir to blend. Using your hands and a ¼-cup measure, form the rice mixture into small pancakes about 2 inches in diameter and ½ inch thick. To prevent the rice from sticking, rinse your hands frequently with cold water.

4. Coat a large nonstick skillet with a thin film of oil. Heat the skillet over medium heat. Add 2 or 3 pancakes to the skillet (do not crowd), and cook until golden brown on one side, about 5 minutes. Using a spatula, carefully turn the pancakes and brown the other side, about 5 minutes. Keep the pancakes warm in an oven set at the lowest temperature while cooking the remaining pancakes. Serve hot.

❋ GRAINS AND BEANS ❋

Corn and Rice with Parmesan

PREPARATION TIME: 10 MINUTES ● COOKING TIME: 15 MINUTES ● SERVES: 4

MAKE THIS DELICATE DISH with the first corn of the season. The corn is not added until the last few minutes, so it is important that it be very tender. Don't substitute frozen, but canned tiny white shoepeg can be used (rinse it first). Jasmine rice, a tender long-grain rice that has a delightfully sweet taste and soft consistency, is delicious. Serve as a side dish, although I also like this as a main course with a fresh tomato and basil salad.

1   tablespoon unsalted butter
1   cup long-grain white rice, preferably jasmine
1¾ cups water
½   teaspoon salt
1   cup (approximately) tender corn kernels (cut from 2 ears husked corn)
1-2 tablespoons grated Parmigiano-Reggiano, or more to taste
1   large basil leaf, rolled tightly and cut into thin slivers (optional)

1. Melt the butter in a large, wide saucepan or a deep skillet with a tight-fitting lid. Add the rice and stir to coat. Add the water and salt and heat to boiling.

2. Stir the rice. Cover and cook over very low heat until the water is almost all absorbed, about 11 minutes. Uncover and sprinkle the corn on top of the rice; do not stir. Cover and continue cooking for 3 minutes, or until the corn is heated and the rice is done.

3. Sprinkle with the cheese and spoon into a serving dish. Don't stir; spooning the rice will distribute the ingredients sufficiently. Garnish with basil, if using.

RISOTTO

DESPITE ITS ITALIAN NAME AND SOPHISTICATED REPUTATION, risotto is neither mysterious nor exotic—it is simply a dish of rice cooked and stirred with broth and other flavorings. Rice, butter or olive oil and chicken broth—basic ingredients found in most kitchens—are typically used to make this creamy, delicious northern Italian dish.

Risotto is cooked in a wide, shallow saucepan or a large, deep skillet and is stirred with a wooden spoon while the broth is slowly added to the rice. From beginning to end, risotto takes less than 30 minutes. It is filling enough to serve as a main course, so with a salad and some bread, you have dinner.

Sounds simple—and it is.

The technique of stirring and the type of rice used—a plump, starchy medium-grain variety—give risotto its rich, almost saucelike consistency. Arborio, Vialone Nano and Carnaroli are the most readily available Italian rices exported to the United States. But medium-grain American rice (grown almost exclusively in California) also makes for a creamy result. Italian rice has a core (sometimes called the pearl) that remains firm to the bite, or al dente, while the American-grown rice cooks up a little more tender. Another difference is the price: imported rice is more expensive than domestically grown.

The success of such a simple dish depends on the pristine quality of its ingredients. Risotto is often flavored with grated Parmigiano-Reggiano, which adds a slightly salty flavor. Therefore, unsalted homemade chicken or meat broth or good-quality reduced-sodium canned chicken broth are highly recommended.

VARIATIONS

RISOTTO, LIKE PASTA, provides a background for any number of additions. The basic recipe is straightforward and simple, but variations requiring fish broth, dried mushrooms or precooked vegetables require a few extra steps. A simple flavoring technique is to stir in fresh or thawed frozen peas, crisp-cooked diced vegetables (carrot, zucchini, yellow squash, red bell pepper), sautéed mushrooms or bits of cooked sausage, meat or fish during the last 5 minutes of cooking. Just before serving, stir in butter and cheese to taste. (Traditionally, cheese is not used with seafood.) To preserve their color and flavor, fresh herbs, like slivered basil leaves, rosemary or thyme leaves and chopped parsley, are added just before serving.

TECHNIQUE

To MAKE A BASIC RISOTTO, sauté a small amount of chopped onion in butter or olive oil or a mixture of both. Then stir in the rice until it is evenly coated with the butter or oil and heated. Add a small amount (about ⅓ cup) of white wine at this point, and allow to boil until it is almost entirely evaporated. Then gradually stir the simmering broth into the rice as it cooks, about ½ cup at a time.

As in all cooking, the right pot is very important. Use a shallow 8- or 10-quart heavy-bottomed pot or a 3-inch-deep heavy-bottomed skillet that will provide plenty of surface for cooking the rice evenly and evaporating the broth, with ample room for stirring. A tall, narrow saucepan makes it too difficult to cook and stir the rice evenly.

It is very important to keep the broth hot (almost simmering) in a separate saucepan. Add the broth with a ladle that holds about ½ cup so you won't have to measure each addition. The heat under the pot should be just high enough to keep the risotto cooking at a lively low boil, but not a hard sputter. Usually, medium heat is best, but this depends on the weight of the pot and the intensity of the heat. Stir with a flat-edged wooden spoon that will get into the corners of the pot and sweep across the bottom with just a couple of strokes.

Once you begin adding the broth, set your timer for 15 minutes. Take little tastes of the risotto frequently after the first 15 minutes to keep tabs on the consistency of the rice. Generally, risotto takes between 20 and 30 minutes to cook.

The next day, if you are lucky enough to have some risotto left over, make delicious little pancakes by stirring in a beaten egg and browning spoonfuls of the mixture in a skillet. Risotto pancakes are great as a snack, an appetizer or a side dish.

Fresh Tomato and Basil Risotto with Ricotta Salata

PREPARATION TIME: 10 MINUTES ◆ COOKING TIME: 30 TO 40 MINUTES ◆ SERVES: 4

I MAKE RISOTTO AT LEAST once during the height of tomato season. There are at least a few unseasonably cool days that make steaming risotto a welcome supper. Ricotta salata, once hard to find in American markets, is now readily available in Italian specialty stores. It is a pressed, lightly salted and aged ricotta with a tangy, yet creamy taste. If you can't find it, substitute grated imported Parmigiano-Reggiano or Pecorino Romano.

1½ cups diced (¼ inch) ripe plum
      tomatoes
2   tablespoons chopped fresh basil
2   tablespoons extra-virgin olive oil
1   garlic clove, crushed through a press
½   teaspoon salt, or to taste
½   cup finely chopped onion
1½ cups medium-grain Italian or
      American rice
⅓   cup white wine (optional)
4-5 cups reduced-sodium canned
      chicken broth, fat skimmed
      from surface, kept simmering
      in a separate saucepan
½   cup diced (¼ inch) ricotta salata
      Freshly ground black pepper, to
      taste

1. Combine the tomatoes, 1 tablespoon of the basil, 1 tablespoon of the oil, the garlic and salt in a small bowl. Stir and set aside at room temperature.

2. Combine the onion and remaining 1 tablespoon oil in a large, wide saucepan or a deep skillet and cook, stirring, until soft, about 3 minutes. Stir in the rice and heat through, about 1 minute. Add the wine, if using, and boil, stirring, until absorbed, about 3 minutes.

3. Add ½ cup of the simmering broth and cook, stirring constantly with a flat-edged wooden spoon, over medium heat until the broth is almost all absorbed. Add another ½ cup of broth. Repeat, adding more broth and stirring, until the risotto is creamy and the rice is plump and tender, with a slight resistance to the bite. After 20 minutes, add the reserved tomato mixture. Cook, stirring, for 2 minutes or longer. Risotto usually takes 20 to 30 minutes total cooking time. (If you run out of broth, finish cooking the risotto with a little boiling water.)

4. Stir in the cheese, salt and pepper. Garnish each serving with the remaining basil.

◆ GRAINS AND BEANS ◆

176

Carrot and Leek Risotto with Fresh Thyme

PREPARATION TIME: 15 MINUTES ❋ COOKING TIME: 25 TO 40 MINUTES ❋ SERVES: 4

I THINK OF THIS as a spring risotto. The carrots make two important contributions: a subtle sweetness and a lovely pale orange color. For the best flavor, use fresh thyme; if it is not available, use parsley, tarragon or chervil. The herbs must be fresh; if not, omit them.

1 cup diced (¼ inch) trimmed and washed leek (1 large leek)

2 teaspoons plus 1 tablespoon unsalted butter

1½ cups medium-grain Italian or American rice

⅓ cup dry white wine (optional)

4-5 cups reduced-sodium canned chicken broth, fat skimmed from the surface, kept simmering in a separate saucepan

1 cup finely chopped carrots (4 carrots; you can use the metal blade of a food processor to chop them)

1½ teaspoons salt, or to taste

¼ cup grated Parmigiano-Reggiano

2 teaspoons fresh thyme leaves, stripped from the stems

1. Combine the leek and 2 teaspoons of the butter in a large, wide saucepan or a deep skillet and cook, stirring, until soft, about 3 minutes. Stir in the rice and heat through, about 1 minute. Add the wine, if using, and boil, stirring, until absorbed, about 3 minutes.

2. Add ½ cup of the simmering broth and cook, stirring constantly with a flat-edged wooden spoon, over medium heat until the broth is almost all absorbed. Add another ½ cup of broth. Repeat, adding more broth and stirring, until the risotto is creamy and the rice is plump and tender, with a slight resistance to the bite. After 20 minutes, add the carrots and salt. Cook, stirring, for 2 minutes or more. Risotto usually takes 20 to 30 minutes total cooking time. (If you run out of broth, finish cooking the risotto with a little boiling water.)

3. Just before serving, cut the remaining 1 tablespoon butter into small pieces. Stir in the cheese and butter. Sprinkle each serving with thyme.

CANNED BEANS

THERE ARE TIMES when I come in the front door, walk into the kitchen and say to myself, "What's for dinner?" If I feel like beans and there aren't any baked and waiting in the refrigerator, I go to my cupboard and peruse my supply of cans.

Compare different brands until you find a good one. The beans should be separate and slightly firm, not broken and mushy. I generally empty the can into a strainer and rinse the beans with tap water and then drain them thoroughly before using, because the juices are slightly salty and "canned" tasting. While they are not more delicious than dried, canned beans are good, very fast, convenient and reputedly easier to digest than their dried counterparts. I like to add my own seasonings, like olive oil, lemon juice, wine vinegar, fresh herbs and freshly ground black pepper.

1 can (19 ounces) beans, drained = 1½ to 1¾ cups

DRIED BEANS

DRIED BEANS AREN'T FAST, but they aren't labor-intensive, either. It takes me less than 5 minutes to combine beans, seasonings and liquid in a casserole. Then I pop them into the oven where they will bake, unattended, for at least 1½ hours. While the beans bake, I can do other things.

An ongoing debate among my fellow cooks is whether it is necessary to soak dried beans before cooking. Sometimes I soak them, and sometimes I don't. Cannellini beans take about 30 minutes longer to cook if they are not soaked first.

Beans contain sugars that cannot be broken down in our digestive systems. When the beans are soaked before cooking, some of these pesky sugars are discarded with the soaking water. If you aren't a frequent bean eater, soak the beans before cooking and consume small servings. If you eat beans often, whether to soak them or not is your choice. Either way, chances are you won't have any problems.

COOKING DRIED BEANS

To PRESOAK DRIED BEANS: Place the beans in a large bowl, and add water to cover by 3 inches. Let stand overnight; drain. Or to quick-soak, place the beans in a large pot and add boiling water to cover. Boil for 2 minutes, and let stand off the heat for 1 hour; drain.

To cook dried beans: Preheat the oven to 325 degrees F. Place the beans in a 3-quart casserole. Add water to cover, a bay leaf, half an onion, a garlic clove and a celery top or parsley sprig. Salt toughens the bean skins; add it after the beans are cooked. Cover tightly, and bake until the beans are tender and the liquid is almost absorbed, about 1½ hours for presoaked beans and 2 hours for unsoaked. Cool.

To season cooked beans: Remove the bay leaf and other seasonings. Add extra-virgin olive oil, salt and freshly ground black pepper to taste. Use in recipes calling for cooked or canned beans.

Soaking time: 1 to 12 hours (optional)

Baking time: 1½ to 2 hours

1 pound (2⅓ cups) dried beans (uncooked) = 4 to 5 cups cooked

BLACK BEANS

THE SPANISH WORDS "FRIJOLES NEGROS" are printed on one side of the plastic bag; on the other side, it says, "black turtle beans." Whatever they are called, I always keep a bag handy in my kitchen cabinet.

Black beans are medium-sized black ovals with a sweet, almost earthy taste. Some say the flavor has a trace of mushroom; I find them rich and meaty. Also called turtle beans, Mexican beans or Spanish black beans, they are a New World bean, as opposed to lentils and chickpeas, which originally came from the Middle East.

Plain cooked black beans are delicious over rice, drained and added to salsa or pureed and served as a dip for vegetables or chips. Jalapeño, ground cumin, chili powder, lime and cilantro are compatible seasonings.

Black Bean and Vegetable Burrito

PREPARATION TIME: **10** MINUTES ● COOKING TIME: ABOUT **20** MINUTES ● SERVES: **4**

A BURRITO IS A FLOUR TACO filled with all sorts of good things, then rolled up. This filling combines black beans with corn kernels, red and green bell peppers, tomato and jalapeño seasoned with ground cumin and chili powder.

4   large (10-inch) or 8 (6-inch)
       flour tortillas
½   cup chopped onion
1   garlic clove, chopped
1   tablespoon vegetable oil
½   teaspoon *each* ground cumin
       and chili powder
½   cup *each* chopped red and
       green bell pepper
½   cup fresh, canned or frozen
       corn kernels, thawed
1   medium carrot, coarsely shredded
1¾   cups rinsed canned or cooked
       dried black beans
½   cup diced fresh or drained
       canned tomato
2   teaspoons finely chopped fresh
       jalapeño, or more to taste
       Salt and freshly ground black
       pepper, to taste
½   cup coarsely shredded
       Monterey Jack cheese

1   cup shredded romaine or
       iceberg lettuce
½   cup sour cream or plain yogurt
¼   cup fresh cilantro leaves

1. Preheat the oven to 350 degrees F. Wrap the tortillas in foil and place in the oven until heated, about 10 minutes.

2. Meanwhile, combine the onion, garlic and oil in a large nonstick skillet. Cook, stirring, over low heat until the vegetables are soft, about 5 minutes. Add the cumin and chili powder; cook for 30 seconds. Add the red and green pepper, corn and carrot, and cook, stirring, for 5 minutes. Add the beans, tomato, jalapeño, salt and pepper. Cook, stirring, until the flavors are blended, about 10 minutes. Remove from the heat. Stir in the cheese.

3. Line up the tortillas on a flat surface. Place a spoonful of the bean mixture in the center of each, dividing evenly. Top each with a portion of the lettuce, a spoonful of the sour cream or yogurt and a few cilantro leaves.

4. Fold the sides of the tortilla over the filling, forming a square package, and roll up. Serve warm.

Marie's Pasta Fagiola

PREPARATION TIME: 15 MINUTES ● COOKING TIME: ABOUT 25 MINUTES ● SERVES: 6

I REMEMBER MY GRANDMOTHER'S rendition of pasta fagiola. She ladled out portions from a large earthenware bowl. It was thick with creamy white cannellini beans, short pasta tubes and a bright green leafy vegetable whose identity now escapes me. I use the dark outside leaves of escarole, which is readily available in my supermarket. The outside leaves are more nutritious than the pale green inside leaves, and because they are tougher, they are more suited to cooking in soup. This dish is wonderful with a generous spoonful of grated Pecorino Romano sprinkled over each serving. (See photograph, page 85.)

½ cup chopped onion
2 garlic cloves, bruised with the
  side of a knife
2 tablespoons extra-virgin olive oil
2 cups rinsed canned or cooked dried
  cannellini (white kidney) beans
2 cups reduced-sodium canned
  chicken broth, or more as needed
1 can (14½ ounces) Italian plum
  tomatoes with juice
1 cup diced carrot
1 cup cut green beans (fresh or frozen)
1 cup frozen small lima beans

2 cups packed outside dark leaves
  of escarole or Swiss chard,
  cut into small pieces
  Salt, to taste
1 cup small elbow macaroni
¼ cup grated Pecorino Romano
  or Parmigiano-Reggiano
  Freshly ground black pepper

1. In a large, wide saucepan, combine the onion, garlic and oil. Cook, stirring, until the onion is soft and golden, about 5 minutes. Add the cannellini beans, broth, tomatoes, carrot, green beans and lima beans. Heat to boiling.

2. Stir in the escarole or Swiss chard and salt; cook, covered, for 5 minutes. Add the macaroni and cook, uncovered, stirring occasionally, until the macaroni and escarole or Swiss chard are very tender, about 15 minutes. Stir in the cheese and a grinding of black pepper. Taste, correct the seasonings and serve.

Cannellini Beans with Arugula and Golden Garlic

PREPARATION TIME: 10 MINUTES ✳ COOKING TIME: 10 MINUTES ✳ SERVES: 4

CANNELLINI BEANS are sometimes called white kidney beans, although I am told that they are different botanically. Cannellini are a large oval with a soft, sweet texture and taste. Like pasta and rice, they are a perfect canvas for the robust Mediterranean flavors of olive oil and garlic. Although I like to use cooked dried beans (for directions on preparing, see page 179), I often substitute canned beans that have been rinsed and drained. This is an excellent side or main dish.

Serve as a main course topped with Soy-and-Ginger-Glazed Salmon Steaks (page 140; the photograph appears on the cover) or Spicy Marinated Shrimp (page 160). Or serve as a part of a vegetable main dish accompanied by roasted peppers. I have also made this dish with the tender inner white leaves from a head of escarole. It is delicious either way.

¼ cup extra-virgin olive oil

2-3 large garlic cloves, cut into thin crosswise slices
     Pinch hot red pepper flakes

2-3 cups rinsed canned or cooked dried cannellini (white kidney) beans
     Salt and freshly ground black pepper, to taste

2 bunches arugula, thoroughly washed, long stems trimmed

½ cup thin lengthwise slivers red onion

1. Combine the oil, garlic and red pepper flakes in a large skillet. Cook slowly over low heat just until the garlic begins to turn golden, 5 to 8 minutes. Stir in the beans to coat with the oil, and heat through. Season with salt and pepper.

2. Add the arugula leaves to the skillet. Stir once or twice to blend. Remove from the heat. Transfer to a serving bowl, top with the onion and serve at once.

Cannellini Beans with Escarole or Broccoli Rabe in Red Pepper Oil: Reduce the garlic to 1 clove in step 1 and crush it through a press. While it is cooking, cook 1 large head of escarole or broccoli rabe (about 1½ pounds), cut into 1-inch lengths, in a large pot of boiling water until almost tender, about 5 minutes. Ladle out and reserve ½ cup of the cooking liquid. Drain the escarole or broccoli rabe in a colander.

Continue as directed in step 2, using the drained escarole or broccoli rabe in place of the arugula and adding the reserved cooking liquid. Omit the onion and season with salt and pepper.

Lentil and Rice Pilaf with Toasted Cumin Seeds

PREPARATION TIME: 5 MINUTES ◆ COOKING TIME: 40 MINUTES

STANDING TIME: 5 MINUTES ◆ SERVES: 4

LENTILS AND RICE have a very similar cooking time, so it is easy to pair the two. In the following recipe, I precook the lentils to soften them a bit before cooking them with the rice. If you are using brown rice, cook the lentils along with the rice and increase the cooking liquid to about 3 cups. Serve as part of a vegetarian meal with Broccoli with Crisp Garlic Slivers (page 245) and Easy Oven-Roasted Red Bell Peppers (page 278).

½ cup brown lentils, rinsed and sorted
2 tablespoons extra-virgin olive oil
½ cup chopped onion
1 garlic clove, finely chopped
1 teaspoon cumin seeds
1 cup long-grain white basmati rice
1 tablespoon dried currants
1¾ cups reduced-sodium canned
    chicken broth
Salt

1. Cook lentils in plenty of boiling water until almost tender, about 15 minutes. Drain and set aside.

2. Heat the oil in a large, wide saucepan. Add the onion and cook, stirring, until tender, about 10 minutes. Add the garlic and cumin seeds, and cook, stirring, for 1 minute.

3. Add the rice, currants and partially cooked lentils; stir to blend. Add the broth and heat to boiling. Add salt to taste. Stir thoroughly; cover and cook over medium-low heat until the liquid is absorbed and the rice is tender, about 15 minutes. Uncover and let stand off the heat for 5 minutes before serving.

LENTILS

REVERED BY THE EARLY Greeks and Romans and mentioned in the Bible, this ancient legume is one of my favorites. Lentils are the fastest-cooking member of the legume family, making them a practical choice when time is of the essence. No soaking is needed. Just boil the lentils gently in plenty of water until they are tender, usually 20 to 30 minutes. Watch them carefully: some brands cook more quickly than others. (If the lentils become mushy, turn them into soup.)

Lentils are a food for all seasons. In the dead of winter, I make lentil soup with mushrooms. In fall and spring, I cook lentils to serve as an accompaniment to broiled salmon or lamb chops. In the summer, I make lentil salad (see page 227).

16-ounce bag lentils = 2½ cups dried = about 7 cups cooked

1 cup dried green or brown lentils = about 3 cups cooked

Simmered Lentils with Vegetables and Herbs

PREPARATION TIME: 15 MINUTES ❋ COOKING TIME: 30 TO 40 MINUTES ❋ SERVES: 6

THESE LENTILS MAKE an easy side dish that serves as both a starch and a vegetable. I cook a whole bag of lentils, because the next day, I eat them as a cold salad, sometimes adding a couple cups of diced cooked potatoes. But the recipe can easily be halved. If you don't have parsnips, omit them.

2 tablespoons extra-virgin olive oil

½ cup diced (¼ inch) carrot

½ cup diced (¼ inch) parsnip

½ cup diced (¼ inch) red bell pepper

1 bag (16 ounces) lentils, rinsed and sorted

1 teaspoon *each* fresh rosemary and thyme or ½ teaspoon *each* dried

2 cups reduced-sodium canned chicken broth

2 cups water

¼ cup chopped fresh Italian (flat-leaf) parsley

½ cup sliced scallion green tops

2 tablespoons sherry wine vinegar
Salt and freshly ground black pepper, to taste

1. Combine the oil, carrot, parsnip and red pepper in a large, deep skillet or a wide saucepan. Cook, stirring, over medium-low heat until the vegetables are tender, about 8 minutes.

2. Add the lentils and dried herbs, if using (add the fresh herbs later); stir to blend. Add the broth and water and heat to boiling. Cover and cook until the lentils are tender, 20 to 30 minutes. Uncover and cook over high heat to evaporate any excess liquid in the bottom of the pan, about 2 minutes.

3. Chop the parsley and the fresh herbs together, if using. Add the herbs and the scallions to the cooked lentils and vegetables. Season with the vinegar, salt and pepper and serve.

Curried Lentils and Vegetables

PREPARATION TIME: 15 MINUTES ❋ COOKING TIME: 40 MINUTES ❋ SERVES: 4

VARY THE VEGETABLES in this simple yet hearty main dish according to whatever you have at home. In addition to or instead of the vegetables listed here, you can use cubed acorn or butternut squash, white potatoes, cauliflower, green beans and/or lima beans.

1 tablespoon extra-virgin olive oil
2 small onions, quartered
1 carrot, trimmed, cut into
   ¼-inch-thick diagonal slices
3 garlic cloves, coarsely chopped
2-3 teaspoons curry powder
1 teaspoon ground cumin
¼ teaspoon turmeric
2 cups reduced-sodium canned
   chicken broth, or more as needed
1 cup brown lentils, rinsed and sorted
1 medium-sized sweet potato, peeled
   and cut into ½-inch cubes
1 thin slice peeled fresh ginger
1 bay leaf
1 cardamom pod
1 cup frozen green peas, thawed
1 cup low-fat plain yogurt
   Salt and freshly ground black
      pepper, to taste
¼ cup fresh cilantro leaves

¼ cup chopped dry-roasted
   unsalted cashews

1. Heat the oil in a large, deep nonstick skillet or wide saucepan. Add the onions and carrot. Cook, stirring occasionally, until tender, about 10 minutes. Add the garlic and cook for 2 minutes. Stir in the curry, cumin and turmeric; cook for 1 minute.

2. Add the broth, lentils, sweet potato, ginger, bay leaf and cardamom. Cook, covered, over medium-low heat until the lentils are tender, about 20 minutes. Check the moisture level halfway through the cooking; add small amounts of additional broth or water as needed to keep the mixture moist.

3. Add the peas; cover and cook over low heat until tender, about 5 minutes. Remove from the heat. Pick out and discard the whole spices. Stir in the yogurt. Season with salt and pepper.

4. Spoon into a serving bowl and top with the cilantro and the cashews.

Basic Soft Polenta

PREPARATION TIME: **10 MINUTES** ❋ COOKING TIME: **30 TO 35 MINUTES** ❋ SERVES: **4**

SOFT POLENTA IS WONDERFUL with meat or vegetable stews, mushrooms cooked with Italian sausage or tomato sauce. To make it even richer, add about 1 cup cubed mozzarella cheese (for a real treat, try it with smoked mozzarella) just before serving. The cheese will partially melt and stretch. If you don't have time to stand and stir, see the variation recommended by friend and cookbook author Michele Scicolone at the end of this recipe. This method uses a double boiler to cook the polenta, eliminating the need for constant stirring. The technique takes 10 to 15 minutes longer but frees you to do other things.

The polenta is excellent chilled, cut into squares and baked until crisp. I like to offer the resulting "toasts" as an appetizer, topped with a spoonful of Olivada (page 25) and a piece of roasted red pepper. Or they can be served with any number of toppings, including Broccoli Rabe with Olive Oil and Garlic (page 249; the photograph appears on page 82) or Pan-Grilled Mushrooms (page 268). Placed under roasted chicken or Cornish hens, polenta toasts sop up the tasty juices.

3 tablespoons unsalted butter
   or extra-virgin olive oil
½ cup finely chopped onion
4 cups cold water or half reduced-
   sodium canned chicken broth
   and half water
1 cup yellow cornmeal
2 tablespoons grated Parmigiano-
   Reggiano
1 teaspoon salt, or to taste

1. Heat the butter or oil in a wide, heavy saucepan. Add the onion and cook, stirring, until golden, about 5 minutes. Add 2 cups of the water and/or broth to the onion and heat to boiling.

2. Combine the cornmeal and the remaining 2 cups liquid until blended. Gradually stir into the boiling liquid. Cook over medium heat, stirring constantly, until the mixture begins to thicken, about 5 minutes.

3. Reduce the heat to low. Cook, stirring often, until the cornmeal is thick enough to clear the sides of the pan, 20 to 25 minutes. Add the cheese and salt. Serve at once. (The polenta will stiffen upon standing; add additional water or broth to soften, if necessary.)

Unstirred Polenta: Begin the soft polenta in the top of a double boiler or a saucepan that can be set inside a second pan containing about 2 inches of simmering water. Prepare the polenta through step 2. Set the polenta pan over boiling water and cook, covered, until the polenta is soft and fluffy, 35 to 40 minutes.

Polenta Toasts: Prepare the polenta as directed in steps 1 and 2. Lightly oil a 13-x-9-inch baking pan and spread the polenta in an even layer. Cool slightly, cover and refrigerate for several hours or overnight, until cold and set. Preheat the oven to 425 degrees F.

Lightly brush a nonstick baking sheet with extra-virgin olive oil. Cut the polenta into 3-inch squares and then into triangles. Carefully transfer to the baking sheet and bake until the bottoms are browned, about 15 minutes. Remove the baking sheet from the oven and carefully turn the toasts over. Bake until the other side is browned, about 10 minutes.

POLENTA

POLENTA, WHICH IS YELLOW CORNMEAL cooked in water or broth and seasoned with butter and freshly grated Parmigiano-Reggiano, has replaced macaroni and cheese at my house as the ultimate comfort food.

Making it is simple, especially if you first dissolve the cornmeal in some of the liquid. This step eliminates the stubborn lumps that you would otherwise have to chase around the pot as you cook the polenta.

If you are impatient or don't have time to stir, it can be cooked just until it is thick enough to pull away from the sides of the pot (about 15 minutes), mixed with milk and cheese and baked in a casserole (see Oven-Baked Polenta with Parmesan and Mozzarella Cheese, opposite page).

Although imported polenta meal is available in some specialty stores, I use plain supermarket-variety American yellow cornmeal.

Oven-Baked Polenta with Parmesan and Mozzarella Cheese

PREPARATION TIME: 5 MINUTES ❋ COOKING TIME: 20 MINUTES

UNATTENDED BAKING TIME: 20 MINUTES ❋ STANDING TIME: 5 MINUTES ❋ SERVES: 4, WITH LEFTOVERS

SERVE THIS RICH BAKED POLENTA as a main dish accompanied by broccoli rabe, Easy Oven-Roasted Red Bell Peppers (page 278), Oven-Roasted Asparagus (omit the Shallot-Mustard Vinaigrette, page 235) or Smothered Spinach (page 285).

2 tablespoons unsalted butter or extra-virgin olive oil
½ cup finely chopped onion
5 cups reduced-sodium canned chicken broth
2 cups yellow cornmeal
1 cup half-and-half or milk, warmed
4 tablespoons grated Parmigiano-Reggiano
1 teaspoon salt
½ pound mozzarella, coarsely shredded (about 2 cups)

1. Preheat the oven to 350 degrees F. Generously butter a shallow 2-quart baking dish.

2. Heat the butter or oil in a large, heavy saucepan. Add the onion and sauté until tender, about 5 minutes. Add 2½ cups of the broth; heat to boiling.

3. Meanwhile, whisk the remaining 2½ cups cold broth into the cornmeal, and stir to blend (this prevents lumps).

4. Slowly stir the cornmeal mixture into the boiling stock. Cook, stirring constantly, over medium-high heat until the mixture begins to boil. (Protect your hand from splattering cornmeal with a towel or pot holder.) Reduce the heat to medium-low and cook, stirring frequently, until the cornmeal is very thick, about 15 minutes.

5. Gradually stir in the half-and-half or milk; add 2 tablespoons of the Parmesan and the salt. Remove from the heat. Spoon half of the polenta into the prepared pan. Sprinkle with half of the mozzarella and 1 tablespoon of the Parmesan. Spread with the remaining polenta and top with the remaining mozzarella and remaining 1 tablespoon Parmesan.

6. Bake until the edges brown and the cheeses are melted and bubbly, about 20 minutes. Let stand for 5 minutes before serving.

SALADS

Main-Dish Salads

Salad of Browned Potatoes with Garlic, Mushrooms,
Red Peppers and Goat Cheese **194**

Chick-Pea, Hard-Cooked Egg and Vidalia Onion Salad **195**

White Bean Salad Platter **196**

Black Bean and Yellow Rice Salad with Fresh Corn and Tomatoes **198**

Chicken Cutlet Salad with Avocado, Tomato and Sweet Onion **200**

Couscous with Lemon Dressing, Roasted Chicken, Mint and Dill **204**

Swordfish, Potato and Celery Salad with Lemon and Parsley **206**

Tuna Salad, Italian Style **207**

Squid, Basil and Tomato Salad **209**

Warm Potato Salad with Sardines and Mustard-and-Lemon Dressing **210**

Spinach, Shrimp and Warm New Potato Salad **211**

Lentil Salad with Italian Sausage and Mustard Vinaigrette **212**

Lentil and Spinach Salad with Crisp Bacon Dressing **213**

Side-Dish Salads

WHEN YOU HAVE MORE TIME

Salad of Browned Potatoes with Garlic, Mushrooms, Red Peppers and Goat Cheese

PREPARATION TIME: 15 MINUTES

COOKING TIME: 30 MINUTES (INCLUDING PREPARATION OF POTATOES) ● SERVES: 4

THIS IS MY IDEA OF SUPPER at the end of a busy day. I sometimes embellish the plates by adding cooked fresh green beans or asparagus and serving Crostini (page 24) on the side.

8 cups washed, trimmed and torn salad greens (chicory, romaine, red leaf lettuce, spinach, Belgian endive and/or watercress)
Skillet-Browned Red Potatoes with Rosemary and Garlic (page 283)
1 package (3½ ounces) shiitake mushrooms or 1 cup thinly sliced white button mushrooms
2 tablespoons finely chopped fresh Italian (flat-leaf) parsley
Salt and freshly ground black pepper, to taste
1 small red bell pepper, quartered, seeds and stems removed, cut into ⅛-x-1-inch slivers

DRESSING

2 tablespoons extra-virgin olive oil
1 tablespoon fresh lemon juice
Pinch salt
4 ounces fresh goat cheese

1. Wrap salad greens in a kitchen towel and refrigerate until ready to serve.

2. Prepare the Skillet-Browned Red Potatoes.

3. Add the mushrooms to the skillet in which the potatoes were cooked and sauté the mushrooms until lightly browned and tender, about 5 minutes. Sprinkle with 1 tablespoon of the parsley, a pinch of salt and a grinding of pepper; transfer to a side dish. Add the red pepper to the skillet and cook, stirring, until lightly browned, about 2 minutes. Sprinkle with the remaining 1 tablespoon parsley, salt and pepper.

4. Make the Dressing: In a large bowl, whisk the oil and lemon juice together; add salt. Add the greens, and toss to coat. Arrange the greens on 4 large plates. Add the goat cheese, distributing evenly.

5. Arrange the potatoes on the plates; top with the mushrooms and red pepper. Serve warm.

Chick-Pea, Hard-Cooked Egg and Vidalia Onion Salad

PREPARATION TIME: 15 MINUTES * COOKING TIME FOR EGGS: 15 MINUTES * SERVES: 4

PERFECTLY HARD-COOKED EGGS, chick-peas and squares of juicy sweet onion are mixed with salad greens and a simple vinaigrette of red wine vinegar, oil and mustard. Make the salad a main event by arranging the ingredients and garnishing with slices of cucumber, tomato wedges, black olives and fresh dill sprigs.

2-4 large eggs

4 cups (lightly packed) torn salad greens (green curly-leaf lettuce is good)

1 can (16 ounces) chick-peas (garbanzo or ceci beans), rinsed, drained

1 large Vidalia onion, trimmed, cut into ½-inch chunks

¼ cup coarsely chopped fresh Italian (flat-leaf) parsley

2 tablespoons snipped fresh dill

DRESSING

⅓ cup extra-virgin olive oil

¼ cup red wine vinegar

1 teaspoon Dijon-style mustard
    Salt and freshly ground black pepper, to taste

½ seedless cucumber, trimmed, cut into ¼-inch slices

1 large tomato, cored and cut into wedges

¼ cup pitted Kalamata olives or other brine-cured black olives
    Sprigs fresh dill, for garnish

1. Place the eggs in a small saucepan; cover with water. Heat to boiling; cover and turn off the heat. Let stand off the heat, covered, for 15 minutes. Rinse under cold water and carefully crack the shells. Peel off the shells.

2. Quarter the eggs, put them in a large bowl and combine them with the salad greens, chick-peas, onion, parsley and dill.

3. Make the Dressing: In a small bowl, whisk together the oil, vinegar, mustard, salt and pepper. Add to the salad and toss gently once or twice.

4. Spoon the salad onto a platter and garnish with the cucumber, tomato, olives and dill.

White Bean Salad Platter

FOR A HEARTIER main dish, garnish this salad with cooked, shelled and deveined shrimp that have been tossed with 2 tablespoons of the vinaigrette dressing.

4 cups rinsed canned or cooked dried
      cannellini (white
      kidney) beans
1 cup slivered red onion
1 cup thin diagonally
      sliced celery
½ cup coarsely chopped
      fresh Italian (flat-leaf) parsley

VINAIGRETTE
   DRESSING
⅓ cup extra-virgin olive oil
¼ cup red wine vinegar, or more
      to taste
1 small garlic clove, crushed
      through a press
½ teaspoon salt, or more to taste
      Freshly ground black pepper,
      to taste

   Curly lettuce leaves
2 ripe tomatoes, cored, cut
      into wedges

1 tablespoon extra-virgin olive oil
   Salt, to taste
2 tablespoons chopped fresh basil
4 hard-cooked eggs, shelled, halved
      (see step 1, page 195)

PLAN AHEAD:

This recipe uses hard-cooked eggs.

1. In a large bowl, combine the beans, onion, celery and parsley.

2. Make the Vinaigrette Dressing: In a separate bowl, whisk the oil, vinegar, garlic, salt and pepper. Add to the beans, and toss. Taste and correct the seasonings.

3. Arrange a border of lettuce on a platter or in a shallow bowl. Spoon the beans into the center. Place the tomato wedges in a small bowl and season with the oil, a pinch of salt and 1 tablespoon of the basil

4. Arrange the tomato wedges and the hard-cooked egg halves around the platter, garnish the eggs with the remaining 1 tablespoon basil and serve.

HARD-COOKED EGGS

THE EGG IS ONE OF THE MOST CONVENIENT and nutritious ways to enhance a menu or round out a dish. I use eggs often—even if it is just one—chopped, sliced or cut into thin wedges and tossed into a salad dressing or a bowl of warm cooked green beans.

Hard-cooking an egg does not require advance preparation or time. It is simply a matter of organization. The method I like to use, which produces a perfectly tender egg rather than an unsightly hard yolk with a greenish purple rim takes about 15 minutes, plus a few minutes cooling under cold running water. It is most often the last ingredient that I add to a prepared dish, so if I start the egg first thing, it can cook along merrily while I get down to the business of chopping, peeling, washing, boiling or whatever else needs to be done. I think hard-cooked eggs taste best when they are still slightly warm. Slice, chop, quarter or cut into thin wedges and use in salads, dressings or vegetable dishes.

Black Bean and Yellow Rice Salad with Fresh Corn and Tomatoes

PREPARATION TIME: 20 MINUTES ❁ COOKING TIME: 15 MINUTES
COOLING TIME: 20 MINUTES ❁ SERVES: 4

FOR A PRETTY VARIATION, omit the tomato from the salad and serve the salad scooped into 8 large hollowed-out tomatoes. It is also delicious spooned onto warm flour tortillas, topped with guacamole, then rolled up.

> **PLAN AHEAD:**
>
> Allow 20 minutes to cool the rice.

YELLOW RICE

⅔ cup long-grain white rice, American basmati or California medium-grain

1 teaspoon vegetable oil

½ teaspoon turmeric

1½ cups water

½ teaspoon salt

DRESSING AND SALAD

⅓ cup fresh lime juice

¼ cup vegetable oil

½ teaspoon salt, or to taste

4 cups rinsed canned or cooked dried black beans

1 large, firm, ripe tomato, cored, diced (¼ inch)

1 cup corn kernels, preferably fresh, uncooked

½ cup packed fresh cilantro leaves

1 scallion, trimmed, thinly sliced

1 tablespoon finely chopped jalapeño Avocado slices and cilantro sprigs, for garnish (optional)

1. Make the Yellow Rice: Combine the rice, oil and turmeric in a large, wide saucepan and cook, stirring, over low heat for 1 minute, or until blended. Add the water and salt; heat to boiling. Stir once. Cover and cook over low heat until the water is absorbed and the rice is tender, about 15 minutes. Uncover and let the rice cool in the pan for about 20 minutes.

2. Make the Dressing: In a large bowl, combine the lime juice, oil and salt; whisk to blend.

3. Add the beans, tomato, corn, cilantro, scallion, jalapeño and cooled rice. Toss to blend. Taste and correct the seasonings.

4. Garnish with avocado slices and sprigs of cilantro, if desired, and serve.

Warm Lentil and New Potato Salad with Sherry Wine Vinaigrette

PREPARATION TIME: 10 MINUTES ✳ COOKING TIME: 30 TO 45 MINUTES

STANDING TIME: 20 MINUTES ✳ SERVES: 4 TO 6

THIS SIMPLE SALAD OF LENTILS and potatoes is dressed with vinegar and oil. Use your best sherry vinegar and extra-virgin olive oil, and the integrity of the remaining ingredients will prevail. This is a large recipe, but I love the leftovers for lunch the next day. If you prefer, you can halve the quantities of ingredients and make a smaller batch.

1   bag (16 ounces) lentils, rinsed
       and sorted
1   celery top
1   bay leaf
1   garlic clove
1   onion slice
1   pound small new potatoes, cut
       into small (⅓ inch) cubes
       (about 2 cups)
    Pinch salt

DRESSING

⅓   cup extra-virgin olive oil
¼   cup sherry wine vinegar or aged red
       wine vinegar, or more to taste
1   teaspoon salt

Freshly ground black pepper,
    to taste

½   cup slivered red onion
½   cup finely chopped fresh parsley

1. Cook the lentils in plenty of boiling, unsalted water along with the celery top, bay leaf, garlic and onion until tender but still firm, 15 to 20 minutes. Drain and let cool. Wipe out the saucepan, fill halfway with water, and add the potatoes and salt. Cover and cook until the potatoes are tender, about 15 minutes; drain.

PLAN AHEAD:

For maximum flavor, let the salad stand for 20 minutes before serving.

2. Make the Dressing: In a large bowl, whisk the oil, vinegar, salt and pepper.

3. Add the cooled lentils, potatoes, onion and parsley. Toss to blend. Let stand for 20 minutes before serving. Taste and correct the seasonings.

Chicken Cutlet Salad with Avocado, Tomato and Sweet Onion

PREPARATION TIME: 15 MINUTES ❧ COOKING TIME: 5 MINUTES ❧ SERVES: 4

SERVE THIS WARM SALAD of chicken, avocado and sweet onion with a side dish such as Basic All-Around Potato Salad (page 222), Yellow Confetti Rice Salad (page 224) or Couscous with Confetti Vegetables (page 225).

2 tablespoons extra-virgin olive oil

1 teaspoon fresh thyme leaves, stripped from the stems, or ¼ teaspoon dried

1 garlic clove, crushed through a press

4 boneless, skinless chicken cutlets (about 6 ounces each)
   Salt and freshly ground black pepper, to taste

1 ripe avocado, halved, pitted, peeled, cut into thin crosswise slices

1 medium tomato, cored, halved, cut into thin half slices

½ sweet yellow onion (Vidalia, Texas sweet, Walla Walla or other), slivered

2 tablespoons fresh lime juice

1 tablespoon cold water

8 loosely packed cups mixed tender salad greens

1. Place 1 tablespoon of the oil, the thyme and garlic on a plate. Add the chicken cutlets and turn to coat. Sprinkle with salt and pepper. Heat a large nonstick skillet over high heat until hot enough to evaporate a drop of water upon contact. Add the chicken and cook until well browned, about 2 minutes. Turn and cook the other side until the chicken is cooked through, about 2 minutes more. Remove to a side dish.

2. Meanwhile, combine the avocado, tomato and onion in a bowl; add 1 tablespoon of the lime juice and salt and pepper to taste; toss to coat. Set aside.

3. Place the remaining 1 tablespoon oil, the water and the remaining 1 tablespoon lime juice in a bowl, add a pinch of salt and whisk to blend. Add the salad greens and toss to coat. Distribute among 4 large dinner plates.

4. Place the avocado mixture in the center of each plate, dividing evenly. Top each with a chicken cutlet. Serve at once.

COOKED CHICKEN FOR SALAD

I OFTEN BAKE EXTRA CHICKEN, knowing that I will need it in a day or two to make salad. But when I decide to make chicken salad on the spur of the moment, I do one of two things:

I buy a cooked chicken on the way home from work. Many deli departments in supermarkets or specialty food shops sell spit-roasted chickens that are fresh, juicy and delicious. These are perfect for salad and worth every cent in time saved. (A 2½-pound chicken equals 3 to 4 cups skinned meat.)

At other times, I quickly sear boneless, skinless chicken cutlets in a nonstick skillet. I flavor the cutlets with olive oil, garlic and perhaps a little fresh or dried thyme (see step 1 of Chicken Cutlet Salad with Avocado, Tomato and Sweet Onion, opposite page). Then I cut these into strips or small pieces. (One 4-ounce chicken cutlet equals about ⅔ cup cubed meat.)

Herb-Marinated Chicken, Shiitake Mushrooms and Roasted Potatoes Vinaigrette

PREPARATION TIME: 20 MINUTES ❋ COOKING TIME: 40 TO 45 MINUTES ❋ SERVES: 4

THIS SALAD SUPPER represents the way I like to eat. It combines seared chicken breasts, shiitake mushroom caps and roasted potatoes that have been seasoned with a light vinaigrette dressing. (See photograph, page 81.)

There are numerous variations on this favorite theme. Sometimes, I add a cluster of steamed green beans, broccoli florets or sugar snap peas. Sautéed cherry tomatoes or roasted red pepper can be tossed in too. For a simpler, lighter version, omit the chicken cutlets.

2 garlic cloves, crushed through a press

2 teaspoons grated lemon or orange zest

1½ teaspoons fresh thyme leaves, stripped from the stems

½ teaspoon salt, or more to taste

¼ teaspoon freshly ground black pepper, or more to taste

4 chicken cutlet halves, pounded thin

3-4 medium russet or Idaho potatoes (about 1 pound), scrubbed

(peeled or unpeeled), cut into ¼-inch-thick slices

1 tablespoon extra-virgin olive oil

VINAIGRETTE

2 tablespoons extra-virgin olive oil

2 tablespoons mild, fruit-flavored red wine vinegar, such as raspberry

1½ teaspoons fresh thyme leaves, stripped from the stems

Salt and freshly ground black pepper, to taste

1 tablespoon extra-virgin olive oil

4 large shiitake mushroom caps (or use 4 white button mushrooms, thinly sliced)

1 red bell pepper, quartered, seeds and stem removed, each quarter cut into thin diagonal slices

¼ cup finely chopped fresh Italian (flat-leaf) parsley

6 cups mixed salad greens

1. Combine the garlic, lemon or orange zest, thyme, salt and pepper on a plate. Add the chicken and rub evenly with the marinade. Set aside while preparing the remaining ingredients.

2. Preheat the oven to 400 degrees F. Place the potatoes in a bowl, drizzle with the oil and sprinkle with salt and pepper; toss to coat. Arrange on a nonstick baking sheet and bake until one side is golden and crisp, about 20 minutes. Carefully turn and bake until tender, about 15 minutes more.

3. Meanwhile, Make the Vinaigrette: In a small bowl, whisk the oil, vinegar, thyme, salt and pepper until blended. Set aside.

4. Heat a large nonstick skillet over medium-high heat until hot enough to evaporate a drop of water on contact. Add ½ tablespoon of the oil and tilt the pan to coat it. Add the chicken cutlets gradually so they keep sizzling, and quickly cook until browned on both sides, about 1 minute per side if the chicken is pounded thin, up to 3 minutes per side if the chicken is thicker. Remove to a side plate.

5. Add the remaining ½ tablespoon oil to the pan. Add the mushrooms and red pepper, and cook for 1 to 2 minutes; sprinkle with salt and pepper and turn. Cook until tender, about 2 minutes more. Transfer to the plate with the chicken. Sprinkle with the parsley.

6. Place the salad greens in a large bowl and toss with half of the vinaigrette. Divide among 4 dinner plates.

7. Cut chicken into thin diagonal slices before arranging on top of the salad. Cut the shiitake mushrooms into ¼-inch strips and arrange them on top of the chicken with the red pepper strips. Sprinkle the potatoes with the remaining vinaigrette and arrange the slices around the rim of the plate, dividing them evenly. Serve.

Couscous with Lemon Dressing, Roasted Chicken, Mint and Dill

PREPARATION TIME: 20 MINUTES * COOKING TIME: 20 MINUTES

COOLING TIME: 20 MINUTES * SERVES: 4 AS A MAIN COURSE

COUSCOUS IS SIMPLY SEMOLINA flour that has been mixed with salt water and then tossed and rubbed into tiny little pellets. In Middle Eastern cuisine, perfectly light, fluffy couscous requires gentle steaming in a special pot called a couscousière. But if you are making a salad, follow the simple and quick method described here. You can use a roasted deli chicken leftover roasted or grilled chicken from a previous meal or a chicken cutlet cooked especially for it.

> **PLAN AHEAD:**
>
> This recipe calls for cooked chicken.

QUICK COUSCOUS

1½ cups quick-cooking couscous

2½ cups boiling water

DRESSING

⅓ cup fresh lemon juice, or more as needed

2 tablespoons extra-virgin olive oil

1 tablespoon cold water

1 garlic clove, crushed through a press

½ teaspoon salt

SALAD

2 cups lightly packed crosswise slices (½-inch) romaine lettuce

2-3 cups coarsely shredded cooked chicken (see step 1, page 200)

1 cup diced (¼ inch) cored plum tomatoes

½ cup finely chopped fresh curly-leaf parsley

½ cup thinly sliced scallions

¼ cup chopped fresh dill, plus sprigs for garnish

2 tablespoons finely chopped fresh mint (optional), plus sprigs for garnish

4-6 large romaine leaves

1 cup halved cherry tomatoes or 2-3 plum tomatoes, quartered

1. **Make the Couscous:** Place the couscous in a large bowl. Add the water; stir to blend. Cover and let stand for 20 minutes. Uncover; fluff with a fork or a chopstick, and let stand, uncovered, until cooled, about 20 minutes.

2. **Meanwhile, Make the Dressing:** In a small bowl, whisk the lemon juice, oil, water, garlic and salt until blended. Add to the cooled couscous; toss to blend. Taste and add more lemon juice, if desired.

3. **Make the Salad:** Add the romaine, chicken, tomatoes, parsley, scallions, chopped dill and chopped mint, if using, to the cooled couscous.

4. Arrange the lettuce leaves on a large platter. Spoon the couscous salad onto the leaves. Garnish with the tomatoes and herb sprigs and serve.

Swordfish, Potato and Celery Salad with Lemon and Parsley

PREPARATION TIME: 10 MINUTES ❈ COOKING TIME: ABOUT 12 MINUTES ❈ SERVES: 4

ALWAYS MAKE THIS SALAD after I have served broiled or grilled swordfish. It is such a rich fish that we never eat all that I prepare, and the leftovers make a welcome addition to lunch or supper the following day. Other cooked fish can be substituted for the swordfish.

1   pound (or more) small red-skinned potatoes, washed, halved or quartered
2   tablespoons extra-virgin olive oil
2   tablespoons fresh lemon juice
1   garlic clove, crushed through a press
2   cups sliced (½ inch) celery, plus a few chopped leaves
½   cup thin wedges red or sweet white onion
¼   cup packed chopped fresh Italian (flat-leaf) parsley
     Salt and freshly ground black pepper, to taste

½   pound (approximately) cooked swordfish, mako shark, halibut or other cooked fish steaks, skin and bones removed
     Assorted mixed salad greens
     Lemon wedges

1. Cook the potatoes in plenty of boiling, salted water until tender, about 12 minutes; drain and cool.

PLAN AHEAD:

This recipe uses cooked fish.

2. Combine the oil, lemon juice, garlic, celery and celery leaves, onion and parsley in a large bowl. Add the potatoes and stir to blend. Sprinkle with salt and pepper. Add the fish and toss once.

3. Line a platter with some salad leaves. Spoon the potato-and-fish mixture on top of the greens. Garnish with lemon wedges and serve immediately.

Tuna Salad, Italian Style

PREPARATION TIME: 20 MINUTES ❀ SERVES: 4

WHEN I WAS GROWING UP, my mother served this salad for Friday night supper after a first course of Ceci e Pasta (page 110).

2 cans (6½ ounces each) tuna packed in oil, drained

3 teaspoons fresh lemon or lime juice

4 teaspoons extra-virgin olive oil

¼ teaspoon freshly ground black pepper

1 celery rib, trimmed, chopped (about ½ cup)

¼ cup chopped red bell pepper

¼ cup chopped green bell pepper

¼ cup chopped red onion

1 small garlic clove, crushed through a press

Red-leaf lettuce (about 6 large leaves), rinsed, drained

1 cucumber, peeled, trimmed, cut into spears

1 medium carrot, peeled, cut into ¼-inch-thick diagonal slices

⅓ cup pimiento-stuffed green olives

2 hard-cooked eggs, peeled, halved (see step 1, page 195)

1. Turn out the tuna onto a plate; do not flake or stir. Sprinkle with 2 teaspoons of the lemon or lime juice and 2 teaspoons of the oil. Sprinkle with the pepper, and let stand.

PLAN AHEAD:

This recipe calls for hard-cooked eggs.

2. Combine the celery, red and green peppers, onion and garlic in a medium bowl; add the remaining 1 teaspoon lemon or lime juice and the remaining 2 teaspoons oil. Toss to blend. Add the tuna; toss once.

3. Arrange the lettuce leaves on a large serving platter. Spoon the tuna mixture into the center. Garnish the platter with the cucumber, carrot, olives and eggs.

SQUID

WHEN I WAS A CHILD, I remember peering on tippy toes into the kitchen sink while my mother cleaned *calamari*, the Italian word for "squid." Though I was fascinated by the tentacles and oozing black ink, it never occurred to me to take a taste of the finished dish.

Somewhere between childhood and adulthood, I met up with crunchy fried rings of squid, juicy grilled stuffed baby squid and delicious squid salad. Now I'm hooked on this Mediterranean favorite.

Squid should be cooked quickly in boiling water for less than 1 minute or slowly simmered for 20 to 30 minutes. Anything in between will produce a texture like rubber bands. Squid is usually sold already cleaned; if it isn't, ask the fish merchant to do it for you, since the procedure is time-consuming and messy.

Squid, Basil and Tomato Salad

PREPARATION TIME: 15 MINUTES ● COOKING TIME: 45 SECONDS ● SERVES: 4

I LIKE THIS COOL SALAD during the summer as part of a seafood buffet. If you are a cilantro lover, substitute it for the basil, or use some of each. Accompaniments could include Spicy Marinated Shrimp (page 160), chilled Mussels in White Wine with Fresh Tomato Salsa (page 162) or any number of vegetable or other seafood salads.

1	pound cleaned small squid
1	bay leaf
1	thick slice onion
1	teaspoon salt
2	cups cubed ripe plum tomatoes
1	cup sliced (½ inch) celery
1	cup diced (½ inch) sweet onion
¼	cup packed torn fresh basil leaves or cilantro
1	garlic clove, crushed through a press
2	tablespoons extra-virgin olive oil
	Salt and freshly ground black pepper, to taste
	Lime wedges

1. Rinse the squid thoroughly inside and out under cold running water; drain well. Cut the bodies into ¼-to-½-inch rings; cut the tentacles into 1-inch lengths. Pat dry between paper towels.

2. Fill a medium saucepan two-thirds full with water. Add the bay leaf, onion and salt. Heat to boiling. Gradually add the squid, stirring, so that the water continues boiling. Cook, stirring, for about 45 seconds, or until the squid pieces turn white (opaque). Drain at once in a colander and rinse with cold running water, tossing the squid until they are cooled. Set aside.

3. Combine the tomatoes, celery, onion, basil or cilantro, garlic, oil, salt and a grinding of pepper in a serving bowl. Add the squid and toss to coat.

4. Transfer to a shallow bowl and garnish with lime wedges. Or refrigerate, covered, until ready to serve.

Warm Potato Salad with Sardines and Mustard-and-Lemon Dressing

PREPARATION TIME: 20 MINUTES ❧ COOKING TIME: 15 TO 20 MINUTES ❧ SERVES: 4

SELECT A LARGE PLATTER, and make an attractive arrangement of the warm potato salad, strips of green bell pepper and red onion, slices of seedless cucumber and dill sprigs. Top with the silvery sardines. Add hard-cooked egg halves to round out this hearty main dish.

> **PLAN AHEAD:**
>
> This recipe uses hard-cooked eggs.

1½ pounds small new potatoes or all-purpose potatoes, peeled

2 cans (3¾ ounces each) Norway Brisling sardines packed in water

5 tablespoons extra-virgin olive oil

2 tablespoons fresh lemon juice

2 teaspoons Dijon-style mustard
Salt and freshly ground black pepper, to taste

1 green bell pepper, quartered, trimmed, cut into narrow strips

1 medium red onion, trimmed, halved lengthwise, cut into thin wedges

½ seedless cucumber, trimmed, thinly sliced

2 tablespoons chopped fresh dill, plus sprigs, for garnish

4-5 large leaves romaine or other leafy greens

2 hard-cooked eggs, peeled, halved (see step 1, page 195)
Lemon wedges

1. Cook the potatoes in boiling, salted water to cover until tender, 15 to 20 minutes. Drain; cool slightly before cutting into generous ¼-inch slices.

2. Meanwhile, carefully lift the sardines from the cans; blot any moisture with a paper towel and set aside.

3. Whisk together the oil, lemon juice, mustard, salt and pepper until blended.

4. Drizzle 1 tablespoon of the oil mixture over the sardines. In a large bowl, combine the potatoes, green pepper, onion, cucumber and chopped dill with the remaining dressing; carefully fold to blend well.

5. Line a serving platter with the greens. Spoon the potatoes into the center. Garnish with the sardines, hard-cooked eggs, dill sprigs and lemon wedges.

❧ SALADS ❧

Spinach, Shrimp and Warm New Potato Salad

PREPARATION TIME: 20 MINUTES ⁕ MARINATING TIME: AT LEAST 15 MINUTES

COOKING TIME: 15 MINUTES ⁕ SERVES: 4

THIS SALAD OF SEARED SHRIMP and small potatoes in a white wine dressing is both good-looking and unusual. Keep in mind that the shrimp can be marinating while the potatoes are cooking, so the preparation and cooking times for the dish are short. The idea for this innovative combination came from Odessa Piper, the chef-owner of L'Etoile, a restaurant in Madison, Wisconsin.

1   pound large shrimp, peeled,
        deveined
4   tablespoons extra-virgin olive oil
1   teaspoon fresh thyme leaves or
        ½ teaspoon dried
1   teaspoon grated lemon zest
1   garlic clove, crushed through a press
        Salt and freshly ground black
            pepper, to taste
2   pounds small new red potatoes,
        halved or quartered
        (½-inch pieces)
½   cup dry white wine
3   tablespoons fresh lemon juice
1   package (10 ounces) fresh spinach,
        rinsed, stems trimmed

1. In a medium bowl, combine the shrimp, 1 tablespoon of the oil, thyme, lemon zest, garlic, a pinch of salt and a grinding of pepper. Stir and marinate for 15 minutes at room temperature or refrigerate for up to 2 hours.

2. Meanwhile, Cook the potatoes in boiling, salted water until tender, about 15 minutes. Drain.

3. Meanwhile, heat a large nonstick skillet over medium-high heat until hot enough to evaporate a drop of water upon contact. Add the shrimp, a few at a time, along with any marinade clinging to the bowl. Quickly sear, turning, until the shrimp are opaque in the center, about 3 minutes. Transfer to a side dish.

4. Add the wine to the hot skillet and boil until reduced by half, about 2 minutes. Off the heat, stir in 2 tablespoons of the oil, 2 tablespoons of the lemon juice, a pinch of salt and a grinding of black pepper; whisk to blend. Pour over the warm potatoes and toss to coat.

5. Toss the spinach with the remaining 1 tablespoon oil and the remaining 1 tablespoon lemon juice, and arrange on 4 dinner plates. Spoon the potatoes into the center and top the salad with the warm shrimp. Serve warm or at room temperature.

Lentil Salad with Italian Sausage and Mustard Vinaigrette

PREPARATION TIME: 15 MINUTES ❧ COOKING TIME: 20 TO 25 MINUTES ❧ SERVES: 4 TO 6

THIS IS A HEARTY SALAD that incorporates meat, starch and vegetables on one platter. To make it vegetarian, substitute mozzarella, Cheddar, Swiss or other cheese for the sausage.

1½ cups dark green or brown lentils, rinsed and picked over

¾ pound Italian pork or turkey sausages, casings removed

½ cup chopped green bell pepper

½ cup chopped red bell pepper

½ cup chopped celery

1 bunch scallions, trimmed, thinly sliced (1 cup)

½ cup chopped fresh Italian (flat-leaf) parsley

DRESSING

½ cup extra-virgin olive oil

3 tablespoons red wine vinegar

2 teaspoons Dijon mustard

1 garlic clove, crushed through a press

½ teaspoon salt

Freshly ground black pepper

Red-leaf lettuce leaves, rinsed, dried

4 ripe, plum tomatoes or 1 large, ripe tomato, cored, cut into wedges

2 hard-cooked eggs, peeled, halved (see step 1, page 195)

8 radishes, rinsed, trimmed

1. Cook the lentils in plenty of boiling, unsalted water to cover until tender, 20 to 25 minutes. Drain; rinse with cool water and set aside.

2. Meanwhile, crumble the sausage into a large nonstick skillet. Cook over medium heat, breaking it up with a spatula, until browned, about 5 minutes; set aside to cool.

PLAN AHEAD:

This recipe calls for hard-cooked eggs.

3. Combine the green and red peppers, celery, scallions and parsley in a large bowl. Add the cooled lentils and sausage.

4. Make the Dressing: Whisk all the ingredients in a small bowl. Toss with the salad.

5. Line a large, shallow serving bowl or a platter with the lettuce leaves. Spoon the salad into the center. Garnish with the tomato wedges, eggs and radishes.

Lentil and Spinach Salad with Crisp Bacon Dressing

PREPARATION TIME: 15 MINUTES * COOKING TIME: 20 TO 25 MINUTES
MARINATING TIME: 20 MINUTES * SERVES: 4

LENTILS tossed with spinach, mushrooms and a crisp bacon dressing make a satisfying meal. Serve with Basic All-Around Potato Salad (page 222).

1   cup dried green or brown lentils,
      rinsed and picked over

DRESSING

⅓   cup plus 1 tablespoon red wine
      vinegar
¼   cup plus 1 tablespoon extra-virgin
      olive oil
1   garlic clove, crushed through a press
      Salt and freshly ground black
      pepper, to taste

1   cup chopped white button
      mushrooms
½   cup red onion, cut into thin slivers
½   red bell pepper, cut into thin slivers
¼   cup finely chopped fresh Italian
      (flat-leaf) parsley
1   bag (10 ounces) fresh spinach,
      rinsed, stems removed,
      torn into pieces
4   strips bacon, cooked crisp, drained,

cut into small pieces
2   hard-cooked eggs, peeled,
      cut into quarters (optional;
      see step 1, page 195)
3   ripe plum tomatoes, quartered

1. Cook the lentils in plenty of boiling, unsalted water until tender, 20 to 25 minutes. Drain; rinse with cool water and set aside. (You should have about 4 cups.)

2. Meanwhile, Make the Dressing: In a medium bowl, whisk the vinegar, oil, garlic and salt and pepper. Set aside 2 tablespoons.

3. Add the mushrooms to the dressing; stir and marinate for 20 minutes.

4. Add the lentils, onion, red pepper and parsley to the dressing; toss to coat. Toss the spinach with the reserved 2 tablespoons dressing. Add half the spinach to the lentils; toss.

5. Place the remaining spinach on a platter or on 4 plates. Top with the lentil salad. Garnish with the bacon. Top the salads with the eggs, if using, and the tomato wedges.

Mixed Greens with Toasted Walnuts and Parmigiano-Reggiano Curls

PREPARATION TIME: **10** MINUTES ● COOKING TIME: **5** MINUTES ● SERVES: **4**

I KEEP A WEDGE OF IMPORTED Parmigiano-Reggiano on hand for many uses, but especially for this favorite salad. I use any mixture of greens, but for special occasions, I splurge on mesclun, a mixture of baby greens available in many specialty produce markets. Walnuts, stored in the freezer, thaw quickly when heated in a dry skillet over medium-low heat.

½ cup broken walnut pieces

¼ cup extra-virgin olive oil

1 tablespoon aged red wine vinegar
    or fresh lemon juice
    Pinch salt
    Freshly ground black pepper,
      to taste

8 cups torn mixed salad greens
    (romaine, watercress, arugula,
    Boston lettuce, red leaf lettuce
    or radicchio)
    Wedge Parmigiano-Reggiano

1. Place the walnuts in a small, heavy skillet, and heat gently over medium-low heat, stirring, until they are warmed and toasted, about 5 minutes. Set aside.

2. In a large bowl, whisk together the oil, vinegar or lemon juice, salt and pepper. Add the salad greens and toss to coat. Distribute among 4 plates. Sprinkle the warm walnuts on top.

3. Using a vegetable peeler, cut large curls of cheese from the wedge directly on top of the salads, adding about 4 or 5 curls per salad. Serve at once.

Mixed Greens and Fresh Herb Salad with Mustard Vinaigrette

PREPARATION TIME: 10 MINUTES ❀ SERVES: 6

THERE IS NOTHING more attractive than a simple salad of mixed greens with leaves of fresh herbs added.

8   cups trimmed, rinsed, torn salad greens (spinach, romaine, curly-leaf or other)
1   cup packed torn fresh basil leaves, dill sprigs and/or mint leaves

DRESSING
2   tablespoons red wine vinegar
1   teaspoon Dijon-style mustard
¼   teaspoon salt
    Freshly ground black pepper
5   tablespoons extra-virgin olive oil

1   cup thinly sliced seedless cucumber

1. Rinse and prepare the salad greens and herbs and refrigerate, wrapped in paper towels or a clean dish towel or stored in a salad spinner until ready to use.

2. Make the Dressing: Combine the vinegar, mustard, salt and pepper in a small bowl. Gradually add the oil, whisking constantly with a small whisk or fork.

3. Place the greens and herbs in a salad bowl and add the cucumber.

4. Just before serving, drizzle the dressing over the salad and toss to coat.

Cabbage Salad with Lemon and Olive Oil

PREPARATION TIME: 10 MINUTES ❖ SERVES: 4

I CAN'T RESIST BEING CREATIVE with something as simple as shredded cabbage. Coleslaw (often erroneously called "cold slaw"), from the Dutch word *koolsla*, meaning "cabbage salad," has been popular in America since the eighteenth century. This late-twentieth-century version is dressed with extra-virgin olive oil, lemon and garlic. I love it freshly made and still crunchy, but some people prefer it after it has been sitting for a day. This is a perfect accompaniment to Spicy Marinated Shrimp (page 160; see photograph, page 83) or grilled salmon that has been seasoned with olive oil, garlic and hot red pepper flakes.

¼ cup extra-virgin olive oil
3 tablespoons fresh lemon juice
1 teaspoon grated lemon zest
1 garlic clove, crushed through a press
½ teaspoon salt
Freshly ground black pepper, to taste
1 bag (16 ounces) thinly sliced cabbage
2 scallions, trimmed, cut into thin diagonal slices

1 small carrot, trimmed, coarsely shredded
1 tablespoon chopped fresh Italian (flat-leaf) parsley

1. In a large bowl, whisk the oil, lemon juice, lemon zest, garlic, salt and pepper until blended.

2. Add the cabbage, scallions, carrot and parsley; toss until well mixed. Cover and refrigerate until ready to serve.

Cabbage Salad with Sesame Oil and Rice Vinegar

PREPARATION TIME: 10 MINUTES ❋ SERVES: 4

PERFECTLY SLICED CABBAGE, both red and green, is now conveniently sold in resealable plastic bags in many produce sections. These packages have encouraged me to use raw cabbage in salads a lot more often.

⅓ cup rice wine vinegar
¼ cup vegetable oil
1 garlic clove, crushed through a press
1 teaspoon sugar
1 teaspoon dark sesame oil
½ teaspoon salt
1 bag (about 16 ounces) presliced cabbage or 6 cups thinly sliced
½ cup slivered green bell pepper
¼ cup slivered red onion (optional)

1. Whisk together the vinegar, oil, garlic, sugar, sesame oil and salt in a large bowl.

2. Add the cabbage, green pepper and onion, if using. Toss to blend. Serve at once or cover and refrigerate until ready to serve.

Tomato, Sweet Onion and Fresh Mint Salad

PREPARATION TIME: 10 MINUTES ● SERVES: 4

SEVERAL YEARS AGO, my friend Rocco brought me a bushel basket of mint, roots and all, and planted it in a patch of earth along my kitchen wall. Today, Rocco's patch continues to grow, and I add mint to many of my salads. For this recipe, the tomatoes must be beautifully ripened and the onion crisp, sweet and mild. Serve with Green Beans with Basil and Mint (page 241) or with grilled chicken or fish.

2   large, ripe tomatoes, cored,
        cut into ½-inch cubes

1   large sweet onion, trimmed,
        cut into ½-inch cubes

2   tablespoons extra-virgin olive oil,
        or more to taste
    Salt and freshly ground black
        pepper, to taste

½   cup packed coarsely chopped
        mint leaves

1. Combine the tomatoes, onion, oil, salt and pepper in a large bowl; toss to coat.

2. Stir in the mint just before serving.

Tomato, Cucumber and Olive Salad with Crumbled Feta Cheese

PREPARATION TIME: 10 MINUTES ❀ STANDING TIME: 20 MINUTES ❀ SERVES: 4

I ALWAYS THINK of this Greek-inspired salad when I am serving grilled lamb or fish. Cut the tomatoes and cucumbers into pieces that match the size of the olives. I usually use black Kalamata olives, because I like the contrast against the red tomatoes. Also, because they have a slit in the side, they are easier to pit. All you need do is press against them with the side of a large chef's knife, and they split open, making the pit easy to remove. Spanish green olives can also be used. They are sometimes sold "cracked," making them simple to pit too.

1. In a large bowl, combine the tomatoes, oil and oregano; toss to blend. Let stand at room temperature for about 20 minutes, or until the tomatoes release their juices. Add the cucumbers and olives.

> **PLAN AHEAD:**
> Allow 20 minutes for the salad to come to room temperature.

2. Line a serving plate with lettuce leaves; add the salad mixture. Sprinkle with the feta. Serve immediately

2-3 pounds ripe plum tomatoes (or regular tomatoes in season), cut into ½-inch cubes

2 tablespoons extra-virgin olive oil, or to taste

1 tablespoon snipped fresh oregano leaves or 1 teaspoon dried

2 cups chopped (½ inch) cucumbers

½ cup pitted brine-cured black or green olives

Curly-leaf lettuce leaves

½ cup crumbled feta cheese

Panzanella

PREPARATION TIME: 10 MINUTES ❃ COOKING TIME: 5 MINUTES

STANDING TIME: 15 MINUTES ❃ SERVES: 4

THIS IS A SALAD for one season only: late summer, when tomatoes are at their peak. Panzanella is an Italian favorite, an ingenious way to use up day-old bread. Toasting the bread is not traditional, but it adds a nice flavor. Serve this hearty salad as part of an all-vegetable dinner along with corn on the cob and grilled eggplant slices and red pepper wedges.

2 pounds ripe, juicy tomatoes
½ cup chopped red onion
½ cup torn fresh basil leaves
¼ cup extra-virgin olive oil,
    or more to taste
1 garlic clove, crushed through a press
    Salt and freshly ground black
        pepper, to taste

4 ½-inch-thick slices day-old
    whole wheat bread (Italian
    or sourdough)

1. In a large bowl, combine the tomatoes, onion, basil, oil, garlic, salt and pepper; toss and let stand at room temperature.

2. Grill, broil or toast the bread and cut into ½-inch cubes. Add to the salad. Toss and let stand for 15 minutes before serving so the bread will absorb some of the juices. Taste and add more oil, salt and/or pepper, as needed.

Warm New Potato Salad with Scallions, White Wine and Olive Oil

PREPARATION TIME: **10 MINUTES** ❈ COOKING TIME: **15 MINUTES** ❈ SERVES: **4**

STUDENTS IN MY COOKING CLASSES tell me that they make this salad all summer long. It is a perfect illustration of my cooking philosophy: keep it simple, use the best ingredients and the dish will be a winner every time.

2 pounds small to medium-sized red potatoes, halved or quartered

½ cup dry white wine

1 bunch scallions, trimmed, thinly sliced

¼ cup extra-virgin olive oil
Salt and freshly ground black pepper, to taste

1. Cook the potatoes in boiling, salted water to cover until tender, about 15 minutes. Drain in a colander and transfer to a serving bowl. Immediately pour the wine over the hot potatoes and toss to blend.

2. Add the scallions, oil, salt and pepper. Toss gently. Serve warm or at room temperature.

Basic All-Around Potato Salad

PREPARATION TIME: **10 MINUTES** ❋ COOKING TIME: **15 TO 20 MINUTES** ❋ SERVES: **4**

SOMEWHERE along the line, I stopped adding mayonnaise to my potato salads. Instead, I use a combination of extra-virgin olive oil and wine vinegar, cider vinegar or lemon juice. This version allows for additions of plenty of chopped raw vegetables.

2 pounds small or medium-sized potatoes, peeled or scrubbed

¼ cup extra-virgin olive oil

2-3 tablespoons red wine vinegar, cider vinegar or fresh lemon juice

1 garlic clove, crushed through a press
Salt and freshly ground black pepper, to taste

POSSIBLE ADDITIONS

2 ribs celery, trimmed (use the green leaves), thinly sliced

3-4 scallions, trimmed, cut into thin slices

1 large carrot, coarsely shredded (on the coarse-shred side of the grater)

½ red bell pepper, cut into thin slivers

½ green bell pepper, cut into thin slivers

½ cup slivered red onion or sweet yellow onion

¼ cup chopped fresh Italian (flat-leaf) parsley and/or basil

1. Cook the potatoes in boiling, salted water to cover until tender, 15 to 20 minutes. Drain and rinse to cool slightly. Halve or quarter the potatoes.

2. In a large bowl, whisk the oil, vinegar or lemon juice, garlic, salt and pepper until blended. Add any of the additions listed above; toss gently. Serve warm or at room temperature.

Sesame Brown Rice Salad with Peanuts

PREPARATION TIME: **10 MINUTES** ❖ COOKING TIME: **45 MINUTES** ❖ SERVES: **4**

THIS SALAD OF RICE AND PEANUTS becomes a main dish with the addition of leftover roasted chicken, pulled into thin shreds, and a handful of steamed broccoli florets. If you like, cooked shrimp or pork can be used in place of the chicken.

1 cup short- or medium-grain brown rice

2½ cups water with a pinch of salt

3 tablespoons vegetable oil

3 tablespoons fresh lime juice, or more to taste

1 teaspoon dark sesame oil

1 small garlic clove, crushed through a press

¼ teaspoon salt

1 large carrot, shredded or finely chopped

2 scallions, trimmed, thinly sliced

⅓ cup chopped unsalted dry-roasted peanuts

Fresh cilantro sprigs, for garnish (optional)

1. Cook the rice in the salted water until tender and all the water is absorbed, about 45 minutes. Transfer to a colander, rinse with cold water, and shake off the excess. (The rice can be cooked ahead and left at room temperature until ready to serve.)

2. Combine the oil, lime juice, sesame oil, garlic and salt in a large bowl. Add the rice, carrot and scallions. Toss to blend; sprinkle with the peanuts. Taste and add more lime juice, if desired. Garnish with cilantro, if using, and serve.

Yellow Confetti Rice Salad

PREPARATION TIME: 10 MINUTES ● COOKING TIME: ABOUT 15 MINUTES

COOLING TIME: 20 MINUTES ● SERVES: 4

TURMERIC TURNS THE RICE bright yellow and, in concert with the cumin, gives it a slightly exotic taste. This is a striking salad, with flecks of scallion, green pepper and red pepper.

1 tablespoon extra-
   virgin olive oil
1 cup long-grain rice
   (such as American
   basmati)
½ teaspoon turmeric
¼ teaspoon ground cumin
1¾ cups water
1 teaspoon salt

DRESSING

2 tablespoons extra-virgin olive oil
2 tablespoons fresh lemon juice,
   or to taste

2 tablespoons thinly sliced scallion
   (both green and white parts)
2 tablespoons *each* finely chopped
   green and red bell pepper

PLAN AHEAD:

Make the rice far enough in advance so it can cool, about 20 minutes.

1. In a wide sauce-pan, heat the oil over low heat. Add the rice and stir to blend. Sprinkle with the turmeric and cumin; stir to coat.

2. Add the water and salt; heat to boiling. Stir once. Cover and cook over medium-low heat, without stirring, until the water is absorbed and the rice is tender, about 15 minutes.

3. Let the rice stand, uncovered, until cooled, about 20 minutes; do not stir.

4. Meanwhile, Make the Dressing: Whisk the oil and lemon juice together.

5. Add the dressing, scallion and green and red peppers to the cooled rice. Stir gently with a fork before serving.

Couscous with Confetti Vegetables

THIS COUSCOUS, MIXED with tiny flecks of brightly colored vegetables, is excellent with Famous Lemon and Basil Chicken (page 113) or with any grilled meat or fish. To make this an all-in-one main dish, add strips of cooked chicken or shrimp along with the vegetables in step 3.

1½ cups quick-cooking couscous
2½ cups boiling water, or as needed
1   teaspoon salt, or as needed

DRESSING

⅓   cup extra-virgin olive oil
¼   cup fresh lemon juice, or as needed
1   small garlic clove, crushed
       through a press

2   cups packed (½ inch) strips of
       romaine or other lettuce
1   carrot, peeled, coarsely shredded
1   small cucumber, peeled, finely diced
       (¼ inch)
¼   cup *each* finely diced (¼ inch) green
       and red bell peppers
¼   cup finely diced (¼ inch) red onion
       or scallion
½   cup fresh corn kernels (cut from
       1 ear of corn; optional)

2   tablespoons finely chopped fresh
       Italian (flat-leaf) parsley

1. Place the couscous in a large bowl and add the boiling water and salt; stir once. Cover and let stand for 20 minutes, or until all the liquid is absorbed.

2. Meanwhile, Make the Dressing: Whisk together the oil, lemon juice and garlic; set aside.

3. Fluff the couscous with a fork. Add the lettuce, carrot, cucumber, green and red peppers, onion or scallion, corn (if using) and parsley; toss to blend. Taste and correct the seasonings with fresh lemon juice and salt. Serve at room temperature.

White Bean and Fennel Salad

PREPARATION TIME: 10 MINUTES ● SERVES: 4

THIS SIMPLE SALAD is delicious paired with tuna salad. It's also nice served as a spread on Crostini (page 24) or as part of an antipasto table or platter.

1   small bulb fennel, tough green tops and bottom trimmed (1 cup thinly sliced celery can be substituted)
2   cups rinsed canned or cooked dried cannellini (white kidney) beans
½   cup thinly slivered red onion
¼   cup chopped fresh Italian (flat-leaf) parsley
1   tablespoon finely chopped fresh oregano leaves or ½ teaspoon dried
3   tablespoons extra-virgin olive oil
2   tablespoons red wine vinegar or fresh lemon juice, or more to taste
Salt and freshly ground black pepper, to taste

1. Cut the fennel into lengthwise quarters. Cut each quarter crosswise into ⅛-inch-thick slices.

2. Combine the beans, fennel, onion, parsley and oregano in a bowl.

3. In a separate bowl, whisk together the oil, vinegar or lemon juice, salt and pepper. Add to the beans; toss to coat. Adjust the seasonings and serve.

VARIATION

Shrimp and Fennel Salad: For a main-dish salad, add 1½ pounds shelled and deveined large shrimp and garnish with lemon wedges.

Lentil and Green Pea Salad with Lemon-and-Herb Dressing

PREPARATION TIME: 15 MINUTES ❋ COOKING TIME: 20 TO 30 MINUTES ❋ SERVES: 8

SWEET GREEN PEAS contrast pleasantly with earthy brown lentils. I serve this for supper with Warm New Potato Salad with Scallions, White Wine and Olive Oil (page 221) and a simple sliced-tomato salad.

16 ounces brown lentils, rinsed and picked over

8 cups water

2 garlic cloves, 1 bruised with the side of a knife, 1 crushed through a press

1 bay leaf

¼ cup extra-virgin olive oil

3 tablespoons fresh lemon juice

1 tablespoon prepared mustard (smooth or grainy)

Freshly ground black pepper

2 cups tiny fresh or frozen green peas, thawed if frozen

1 cup chopped celery

½ cup coarsely shredded carrots

½ cup finely chopped red onion

¼ cup chopped fresh Italian (flat-leaf) parsley

1 tablespoon chopped celery leaves

½ teaspoon salt, or to taste

Lettuce leaves
Cherry tomatoes, for garnish

1. Combine the lentils, water, bruised garlic and bay leaf in a large saucepan. Cover and heat to boiling over high heat. Uncover and boil, stirring occasionally, until the lentils are tender to the bite, 20 to 30 minutes. Drain and rinse with cool water; discard the bay leaf.

2. Whisk the oil, lemon juice, mustard, crushed garlic and pepper to taste in a large bowl. Add the well-drained lentils, peas, celery, carrots, onion, parsley and celery leaves. Toss to coat. Taste and adjust the seasonings, adding the salt.

3. Line a large, deep platter with lettuce leaves. Spoon the lentil salad into the center. Garnish with the cherry tomatoes and serve.

Tomato and Bulgur Salad

PREPARATION TIME: 10 MINUTES ● STANDING TIME: 15 MINUTES ● SERVES: 4

BULGUR IS BEST KNOWN to the American palate as the star of a Middle Eastern salad called tabbouleh, which is a mixture of soaked bulgur, chopped onion, parsley, mint and lemon juice. To this bulgur salad, I add tomatoes and olives and a dressing made with tahini, which is a rich, intensely flavored puree of sesame seeds. I like it for lunch or as part of a plate served with sliced cucumbers, grilled eggplant and red peppers.

SALAD

½   cup bulgur

1   cup boiling water

1   tablespoon extra-virgin olive oil

2   cups diced (¼ inch) firm, ripe plum tomatoes

½   cup diced (¼ inch) red onion

¼   cup finely chopped fresh Italian (flat-leaf) parsley

2   garlic cloves, finely chopped or crushed through a press

15   Kalamata olives or other brine-cured black olives, pitted, coarsely chopped

DRESSING

2   tablespoons tahini (sesame paste)

1   tablespoon cold water

2   tablespoons fresh lemon juice, or more to taste

2   tablespoons extra-virgin olive oil, or more to taste

¼   teaspoon ground coriander

Salt and freshly ground black pepper, to taste

1. Make the Salad: Place the bulgur in a medium heat-resistant bowl. Stir in the water and let stand, uncovered, until softened, about 15 minutes. Transfer to a strainer and drain off any excess water; cool. Return the bulgur to the bowl and toss with the oil. Add the tomatoes, onion, parsley, garlic and olives.

2. Make the Dressing: In a small bowl, stir the tahini and water until blended. Add the lemon juice, oil, coriander, salt and pepper.

3. Add to the salad and stir to blend. Taste and add more lemon juice, oil, salt and pepper as needed.

Black Bean and White Corn Salad

PREPARATION TIME: 15 MINUTES • COOKING TIME: 30 SECONDS • SERVES: 4 TO 6

THIS SALAD MAKES A TERRIFIC main dish with the addition of cooked shrimp or strips of chicken. Otherwise, serve it as a side dish or a vegetarian main dish.

1¾	cups rinsed canned or cooked dried black beans
1½	cups fresh white corn kernels, cut from the cob (or crisp vacuum-packed canned white shoepeg corn), drained, rinsed
1	cup diced (¼ inch) ripe plum tomatoes
1	cup diced (¼ inch) ripe avocado
½	cup chopped scallions
½	cup chopped fresh cilantro leaves, plus sprigs for garnish
1	tablespoon minced seeded jalapeño
1	teaspoon ground cumin
3	tablespoons fresh lime juice, or more to taste
2	tablespoons extra-virgin olive oil
1	garlic clove, crushed through a press
½	teaspoon salt
2	cups crisp romaine or iceberg lettuce, shredded

1. Combine the beans, corn, tomatoes, avocado, scallions, cilantro leaves and jalapeño in a large bowl.

2. Sprinkle the cumin in a small skillet and set over low heat. Heat, stirring, until fragrant, about 30 seconds. Remove from the heat. Add the lime juice, oil, garlic and salt; whisk to blend.

3. Add the dressing to the bean mixture and toss. Spread the lettuce on a deep platter or on 4 individual salad plates and spoon the bean salad into the center. Garnish with the cilantro sprigs and serve.

Arugula, Pear, Parmesan and Walnut Salad

PREPARATION TIME: **10 MINUTES** ● COOKING TIME: **3 MINUTES** ● SERVES: **4**

THIS SALAD IS PERFECT in the fall, when pears are at their best. I like to use either crisp, crunchy brown-skinned Boscs or the softer, sweeter Bartletts.

1	garlic clove, halved
1	tablespoon honey
1	tablespoon fresh lemon juice
	Pinch salt
1	Bartlett, Bosc or other ripe pear, quartered, cored, cut into thin lengthwise slices
1-2	bunches arugula, rinsed, long stems trimmed (about 4 cups)
⅓	cup broken walnuts
	Small wedge Parmigiano-Reggiano

1. Rub the surface of a large mixing bowl with the cut side of the garlic; reserve for another use. Add the honey, lemon juice and salt; whisk to blend. Add the pear; turn to coat.

2. Heat the walnuts in a small dry skillet, stirring until warm, about 3 minutes.

3. Just before serving, add the arugula to the bowl; toss to coat with the dressing. Divide the salad among 4 plates, distributing the pears evenly on top of the arugula. Sprinkle with the walnuts. Using a vegetable peeler or cheese server, cut curls of cheese from the wedge and arrange on top of the salad.

Salad of Prosciutto, Figs, Greens and Parmigiano-Reggiano

PREPARATION TIME: 15 MINUTES ❋ COOKING TIME: 3 MINUTES ❋ SERVES: 4

IN SUMMER AND EARLY FALL, when fresh figs are in my market, I find as many different ways as possible to incorporate these sensually luscious fruits into my meals. This apt combination reflects the cultural and culinary affinity of figs, prosciutto and Parmigiano-Reggiano.

1   garlic clove, halved
8   cups mixed greens (arugula,
       romaine, chicory, radicchio,
       endive or others)
¼   cup slivered red onion
1   tablespoon extra-virgin olive oil
1   teaspoon fresh lemon juice
     Salt and freshly ground black
       pepper, to taste
8   fresh ripe figs, quartered
       (see page 306)
¼   cup coarsely chopped walnuts
8-12 thin slices prosciutto,
       preferably imported
     Wedge Parmigiano-Reggiano

1. Rub the inside of a large bowl with the cut side of the garlic; reserve for another use. Add the salad greens, onion, oil, lemon juice, a sprinkling of salt and a grinding of black pepper. Toss to coat. Spread the salad on a large oval platter or distribute among 4 dinner plates.

2. Arrange the fig pieces around the edges of the platter or plates. Heat the walnuts in a small, dry skillet, stirring, over low heat until they are warmed and toasted, about 3 minutes. Sprinkle over the salad.

3. Drape the slices of prosciutto over the salad. Using a vegetable peeler or cheese server, cut thin curls of the cheese and arrange on top. Serve immediately.

VEGETABLES

FAST

WHEN YOU HAVE MORE TIME

Vegetables Can Make a Meal

Menu I

Oven-Roasted Asparagus (without the vinaigrette) *(page 235)*

Pan-Grilled Mushrooms *(page 268)*

Favorite Oven-Baked Potatoes with Olive Oil,
Garlic and Herbs *(page 284)*

(See photograph, page 34.)

Menu II

Oven-Roasted Vegetable Plate with Herb Dressing *(page 296)*

Cannellini Beans with Arugula and Golden Garlic *(page 183)*

Menu III

Warm Sautéed Tomato Slices with Melted Cheese *(page 289)*

Green Beans with Basil and Mint *(page 241)*

Broccoli with Crisp Garlic Slivers *(page 245)*

Menu IV

Skillet-Browned Red Potatoes with
Rosemary and Garlic *(page 283)*

Easy Oven-Roasted Red Bell Peppers *(page 278)*

Escarole with Vinegar and Olive Oil *(page 263)*

Oven-Roasted Asparagus with Shallot-Mustard Vinaigrette

PREPARATION TIME: 10 MINUTES ● COOKING TIME: 10 TO 20 MINUTES ● SERVES: 4

THE DRY HEAT OF OVEN-ROASTING intensifies asparagus flavor. After it is almost tender, I place big curls (cut with a vegetable peeler) of Parmigiano-Reggiano over the asparagus and continue to roast just until the cheese melts, 2 or 3 minutes more.

A range of oven temperatures is given here because you may want to roast fish, chicken or another dish at the same time. If you are cooking the asparagus alone, roast it for 10 to 12 minutes at 500 degrees. If you want to roast at 400 to 450 degrees, the asparagus will take 15 to 20 minutes to become tender. Stir the asparagus halfway through the roasting time.

1 large bunch (about 1 pound) asparagus, trimmed and washed
2 tablespoons extra-virgin olive oil
1 garlic clove, thinly sliced
1 tablespoon red wine vinegar, or more to taste
½ teaspoon Dijon-style mustard
2 tablespoons very finely chopped shallots
½ teaspoon minced fresh thyme leaves, stripped from the stems, plus more for garnish (optional)

Pinch salt
Freshly ground black pepper

1. Preheat the oven to 400 or 500 degrees F. Place the asparagus in a large (13-x-9-inch) baking dish, add 1 tablespoon of the oil and the garlic; toss to coat. Roast until crisp-tender, 10 to 20 minutes, depending on the size of the asparagus, stirring once. Remove from the oven and let stand at room temperature until ready to serve.

2. Whisk together the remaining 1 tablespoon oil, vinegar, mustard, shallots and thyme. Season to taste with salt and pepper.

3. Arrange the asparagus on a large platter or distribute among individual salad plates. Pour the dressing evenly over the asparagus and toss to coat. Garnish with the thyme leaves, if using.

ASPARAGUS

WHEN BUYING ASPARAGUS, examine the tips carefully. They shouldn't be dry and curled or soft and mushy. I like asparagus with slender-to-medium-sized stems. But larger ones that look bright green and sparkling can also be good. Just make sure to adjust the cooking time; fatter asparagus will take longer.

CLEANING ASPARAGUS

Hold a spear in one hand; take the stem end in your other hand, and bend until it snaps— it will break at the most tender spot. Once the stems are snapped, the asparagus will be different lengths. If the asparagus spears are medium to thick, use a vegetable peeler to remove the larger scales near the base. If they are pencil-thin, this is not necessary. Soak the asparagus in a large bowl or a pan (a loaf pan is good) of cool water for at least 10 minutes. If they are very sandy, repeat the soaking, using warm water; drain and crisp them in cold tap water.

Asparagus with Warm Chopped Egg, Lemon, Capers and Olive Oil

PREPARATION TIME: 10 MINUTES ● COOKING TIME: 5 TO 6 MINUTES ● SERVES: 4

FOR THIS SPRING SALAD, I pair subtle asparagus with the rich, buttery taste of warm hard-cooked egg and the tang of lemon juice. Sometimes, I serve this dish as a main course, doubling or tripling the recipe so that each person gets ½ pound of asparagus. It makes a lovely meal preceded by Curried Carrot Soup (page 45) and followed by a dessert of fresh fruit and cheese or strawberries dipped in vanilla-laced confectioners' sugar (page 312).

1-1½	bunches (about 1½ pounds) asparagus, washed and trimmed
	Pinch plus ½ teaspoon salt
3	tablespoons extra-virgin olive oil
3	tablespoons fresh lemon juice
1	tablespoon cold water
1	small garlic clove, crushed through a press
½	teaspoon fresh thyme leaves, stripped from the stems
	Freshly ground black pepper, to taste
1	warm hard-cooked egg, peeled and finely chopped (see step 1, page 195)
½	tablespoon capers, rinsed and patted dry

1. Fill a large, wide skillet with about 1 inch of water; heat to boiling. Add the asparagus and a pinch of salt, cover and cook until just tender, 5 to 6 minutes. Drain; arrange on a large platter.

2. Combine the oil, lemon juice, water, garlic, thyme, pepper and ½ teaspoon salt in a small bowl; whisk to blend. Stir in the egg. Spoon over the asparagus and serve at room temperature.

> **PLAN AHEAD:**
> This recipe calls for a hard-cooked egg.

GREEN BEAN KNOW-HOW

JULIA CHILD, THE MUCH-LOVED, much-quoted and much-admired chef and culinary personality, changed my life the day I saw her plunge a colander of fresh green beans into a pot of boiling water. My nutrition education had taught me that all vegetables should be steamed, or they would lose their nutrients. So I dutifully steamed my beans, even though they often came out tough and tasteless. As a result, I avoided them as often as possible. But thanks to Julia Child, I learned that boiling green beans in lots of salted water renders them plump, tender and very tasty.

Don't spend time trimming both the stem and blossom ends of a green bean. Line the beans up on a cutting board with all the stem ends even and slice them off. Leave the gracefully tapered blossom ends alone.

Warm Green Beans and Red Potatoes with Basil Vinaigrette

PREPARATION TIME: 10 MINUTES ● COOKING TIME: 20 TO 25 MINUTES ● SERVES: 4

THIS WARM SALAD is standard fare at my house from May through September. (Leftovers are great cold.) For an easy supper menu, I often serve this with Famous Lemon and Basil Chicken (page 113), either hot off the stove or at room temperature. Cooking the potatoes and green beans in the same pot not only saves cooking time but clean-up time as well.

1½   pounds small (about 2½ inches in diameter) red potatoes, washed
1   teaspoon salt
¾   pound tender green beans, rinsed, trimmed, halved crosswise

BASIL VINAIGRETTE
3   tablespoons extra-virgin olive oil
3   tablespoons red wine vinegar
¼   cup chopped fresh basil or parsley
      Salt and freshly ground black pepper, to taste

½   cup slivered red onion

1. Place the potatoes in a large saucepan. Fill the pan three-quarters full with water; add the salt. Cook, covered, until the potatoes are not quite tender when pierced with a skewer, about 15 minutes. Add the green beans to the water with the potatoes; cook, uncovered, until crisp-tender, 5 to 10 minutes. Drain in a colander.

2. Make the Basil Vinaigrette: In a large salad bowl, whisk the oil, vinegar, basil or parsley, salt and pepper until blended.

3. When the potatoes are cool enough to handle, cut them into slices or half circles and add them to the vinaigrette. Add the beans and onion, and toss to blend. Serve while still warm or at room temperature.

Green Beans with Two Red Peppers

PREPARATION TIME: **10 MINUTES** ❁ COOKING TIME: **10 MINUTES** ❁ SERVES: **4**

THESE BEANS, dressed with warm olive oil, are colorful and tasty. For rich, roasted flavor, cook the bell peppers until the edges turn brown.

1½   pounds tender green beans,
         stem ends trimmed

2   teaspoons salt

2   tablespoons extra-virgin olive oil

½   cup slivered red bell pepper

½   teaspoon hot red pepper flakes,
      or to taste

1   garlic clove, cut into thin slivers

1   tablespoon coarsely chopped fresh
      Italian (flat-leaf) parsley
      (optional)

1. Heat a large pot of water to boiling. Add the green beans and salt; stir until the water returns to a boil. Boil the beans until tender but still bright green, about 8 minutes. Drain immediately.

2. Meanwhile, heat the oil, red bell pepper and red pepper flakes in a medium skillet. Cook, stirring, over medium heat until the bell pepper begins to brown on the edges, about 5 minutes. Reduce the heat to low, add the garlic and cook, stirring, until softened, about 2 minutes.

3. In a serving bowl, toss the hot beans and the oil mixture together. Add the parsley, if using.

Green Beans with Basil and Mint

I SERVE THIS DISH all summer long, when beans and basil are at their peak. Sometimes, I add red onion or thin slivers of sweet yellow onion or thin wedges of red or yellow tomato. It is pretty and simple and a little elegant. For maximum flavor, add the beans to the basil, mint and olive oil when they are piping hot.

1½ pounds tender green beans, stem ends trimmed

2 teaspoons salt

⅓ cup fresh basil leaves, coarsely chopped or torn into pieces

¼ cup fresh mint leaves, coarsely chopped or torn into pieces

2 tablespoons extra-virgin olive oil

1 garlic clove, bruised with the side of a knife

Salt and freshly ground black pepper, to taste

1. Heat a large pot of water to boiling. Add the green beans and salt; stir until the water returns to a boil. Boil the beans until tender but still bright green, about 8 minutes. Drain immediately.

2. Combine the basil, mint, oil and garlic in a large bowl. Add the hot beans, salt and pepper. Serve warm or at room temperature.

Warm Beet Salad with Wilted Greens

PREPARATION TIME: 15 MINUTES ● COOKING TIME: 20 MINUTES ● SERVES: 4

IF BEET GREENS aren't plentiful or fresh enough, substitute the dark green outside leaves of a head of romaine lettuce. I love this vegetable side dish served with Favorite Meat Loaf (page 136).

1½ pounds beets

4 tablespoons extra-virgin olive oil

2 tablespoons plus 2 teaspoons apple cider vinegar

Salt and freshly ground black pepper, to taste

4 cups large pieces (1 x 2 inch) torn beet greens and/or dark outside leaves romaine lettuce, rinsed and drained

1 scallion, trimmed, cut into ¼-inch-thick diagonal slices

1 small tender inside celery rib, cut into ¼-inch-thick diagonal slices

1. Trim the tops from the beets, leaving about 2 inches of stem attached. If the tops are young and tender, trim the long stems, rinse thoroughly and add to the romaine leaves in step

3. Cook the beets in boiling, salted water to cover until tender, about 20 minutes. Drain and set aside until cool enough to handle. Peel off the skins and cut into 1-inch chunks.

2. Meanwhile, whisk 3 tablespoons of the oil, 2 tablespoons of the vinegar and salt and pepper in a large bowl. Add the beets and toss to coat. Set aside.

3. Place the romaine leaves and/or young beet tops with the water still clinging to the leaves in a large skillet with a lid. Turn the heat to medium and when the mixture begins to steam, after about 2 minutes, uncover and stir. Drain off any excess liquid. Add the remaining 1 tablespoon oil, 2 teaspoons vinegar, salt and pepper to the skillet; toss to coat.

4. Spread the romaine and/or beet leaves in an even layer on a platter. Add the scallion and celery to the beet mixture; toss and spoon onto the cooked greens. Serve warm or at room temperature.

Oven-Roasted Beets with Orange Gremolata

PREPARATION TIME: 10 MINUTES ● COOKING TIME: 1 TO 1½ HOURS ● SERVES: 4

LIKE ASPARAGUS, beets benefit from being roasted in the oven. These oven-roasted beets can be dressed in any number of ways. Cut them into wedges, and toss with a simple red wine vinaigrette or drizzle with basil oil or serve with mayonnaise. Or top them with a zesty mixture of orange, parsley and garlic stirred into a little olive oil, as in this recipe.

1-1½   pounds medium-sized beets (4-6)

ORANGE GREMOLATA

⅓   cup packed fresh Italian (flat-leaf)
        parsley leaves
2½   strips (½ x 2 inches) orange zest
        (remove with a vegetable peeler)
1   garlic clove, chopped
        Salt and freshly ground black
        pepper, to taste
⅓   cup extra-virgin olive oil

1. Preheat the oven to 350 degrees F.

2. Trim the beet tops down to the base (reserve the tops separately if they are relatively unblemished and cook as a side dish; see Warm Beet Salad with Wilted Greens, opposite page). Trim the long root from each beet and discard. Wash and dry the beets. Wrap them individually in foil and roast in the oven until tender, 1 to 1½ hours. When the beets are cool enough to handle, unwrap them and rub off the skins. They are now ready to dress and serve. Slice them into ¼-inch-thick crosswise slices.

3. Make the Gremolata: Combine the parsley, orange zest, garlic, salt and pepper in a food processor and process until finely chopped. Add the oil and process just to blend. Or, if you prefer, gather the parsley, orange zest and garlic into a little pile on a cutting board and finely chop with a large knife. Transfer to a small bowl and stir in the salt and pepper and oil.

4. Arrange the beets, overlapping, on a large platter. Top with the gremolata. Serve at room temperature.

BROCCOLI

Broccoli is a staple in my kitchen. Usually, I steam it until tender (I don't like it undercooked) and serve it plain, dressed with a little olive oil and garlic. I also like it tossed in a stir-fry and added to a salad or even a frittata.

BROCCOLI TWO WAYS

To serve broccoli plain, trim about 1 inch of the tough woody ends off the stems. Then cut the stems lengthwise into portions. The spears can be steamed and served plain or with olive oil or butter and lemon wedges.

To prepare broccoli for stir-fries, salads or other dishes, trim the woody ends off the stems. Trim the florets with about 1 inch of the tender stems attached. Trim the thick skin off the stems with a small knife, especially toward the base. Slice the stems into rounds or cut into lengthwise sticks, then stack and cut crosswise into small pieces.

Broccoli with Crisp Garlic Slivers

PREPARATION TIME: 10 MINUTES ❋ COOKING TIME: 8 MINUTES ❋ SERVES: 4

THIS IS FOR GARLIC LOVERS. Plain steamed broccoli becomes exciting when topped with slivers of crisp-fried garlic. For a simpler version, put a garlic clove through a press and heat it in oil until it sizzles. (You can add hot red pepper flakes too.) Toss the garlic-flavored oil with the steamed broccoli and serve with lemon wedges.

1   bunch broccoli, trimmed, thick
        stalks peeled, tops cut into
        2-inch pieces
3   tablespoons extra-virgin olive oil
1   tablespoon thin garlic slices
        Pinch hot red pepper flakes,
        or more to taste (optional)
        Salt, to taste

1. Place a vegetable steamer in a large, wide saucepan above 1 to 2 inches of water. Cover and heat to boiling. Add the broccoli; cover and cook until tender, about 8 minutes.

2. Meanwhile, combine the oil, garlic and red pepper flakes, if using, in a small skillet. Heat over very low heat, stirring constantly, until the garlic begins to sizzle and turn golden, about 2 minutes. Remove from the heat and remove the garlic from the oil with a slotted spoon. Set aside. (This is important because the garlic will continue to cook in the hot oil, and if it gets too brown, it will taste bitter.) Reserve the oil.

3. Transfer the cooked broccoli to a serving dish. Sprinkle with salt, drizzle with the garlic-flavored oil and top with the crisp garlic slices. Serve at once.

Ginger Stir-Fried Broccoli with Soy Almonds

PREPARATION TIME: 10 MINUTES ● COOKING TIME: 7 MINUTES ● SERVES: 4

THIS MAKES A LOVELY main course served with a brown rice pilaf or plain cooked brown rice.

PLAN AHEAD:

This recipe uses Soy Almonds.

1 bunch broccoli, woody part of stems trimmed, cut into ½-inch-thick slices, florets cut into 1-inch lengths
1 tablespoon vegetable oil
1 tablespoon grated peeled fresh ginger
1 garlic clove, crushed through a press
½ cup Soy Almonds (page 12)
Salt, to taste

1. Steam the broccoli in a vegetable steamer set over boiling water until tender, about 6 minutes. Remove the steamer from the pan.

2. Heat a large nonstick skillet over medium-high heat until hot enough to evaporate a drop of water upon contact. Add the oil, ginger and garlic and stir-fry for 20 seconds. Add the broccoli and stir-fry until coated with the seasonings. Stir in the almonds, season with salt and serve.

Broccoli with Potatoes and Tomatoes

PREPARATION TIME: 10 MINUTES ❋ COOKING TIME: 25 MINUTES ❋ SERVES: 4

THIS PRETTY, FRESH-TASTING and original side dish will perk up your winter menus.

2 pounds potatoes, peeled, cut into large chunks

2 cups water

1 bunch broccoli, trimmed, cut into 1-to-2-inch pieces

1 tablespoon extra-virgin olive oil

1 garlic clove, thinly sliced

2 small vine-ripened tomatoes, cored, cut into 1-inch cubes, or 1 cup halved cherry tomatoes

1 tablespoon grated Parmigiano-Reggiano

1. Combine the potatoes and the water in a large, wide saucepan. Cover and cook over low heat until potatoes are almost tender, about 15 minutes. Add the broccoli, cover and cook until tender, about 8 minutes.

2. Place a colander over a bowl and drain the potatoes and broccoli, saving the cooking liquid. Wipe out the saucepan and add the oil and garlic.

3. Cook the garlic in the oil over low heat just until it begins to sizzle and turn golden, about 1 minute. Add the potatoes and broccoli and stir to coat.

4. Add about ½ cup of the reserved cooking liquid. Add the tomatoes and toss to distribute evenly. Sprinkle with the cheese. Serve at once.

BROCCOLI RABE

WHEN I WAS A CHILD, the only broccoli I knew was broccoli rabe with olive oil and garlic. We called the vegetable "robbies," and although Mom admonished us to eat our robbies because they were filled with iron and would make us big and strong, I secretly thought they were bitter and awful. Fortunately, as an adult, I became a broccoli rabe fan.

To prepare broccoli rabe, trim off and discard about 1 inch of the toughest part of the stems. Working from the flowered end, trim the florets, leaving 1 to 2 inches of the thin, tender stems attached to the flowers. Peel off any tough outer skin from the remaining stems, which are thinner and more pliable than regular broccoli, and cut them into 1-inch lengths.

I like broccoli rabe cooked in plenty of boiling, salted water until it is almost tender, about 6 minutes. Then I drain it and sauté it in olive oil and garlic. The boiling tempers the bitterness, and it also softens the fibers, making the robbies more palatable and tender.

Broccoli Rabe with Olive Oil and Garlic

PREPARATION TIME: 5 MINUTES ● COOKING TIME: 11 TO 15 MINUTES ● SERVES: 4

MAKE CLEANUP EASY by using the same pan for heating the oil and garlic that was used for boiling the broccoli rabe. I often serve this on Polenta Toasts (page 190; see photograph, page 82.)

1 bunch (about 1½ pounds) broccoli rabe, rinsed, thick ends of stems trimmed, cut into 2-inch lengths
   Salt, to taste
2 tablespoons extra-virgin olive oil
1 garlic clove, cut into thin slivers
   Pinch hot red pepper flakes

1. Fill a large, wide saucepan with water; heat to boiling. Add the broccoli rabe and salt; boil until tender, 6 to 8 minutes. Drain immediately. Wipe the pan dry.

2. Add the oil, garlic and red pepper flakes to the saucepan. Heat over low heat, stirring, until warmed and garlic begins to sizzle, about 5 minutes.

3. Stir the broccoli rabe into the warm oil to coat. Serve at once.

Sweet and Sour Cabbage

THIS CABBAGE IS SLOWLY BRAISED in olive oil and garlic and finished with a sprinkling of sugar and a dash of apple cider vinegar. It is delicious with a roasted pork loin, baked fish or grilled chicken.

2 tablespoons extra-virgin olive oil

1 garlic clove, crushed through a press

4 cups thinly sliced green cabbage

1 tablespoon sugar, or more to taste

2 tablespoons apple cider vinegar,
   or more to taste

Salt and freshly ground black
   pepper, to taste

1. Combine the oil and garlic in a large, deep skillet and heat over medium heat until the garlic begins to sizzle, about 1 minute. Add the cabbage all at once and stir until coated with the oil. Cover and cook for 3 minutes, or just until the cabbage begins to wilt.

2. Turn the heat to high, sprinkle the cabbage with the sugar and vinegar and stir to coat. Add salt and pepper. Taste and correct the seasonings and serve.

Stir-Fry of Cabbages with Asian Flavor

PREPARATION TIME: 15 MINUTES ● COOKING TIME: 5 MINUTES ● SERVES: 4

THIS DISH HAS JUST ENOUGH soy sauce, sesame oil, ginger and garlic to suggest Asia without overwhelming the vegetables. I like to serve this with broiled salmon or tuna.

1 tablespoon white vinegar

2 teaspoons soy sauce

1 teaspoon sugar

1 teaspoon cornstarch

1 teaspoon dark sesame oil

2 cups thinly sliced green cabbage

2 cups thinly sliced napa (Chinese celery) cabbage

2 cups thinly sliced bok choy (Chinese cabbage)

1 cup diced red cabbage

2 tablespoons vegetable oil

½ teaspoon finely chopped peeled fresh ginger

¼ teaspoon finely chopped garlic
   Pinch hot red pepper flakes (optional)

1. Stir the vinegar, soy sauce, sugar, cornstarch and sesame oil together until blended. Set aside.

2. Toss the cabbages together in a large bowl; set aside.

3. Heat a wok or a large, heavy skillet over high heat until hot enough to evaporate a drop of water upon contact. Add the vegetable oil, ginger and garlic; stir-fry for 10 seconds. Add the cabbage all at once and stir-fry just until the cabbage begins to wilt, about 3 minutes.

4. Stir the reserved vinegar mixture to blend and add to the skillet all at once; add the red pepper flakes, if using. Stir to coat. Stir-fry for 1 minute to heat through and serve.

Oven-Roasted Carrots with Lemon and Olives

PREPARATION TIME: **10 MINUTES** ● COOKING TIME: **55 MINUTES** ● SERVES: **4**

I F YOU CAN FIND THEM, use peeled and trimmed baby carrots for this recipe. Otherwise, substitute regular carrots that you have trimmed, peeled and cut into 2-inch lengths. If the carrots are fat, halve them lengthwise as well.

1   bag (1 pound) baby carrots, rinsed

4   garlic cloves, bruised with the
      side of a knife

4   paper-thin slices lemon, halved

2   tablespoons extra-virgin olive oil

2   tablespoons coarsely chopped pitted
      Kalamata or other brine-cured
      black olives

   Salt and freshly ground black
      pepper, to taste

1. Preheat the oven to 400 degrees F. Combine the carrots, garlic, lemon and oil in a shallow 13-x-9-inch baking dish. Stir to blend.

2. Bake, stirring occasionally, until the carrots are tender and lightly browned, about 45 minutes. Add the olives. Bake for 10 minutes longer. Sprinkle with salt and pepper and serve.

Roasted Carrots and Parsnips

PREPARATION TIME: 10 MINUTES ● COOKING TIME: 55 MINUTES ● SERVES: 4

PARSNIPS AND CARROTS are similar in flavor and are delicious when roasted together. Tarragon goes well with both of these vegetables.

1   bag (1 pound) carrots, trimmed,
       peeled, cut into 1-inch-thick
       diagonal slices
1   bag (1 pound) parsnips, trimmed,
       peeled, cut into 1-inch-thick
       diagonal slices
2   tablespoons extra-virgin olive oil
       Salt and freshly ground black
          pepper, to taste
1   tablespoon fresh tarragon leaves,
       snipped from the stems,
       or a pinch of dried

1. Preheat the oven to 400 degrees F. Combine the carrots, parsnips and oil in a shallow 13-x-9-inch baking dish. Sprinkle with salt, pepper and half of the fresh tarragon, if using, or all of the dried. Stir to blend.

2. Bake, stirring occasionally, until the vegetables are tender and lightly browned, about 55 minutes. Add the remaining fresh tarragon, if using, just before serving.

Lorena's Fried Cauliflower

PREPARATION TIME: 20 MINUTES ● COOKING TIME: 20 MINUTES ● SERVES: 4 TO 6

LORENA ALESSIO, friend and architecture student from Turin, Italy, boarded with us in Brooklyn, New York, during a semester at a nearby college. Lorena shopped and cooked almost every day. Often while she cooked, she would nonchalantly pick up the telephone and call her mother in Turin. With the telephone tucked under her ear, she would follow her mother's verbal recipe while juggling pots, pans, spoons and spatulas. This is one of her recipes. Serve as a vegetable side dish or as finger food with drinks before dinner.

1	head cauliflower, rinsed, trimmed, separated into large florets
2	large eggs
	Salt and freshly ground black pepper, to taste
1-1½	cups fine dry bread crumbs
½	cup grated Parmigiano-Reggiano
	Extra-virgin olive oil
	Lemon wedges

1. Steam the cauliflower in a vegetable steamer set over 1 inch of boiling water until crisp-tender, about 4 minutes. Lift from the water and let cool.

2. Beat the eggs in a shallow bowl with a pinch of salt and a grinding of black pepper. Combine the bread crumbs and cheese in a pie plate or a shallow bowl.

3. Dip the cauliflower into the beaten eggs; shake off the excess. Coat with the bread-crumb mixture; shake off the excess. Place on a work surface covered with a sheet of foil or waxed paper.

4. Pour the oil into a large, deep skillet to a depth of 1 inch. Heat over medium heat until a cube of bread added to the hot oil sizzles and becomes golden brown, about 1 minute.

5. Fry the breaded cauliflower in batches, turning until golden on all sides, about 5 minutes per batch. Adjust the heat as necessary to maintain a gentle sizzle. Remove with a slotted spoon to a double thickness of paper toweling to drain. Keep warm on a heatproof plate in an oven at the lowest setting until all the cauliflower is fried. Serve hot with lemon wedges.

Cauliflower with Anchovy Sauce

PREPARATION TIME: 15 MINUTES ● COOKING TIME: UP TO 20 MINUTES ● SERVES: 6

CAULIFLOWER AND ANCHOVIES are a classic combination. I always encourage people to try cooking with anchovies, especially if they think of them as a strong-tasting fish. In sauces, anchovy melts to a paste and mellows, contributing a distinctive, slightly salty flavor.

1   head cauliflower, rinsed, trimmed, left whole

3   tablespoons extra-virgin olive oil

3   tablespoons unsalted butter

1   small garlic clove, crushed through a press

3   anchovy fillets, well drained and patted dry

1   hard-cooked egg (see step 1, page 195)

1   teaspoon fresh lemon juice

1   teaspoon small capers, rinsed and drained

1   teaspoon finely chopped fresh parsley

1. Steam the cauliflower in a vegetable steamer over boiling water until tender when pierced with a skewer. A small cauliflower will take between 12 and 15 minutes, a large cauliflower up to 20 minutes.

2. Meanwhile, heat the oil and butter in a small, heavy saucepan over medium-low heat. When the foam subsides, add the garlic and cook until fragrant, about 1 minute. Stir in the anchovy fillets; mash with the back of a fork until dissolved. Set aside off the heat.

> **PLAN AHEAD:**
>
> This recipe uses a hard-cooked egg.

3. Separate the white and yolk of the hard-cooked egg. Finely chop the egg white; set aside. Press the yolk through a sieve with the back of a spoon; set aside separately.

4. Just before serving the cauliflower, quickly reheat the anchovy sauce. Stir in the chopped egg white, lemon juice and capers. Place the cauliflower on a platter; pour the anchovy sauce over the top. Sprinkle with the reserved egg yolk and the parsley.

Corn on the Cob

I WAIT ALL YEAR for the corn season to arrive, and when it finally does, we eat corn every day. Sometimes, I just pull back the husk and eat it on my way home from the farmer's market. I love it raw, sweet and crunchy and often cut it from the cob and add it, without cooking, to salads and soups.

Of course, there is nothing like sweet (unsalted) butter slathered on a steaming ear, but just as often, we reach for the bottle of extra-virgin olive oil and drizzle on a little. The following recipes for flavored olive oil and butter are nice for a change of taste.

Basic Cooking for Corn on the Cob

CORN HAS CHANGED A LOT in the last decade. Each season, it seems sweeter and more tender than the season before, requiring less and less cooking. This is my basic recipe for cooking corn on the cob: Place the husked corn on a vegetable steaming rack set over 1 inch of boiling water in a large, wide saucepan. Cover and cook for 3 to 5 minutes, depending on the variety.

Garlic Oil for Fresh-Cooked Corn

PREPARATION TIME: 2 MINUTES

COOKING TIME: 2 MINUTES

MAKES ENOUGH FOR 8 EARS

2   tablespoons extra-virgin olive oil
1   garlic clove, crushed through a press
    Freshly ground black pepper, to
    taste (optional)

COMBINE THE OIL and garlic in a small skillet. Heat, stirring, over low heat just until the garlic begins to sizzle, about 2 minutes. Remove from the heat. Using a brush, spread the garlic oil on a steaming ear of corn. Add a grinding of black pepper, if desired.

Cumin Butter for Fresh-Cooked Corn

PREPARATION TIME: 2 MINUTES

COOKING TIME: LESS THAN 1 MINUTE

MAKES ENOUGH FOR 8 EARS

1   teaspoon ground cumin
4   tablespoons butter (preferably
    unsalted), softened

PLACE THE CUMIN in a small skillet, and heat slowly over very low heat just until fragrant, about 20 seconds. Remove from the heat. Combine the cumin and butter in a small bowl and stir together with a fork. Serve with the corn.

GETTING THE MOST FROM DRIED SPICES

HEATING DRIED SPICES VERY SLOWLY in a small, dry skillet over low heat releases their oils and makes them more aromatic. Try this technique the next time you decide to add curry powder to potato salad, paprika to a vinaigrette or ground cumin to a cold soup or salsa.

Corn and Lima Beans with Cream, Tomatoes and Basil

PREPARATION TIME: 15 MINUTES ● COOKING TIME: 10 MINUTES ● SERVES: 4

THIS RECIPE TAKES ALMOST everything I love about August and stirs it together in one pot. Although I admire the fresh limas at the farmstand, they are labor-intensive to shell, so I usually resort to frozen limas (which I love) for this dish.

1   tablespoon unsalted butter
½   cup slivered red onion
2   cups thawed frozen Fordhook lima
       beans (or fresh, if you desire)
2   cups fresh raw corn kernels
       (cut from 4 or more cobs)
½   cup heavy cream
1   ripe tomato, cored, seeded, cut into
       ½-inch pieces (about 1 cup)
     Salt and freshly ground black
       pepper, to taste
2   tablespoons thin slivers fresh basil

1. Melt the butter in a medium skillet over medium-low heat. Stir in the onion and cook, stirring, until wilted but not browned, about 3 minutes. Add the lima beans and the corn; cover and cook for 5 minutes.

2. Add the cream and heat just to boiling. Stir in the tomato, salt and pepper and simmer gently for 2 minutes. Sprinkle with the basil before serving.

EGGPLANT

I HAVE A PASSION FOR EGGPLANT, especially the firm, deep purple beauties available in local markets at the height of the season. Because I love the look of the skin, I never completely peel eggplant. Instead, I randomly remove wide strips with a vegetable peeler, leaving the partly peeled vegetable looking like a zebra.

My mother always salted, weighted and drained eggplant before frying it in olive oil, and for years, I did the same. She claimed the salt removed the bitterness. What the salt does is draw out the moisture, so when the eggplant is fried, it becomes more crisp. As for the bitterness, I suspect that like people, some eggplants are sweet and mellow—and some are not. I have on occasion salted and drained it only to have it remain slightly bitter-tasting. As a rule, though, the only time I bother to salt eggplant is when I intend to fry it.

Baking eggplant in a hot oven is not only a less tedious but a lower-fat method of preparing it. Cut the eggplant into slices, brush with a thin film of olive oil and bake in a 425-degree oven until browned on both sides. The browned and tender eggplant slices are then ready for your favorite recipes.

Baked Eggplant, Tomato and Basil Salad

PREPARATION TIME: **10** MINUTES ❖ BAKING TIME: **20** MINUTES ❖ SERVES: **4**

THIS IS A RECIPE MEANT FOR the height of the eggplant, tomato and basil season. Any other time, the ingredients just aren't wonderful enough for the flavors to soar. Serve as a first course or as a side dish with grilled meat, fish or poultry.

4 tablespoons extra-virgin olive oil

1 garlic clove, crushed through a press

1 eggplant (1-1¼ pounds), trimmed, cut into 8 thick slices

1-2 tablespoons red wine vinegar

¼ teaspoon salt, or more as needed
Freshly ground black pepper

2-3 large ripe tomatoes, cored, cut into 8 thick slices

6 large basil leaves

1. Preheat the oven to 425 degrees F. Combine 2 tablespoons of the oil and the garlic in a small bowl and lightly brush both sides of the eggplant slices. Arrange in a single layer on a baking sheet. Bake until browned and tender, turning the slices once, about 10 minutes per side. Remove from the oven and cool.

2. Meanwhile, whisk 1 tablespoon of the oil and the vinegar until blended; add salt and pepper to taste. Sprinkle on the eggplant.

3. Sprinkle the tomato slices with a pinch of salt and the remaining 1 tablespoon oil. On a large platter, arrange slightly overlapping circles of tomato and eggplant slices.

4. Stack the basil leaves on a work surface. Working from the stem end, roll them up tightly. Cut the roll into thin crosswise slices, making long, thin strips of the basil. Sprinkle over the top of the salad. Serve at room temperature.

Herb-Marinated Baked Eggplant Slices

PREPARATION TIME: 10 MINUTES ❋ COOKING TIME: 20 MINUTES ❋ SERVES: 4

BAKING EGGPLANT IS A NO-FUSS, efficient way of cooking this favorite vegetable. Look for eggplants that are plump and heavy, with taut, shiny skin. If they are old and dehydrated, their flavor will be bitter.

My mother always peeled eggplant in strips so that it was purple-and-white striped when she was done. Leaving some of the skin intact is attractive and gives support to the flesh.

3   tablespoons extra-virgin olive oil

1   garlic clove, crushed through a press

1   eggplant (1-1¼ pounds), trimmed, peeled, cut into 12 slices ¼ inch thick

½   teaspoon fresh rosemary leaves, stripped from the stems, or ½ teaspoon dried

¼   teaspoon fresh thyme leaves, stripped from the stems, or ¼ teaspoon dried

¼   teaspoon fresh oregano leaves, stripped from the stems, or ¼ teaspoon dried

¼   teaspoon salt
     Freshly ground black pepper

1-2   tablespoons red wine vinegar

1. Preheat the oven to 425 degrees F. Combine 2 tablespoons of the oil and the garlic in a small bowl and lightly brush both sides of the eggplant slices. Arrange in a single layer on a non-stick baking sheet. Combine the rosemary, thyme, oregano and salt in a small bowl; sprinkle the top of each eggplant slice evenly with the herbs. Add a grinding of black pepper.

2. Bake the eggplant until browned and tender, turning the slices once, about 10 minutes per side. Whisk the remaining 1 tablespoon oil and the vinegar until blended; sprinkle on the eggplant. Serve warm or at room temperature.

Oven-Braised Fennel with Melted Parmigiano-Reggiano

PREPARATION TIME: 10 MINUTES ❀ SOAKING TIME: 30 MINUTES

BAKING TIME: 35 TO 40 MINUTES ❀ SERVES: 4

WHEN I WAS A CHILD, one of the vegetables I loved was fennel. In Italian, fennel is called *finocchio*, but all the youngsters in the family called it "finook." It was a holiday food, always served raw, cut into sticks and presented in Mom's best cut-glass relish dishes, along with celery sticks, radishes and olives.

> **PLAN AHEAD:**
>
> Allow ½ hour for the fennel to soak in ice water.

Now that I am the cook in the family, I have discovered the delicate flavor and silken texture of cooked fennel. I like it oven-braised with slivers of Parmigiano-Reggiano melted on top. Fresh fennel quickly loses its moisture and juicy taste when refrigerated. Soaking it in ice water will quickly restore its freshness.

2 large fennel bulbs
½ cup reduced-sodium canned
   chicken broth or water
1 tablespoon unsalted butter,
   cut into small pieces
8 thin curls Parmigiano-Reggiano
   Freshly ground black pepper

1. Trim the base of the fennel bulbs. Cut across the top of each to remove the darker green portion of the ribs and the fernlike tops. Cut the fennel lengthwise into quarters. Place the fennel in a large bowl and cover with water and ice cubes. Let soak for 30 minutes.

2. Preheat the oven to 400 degrees F.

3. Drain the fennel and arrange in a 13-x-9-inch or other shallow baking dish. Add the broth or water. Dot with the butter. Cover with foil and bake until the fennel is tender when pierced with a fork, 30 to 35 minutes.

4. Arrange the cheese evenly over the fennel. Bake until the cheese melts, about 5 minutes. Add a grinding of black pepper. Serve immediately.

Escarole with Vinegar and Olive Oil

PREPARATION TIME: **10** MINUTES ❋ COOKING TIME: **20** MINUTES ❋ SERVES: **4**

OTHER KIDS GREW UP ON canned peas; I grew up on escarole. Escarole was served both cooked and raw. The tough outside leaves were braised until soft and tender and served with olive oil, garlic and a splash of vinegar. The tender inside leaves were used in the salad bowl. Today, I still love this green, especially when it is braised. This is Mom's recipe.

1 large bunch escarole (about 1¾ pounds), rinsed, trimmed, torn into small pieces
  Salt
1 tablespoon extra-virgin olive oil
1 garlic clove, halved
1 tablespoon red wine vinegar, or more to taste
  Freshly ground black pepper, to taste

1. Fill a large pot halfway with water, heat to boiling and add a pinch of salt. Stir in the escarole. Cover and cook until very soft and tender, about 15 minutes. Drain and press with the back of a spoon to remove any excess moisture.

2. Place the oil and garlic in a medium skillet; heat just until the garlic begins to sizzle, about 1 minute. Remove and discard the garlic. Add the drained escarole and heat, stirring, until coated with the oil. Add the vinegar, more salt and pepper, stir to blend and serve at once.

VARIATION

Escarole and Potatoes with Vinegar and Olive Oil: Boil 1 pound cubed peeled potatoes until tender. Drain and add to the oil and garlic along with the escarole in step 2.

LEEKS

ALTHOUGH THEY ARE MEMBERS OF THE ONION FAMILY, leeks have a sweet, gentle taste, not at all like that of an onion. In fact, they look more like overgrown scallions, but without the sharp, hot taste.

The white part, which is the edible portion, is kept that way by a process called hilling—which is simply mounding the soil up around the leek to keep it "blanched," or white. For this reason, leeks can be very sandy and need to be carefully washed to remove the grit from between the layers. Trim the root end and the dark green tops from the leeks. Peel off one or two of the outside layers. Place in a bowl filled with lukewarm water. Let the leeks soak for a while, and inspect some of the layers to see if they are still sandy. If they are, split them lengthwise with a large sharp knife and soak in clean water. The final rinsing can be in cold tap water.

Braised in a little broth or water, leeks will be tender—but not mushy—in 10 to 12 minutes. Or you can oven-roast them, as in the following recipes.

Leeks are large, so 1 or 2 per person is usually sufficient. If they are slender or immature, serve 2 or 3 per person.

Oven-Braised Leeks

PREPARATION TIME: 10 MINUTES ❋ COOKING TIME: 25 TO 30 MINUTES ❋ SERVES: 4

SERVE THESE LEEKS at room temperature as part of a first course of assorted vegetables, with a splash of lemon juice or mild vinegar, or serve warm as a side dish. If the leeks are large, cut a slit through the base so the rinse water can reach between the leaves; this will also hasten the cooking.

8   medium-sized leeks, roots, green tops and outside leaves trimmed, thoroughly rinsed in warm and cold water
1   tablespoon extra-virgin olive oil or 2 tablespoons reduced-sodium canned chicken broth
1   strip (½ x 2 inches) lemon zest, twisted to release the flavor
    Pinch dried thyme or sprig fresh (optional)
    Salt and freshly ground black pepper

1. Preheat the oven to 350 degrees F. Arrange the leeks in one layer in a 13-x-9-inch baking dish. Drizzle with the oil or broth. Add the lemon zest and thyme, if using. Cover with foil.

2. Bake until the leeks are fork-tender, 25 to 30 minutes. Season with salt to taste and a grinding of black pepper and serve.

Oven-Braised Leeks with Tomato and Orange Vinaigrette

PREPARATION TIME: 20 MINUTES ❋ COOKING TIME: 25 TO 30 MINUTES ❋ SERVES: 4

BECAUSE LEEKS ARE OFTEN available during the peak of tomato and basil season, I like them together. This simple composition of tender leeks with a dressing of fresh tomato, basil and a little orange zest is attractive and refreshing. Serve it as a first course or as a side dish with fish.

8   medium-sized leeks, roots, green tops and outside leaves trimmed, thoroughly rinsed in warm and cold water

1   tablespoon extra-virgin olive oil or 2 tablespoons reduced-sodium canned chicken broth
     Salt and freshly ground black pepper

VINAIGRETTE

½   cup finely chopped seeded fresh or good-quality canned tomato

1   tablespoon mild white wine vinegar or cider vinegar

1   tablespoon slivered fresh basil

½   teaspoon finely shredded orange zest
     Pinch salt, or to taste

1. Preheat the oven to 350 degrees F. Arrange the leeks in one layer in a 13-x-9-inch baking dish. Drizzle with the oil or broth. Cover with foil.

2. Bake until the leeks are fork-tender, 25 to 30 minutes. Season with salt to taste and a grinding of black pepper. Uncover and cool to room temperature.

3. Make the Vinaigrette: Combine the tomato, vinegar, basil, orange zest and salt in a small bowl; stir to blend. Taste and correct the seasonings.

4. Arrange the leeks on 4 salad plates or a large platter. Spoon the vinaigrette over them and serve.

VARIATION

Leeks with Mustard Vinaigrette: Prepare the leeks as directed in steps 1 and 2; cool. Whisk together 2 tablespoons extra-virgin olive oil, 1 tablespoon red wine vinegar and ½ teaspoon Dijon mustard until blended. Drizzle over the cooled leeks and serve as a first course or a side-dish salad.

MUSHROOMS

ONCE EXOTIC FARE, mushrooms are now standard in most refrigerators. My supermarket carries at least three or four varieties from which to choose. Many can be used interchangeably.

White Button Mushroom (Agaricus): The most widely available variety, ranging in color from creamy white to light brown and in size from small to very large. It has a mild flavor, especially when the underside of the cap is closed. When the mushroom matures, this part opens, exposing the dark brown gills. The older mushrooms taste richer.

Crimini (also called Italian brown mushroom): Related to Agaricus, except that the cap is brown. The flavor is deeper, denser and more earthy than that of the white mushroom.

Shiitake (also called oak or Black Forest mushroom): Once available only in dried form, imported from Asia, the shiitake is now cultivated in the United States and sold fresh in supermarkets and specialty stores. The flavor is rich and woodsy. Shiitakes are relatively expensive, but a little goes a long way. Discard the stems; they are inedible.

Oyster Mushroom (Pleurotus): A graceful, tender mushroom with a soft brown or gray color, shaped like an oyster shell. The flavor is mild, and the texture is delicate. These cook quickly and should be simply tossed in a hot skillet with olive oil or melted butter and herbs.

Portobello Mushroom: Enormous, often up to 5 inches in diameter, this mushroom is great as a meat substitute. Trim the stem, finely chop, and cook, along with the cap, in olive oil with garlic and herbs. They are delicious served on toasted bread with salad greens as a main-dish salad or an appetizer.

Enoki Mushroom: Growing in small clusters, with a long stem and a tiny budlike cap, these mushrooms are creamy white and very delicate. They are best added to salads, because they are slightly crunchy when raw. They are also pretty as a garnish on soups.

Pan-Grilled Mushrooms

PREPARATION TIME: 10 MINUTES ❋ COOKING TIME: 10 MINUTES ❋ SERVES: 4

PORTOBELLO MUSHROOMS are perfect for this recipe, but thick-sliced crimini or large white button mushrooms can be substituted, if preferred.

2-4	large Portobello mushrooms, ends of stems trimmed
¼	cup packed fresh Italian (flat-leaf) parsley
1	teaspoon fresh oregano leaves, stripped from the stems
1	teaspoon fresh thyme leaves, stripped from the stems
1	garlic clove, chopped
2	tablespoons extra-virgin olive oil, or more as needed
	Salt and freshly ground black pepper, to taste

1. Remove the mushroom stems and finely chop. Set caps aside, and reserve chopped stems.

2. Combine the parsley, oregano, thyme and garlic on a cutting surface and finely chop.

3. Heat the oil in a large nonstick skillet. Add the mushrooms, caps down, and cook, without turning, until lightly browned, about 5 minutes.

4. Sprinkle the reserved chopped stems and the herb mixture over the mushroom caps. Season with salt and pepper. Carefully turn the mushroom caps, and cook, adding a tiny bit more oil if the mushrooms seem dry, until they are tender, about 5 minutes more. Serve on a platter or as part of an antipasto menu.

Mushrooms with Melted Parmigiano-Reggiano

PREPARATION TIME: 10 MINUTES ● COOKING TIME: 10 MINUTES ● SERVES: 4

THIS RECIPE WAS BORN of necessity. It was dinnertime, and I hadn't even thought about it. In the refrigerator were two containers of mushrooms, a hunk of Parmigiano-Reggiano cheese and some fresh parsley and thyme. Serve this with toasted bread and a green salad.

¼   cup extra-virgin olive oil,
      or more as needed
2   boxes (10 ounces each) large white
      button or crimini mushrooms,
      wiped clean, cut into ¼-inch-
      thick slices (leave the stems on)
      Salt and freshly ground black
      pepper, to taste
2   garlic cloves, minced or crushed
      through a press
3   tablespoons chopped fresh parsley
1   teaspoon fresh thyme leaves,
      stripped from the stems,
      or ½ teaspoon dried
      Wedge Parmigiano-Reggiano
4   thick slices bread, cut from
      sourdough or whole-grain round
      peasant loaf

1. Heat the oil in a large nonstick skillet until very hot. Add the mushrooms and sauté, stirring often, over high heat until they are lightly browned, about 5 minutes.

2. Add a generous pinch of salt, a grinding of pepper, garlic, parsley and thyme. Sauté, stirring, over medium heat for about 2 minutes more. Spread the mushrooms in an even layer, and press them lightly with the back of a spatula. Reduce the heat to medium-low.

3. Shave large curls of cheese over the top of the mushroom "pancake," covering the surface generously. Cover the skillet and cook just until the cheese melts, about 3 minutes.

4. Meanwhile, toast the bread under a broiler or in a toaster. Wrap in a towel to keep warm.

5. To serve, slide the mushroom pancake onto a platter or serve it from the skillet, distributing the portions evenly over the slices of warm toast.

ABOUT ONIONS

BERMUDA ONIONS

These large, flat onions come with white, tan or even red skin. They are mild and sweet and are perfect for slicing and eating raw.

SPANISH ONIONS

Often mistakenly called Bermuda onions, these are tan-colored jumbo onions. Very juicy, they are mild and sweet in flavor.

RED OR ITALIAN ONIONS

These are medium- or large-sized round red- or purple-skinned onions with a strong flavor.

YELLOW ONIONS

More golden than tan in color, they look like smaller versions of Spanish onions. They are round and are considered an all-purpose cooking onion. They are stronger in flavor than Spanish onions.

MAUI, VIDALIA AND WALLA WALLA

Unusually sweet and juicy, these onions are named for the locations in which they are grown—Maui, Hawaii; Vidalia, Georgia; and Walla Walla, Washington. The Maui and Vidalia are flat and round (like the Bermuda), and the Walla Walla, which can be very large, is round.

SMALL WHITE ONIONS

These miniature onions are small and sweet and are especially good when peeled and browned in olive oil or butter. The fastest way to peel small white onions is to plunge them into a saucepan of boiling water and let them simmer for about 5 minutes. Drain in a colander, and rinse them with cold water. With a paring knife, cut off the root end, and the loose outer layers will easily peel off.

Caramelized Small Onions

PREPARATION TIME: 15 MINUTES ❋ COOKING TIME: 16 MINUTES ❋ SERVES: 4

I PREFER COOKED ONIONS to raw. Instead of boiling them, I like to cook them slowly in olive oil until their natural sugar caramelizes and turns them the color of fresh-mowed straw. These onions are attractive stirred into a stew or served as a side dish with meat or game.

1   basket (about 1 pound) small white or purple onions (or half white and half purple)
1   tablespoon extra-virgin olive oil
1   teaspoon snipped fresh sage, marjoram or oregano leaves, or a pinch of dried
Salt and freshly ground black pepper, to taste

1. Peel the onions (see opposite page). This can be done in advance and the onions refrigerated until it is time to cook and serve them.

2. Heat the oil in a large nonstick skillet over medium-high heat. Add the onions and cook, shaking the pan and turning them, until golden brown, about 10 minutes. Add the herb of choice along with the salt and pepper. Cover the skillet, reduce the heat to low and cook until the onions are tender when pierced with the tip of a knife, about 5 minutes more. Uncover and cook for 1 minute on high heat to boil off any juices. Serve immediately.

VARIATION

Add 1 tablespoon red wine vinegar or apple cider vinegar during last 1 minute of cooking; stir to coat evenly.

Oven-Roasted Sweet Onions

PREPARATION TIME: 10 MINUTES ❧ COOKING TIME: 1 TO 1½ HOURS ❧ SERVES: 4

I LIKE TO SAVE THIS RECIPE for spring, when the first onions such as Vidalia or Texas sweets appear in my market. But any medium- to large-sized onions—even red ones—work well.

4   medium, uniformly sized onions, peeled, left whole
     Extra-virgin olive oil
     Salt and freshly ground black pepper, to taste
     Fresh herb of choice (sage leaves, oregano, marjoram, thyme or rosemary) or a pinch of dried

1. Preheat the oven to 350 degrees F. Cut a 6-inch-long piece of foil for each onion. Cut a slice from the top of each onion. Place an onion, top side up, on each piece of foil. Top each with a drizzle (about ½ tablespoon) of oil, a pinch of salt, a grinding of black pepper and a sprinkle (about ½ teaspoon or less) of the snipped fresh or pinch dried herb of your choice (or use two or three).

2. Wrap each onion tightly in the foil and place in the oven. Bake until the onions are very tender when pierced with a skewer, 1 to 1½ hours, depending on their size. Let cool slightly before unwrapping.

3. Unwrap the onions over a plate to catch the juices. Spoon the juices back over the onions and serve warm or at room temperature.

Green Peas with Bacon and New Potatoes

PREPARATION TIME: 5 MINUTES ❀ COOKING TIME: 10 TO 12 MINUTES ❀ SERVES: 4

AS A YOUNG BRIDE, I thought peas were boring, and as I slowly intro-duced my new husband to the ar-ray of colorful and flavorful vegetables from my Italian mother's kitchen, peas began to disap-pear from our menus. But I do like tiny green peas, especially when they are fresh in the mar-ket. Even the frozen ones taste sweet cooked with bacon and potato in the following recipe.

1 bacon strip, finely diced
1 tablespoon extra-virgin olive oil
1 cup diced (¼ inch) unpeeled
    red potato
2 cups fresh or frozen green peas
    Salt and freshly ground black
        pepper, to taste

1. Combine the bacon, oil and potato in a large nonstick skillet. Cook, stirring, until the bacon and potato begin to brown. Cover and cook for 5 minutes, until the potato is tender.

2. Stir in the peas. Cook, covered, until the peas are tender, 5 to 8 minutes. Season with salt and pepper and serve.

Sugar Snap Peas

I RARELY SEE SUGAR SNAP PEAS in my supermarket, but come summer, they are abundant at local farmstands. Sugar snaps are fabulous when eaten raw. If you can discipline yourself to save them for supper, they make a lovely side dish steamed and tossed with a little olive oil (or melted butter) and fresh mint. When the supply of sugar snaps is limited, I steam the few I have on hand, chill them in ice water, drain well and toss into a tomato-and-lettuce salad.

1   pound sugar snap peas, stem ends
        snapped, strings pulled
2   teaspoons extra-virgin olive oil
        or melted unsalted butter,
        or more to taste
1   tablespoon chopped fresh mint
        Salt, to taste

1. Place the sugar snaps on a steaming rack set over 1 inch of boiling water. Steam, covered, until crisp-tender, 2 to 3 minutes. Rinse with water to cool. Drain well and transfer to a serving bowl.

2. Drizzle with oil or butter, then sprinkle with the mint and salt. Serve at room temperature.

JARRED ROASTED RED PEPPERS

IT'S A GOOD IDEA to keep jarred roasted peppers on hand for use in a pinch. When buying them, scan them carefully to make sure they show a little bit of charring here and there, which gives them a toasted taste. At home, open the jar and drain off all the juices. Rinse the peppers well to get rid of some of the salts and other preservatives.

I add my favorite brand of extra-virgin olive oil and a piece of garlic crushed through a press or bruised with the side of a knife, along with salt, freshly ground black pepper and snips of fresh herb leaves, especially thyme and oregano. Garnished with a few black olives and sprigs of fresh herbs, these peppers are an acceptable substitute for the real thing.

Mom's Roasted and Peeled Red Peppers

PREPARATION TIME: 5 MINUTES ● COOKING TIME: 15 TO 20 MINUTES
COOLING TIME: 1 HOUR ● PEELING TIME: 2 MINUTES FOR EACH PEPPER

MY MOTHER, MARIE MATARAZA, is still cooking for family and friends at the grand age of 84. She roasts and peels her own peppers. Because they keep for only two or sometimes three days before turning sour, she freezes them by layering them between squares of foil so she can gently peel them apart as they thaw without tearing them.

Mom always serves her roasted red peppers sprinkled with capers as an antipasto. The salty tang of the capers contrasts nicely with the deep, sweet taste of the peppers. (Capers should always be placed in a small strainer and rinsed with water before using to wash off excess salt.)

Roast as many red peppers as you will have the time to peel and seed. I usually do at least four, since it hardly seems worthwhile to do fewer. Even when she was a "difficult teen," our daughter loved to peel peppers, so I would roast them, wrap them in foil to cool and leave them in the kitchen for her to peel later. They can sit around for a few hours without suffering. Be sure to cool them in foil (not a paper bag) so you can save all the precious juices.

> **PLAN AHEAD:**
>
> The roasted peppers will need about 1 hour to cool before they are peeled.

Large, unblemished red bell peppers, washed and dried

1. Position the broiler rack about 2 inches from the heat source and preheat the broiler.

2. Place a large piece of foil on a baking sheet. Arrange the peppers, shoulder to shoulder, in neat rows on the foil. Broil, turning frequently with tongs, until they are evenly charred, 15 to 20 minutes. Remove the pan from the broiler.

3. Fold the foil up over the peppers and seal. Let stand until cool enough to handle, about 1 hour. As the peppers cool, the skins will loosen and lift off easily.

4. Working over the foil to catch the juices, peel the loosened skin with a small paring knife. Separate the peppers into halves or quarters, following their natural contours. Lift out the seeds and the stem; pull out any thick white ribs. Flick off any remaining seeds with the tip of the knife. Never rinse the peppers under water; it will wash away all the good flavors.

5. Transfer the peppers to a bowl. Place a large strainer over the bowl. Empty the contents of the foil into the strainer and strain the juices, pressing down to extract as much flavor as possible.

6. Refrigerate until ready to use or serve. Freshly roasted and peeled peppers will keep in the refrigerator for 2 or 3 days before they sour.

VARIATIONS

Yellow bell peppers can also be roasted and peeled, although they are less sweet and sometimes (depending on the variety) less fleshy. If they are available, I buy one or two and roast them along with a batch of red peppers. They make a colorful addition.

Roasted Red Pepper Puree

PREPARATION TIME: 20 TO 25 MINUTES
MAKES: ABOUT ½ CUP

Use this as a spread for sandwiches, Crostini (page 24) or Polenta Toasts (page 190) or stirred into soup.

1-2	large red bell peppers
½	garlic clove, chopped
1-3	teaspoons extra-virgin olive oil
	Salt and freshly ground pepper

1. Roast, cool and peel the peppers as directed on the opposite page.

2. Place the peppers and garlic in a food processor and process until finely chopped. With the motor running, add the oil, a few drops at a time until emulsified.

3. Add salt and pepper to taste.

Easy Oven-Roasted Red Bell Peppers

PREPARATION TIME: 10 MINUTES ● COOKING TIME: 45 TO 55 MINUTES ● SERVES: 4

WHEN I AM IN NEED of a roasted-pepper fix but lack the time and energy to make them from scratch, I simply roast them in a hot oven until their skins are charred, and serve them with the skins on. These are especially good with the Pork Loin with Fennel and Garlic (page 135), but they also make a fine addition to an antipasto platter or a sandwich.

2-3   large red bell peppers, quartered, stems and seeds removed

2   tablespoons extra-virgin olive oil

1-2   garlic cloves, bruised with the side of a knife

1-2   sprigs fresh thyme (optional)
Salt and freshly ground black pepper, to taste

1. Preheat the oven to 400 degrees F. Arrange the peppers in a large shallow baking dish (about 13 x 9 inches), and drizzle with the oil; toss to coat. Add the garlic and the thyme, if using.

2. Roast for 45 to 55 minutes, turning occasionally, until the edges begin to char and the peppers are tender. Remove from the oven. Sprinkle with salt and pepper. Serve warm or at room temperature.

Grilled Red Bell Peppers and Eggplant

PREPARATION TIME: 5 MINUTES ⁕ COOKING TIME: 15 TO 20 MINUTES ⁕ SERVES: 4

A VARIETY OF FRESH SUMMER vegetables can be used in this recipe. I often grill small, tender zucchini and crookneck yellow squash that have been halved lengthwise. The grilling time varies with the intensity of the heat and the tenderness of the vegetables. Keep a large platter handy, and transfer the vegetables to it as they cook.

2 tablespoons extra-virgin olive oil, or more as needed

1 garlic clove, crushed through a press

2 red bell peppers, quartered, seeds and stems removed

2 baby eggplants (or long, thin Japanese eggplants), halved lengthwise

Salt and freshly ground black pepper, to taste

Fresh thyme or rosemary leaves, stripped from the stems

1. Preheat the grill.

2. Combine the oil and garlic in a small bowl. Brush the peppers and eggplants lightly with the oil.

3. Grill the vegetables until charred and tender, turning often, for 15 to 20 minutes, depending on the heat of the grill. Sprinkle with salt, pepper and fresh thyme or rosemary before serving. Serve warm or at room temperature.

VARIATION

Cool the vegetables slightly and coarsely chop. Add ½ cup chopped fresh tomato and ¼ cup chopped pitted brine-cured black olives such as Kalamata. Serve with grilled chicken, steak or fish.

Rough-Mashed Potatoes with Garlic

PREPARATION TIME: 20 MINUTES ● COOKING TIME: 20 TO 25 MINUTES ● SERVES: 4

SANDRA GLUCK, a friend and colleague, taught me to make this dish. I prefer my mashed potatoes somewhat lumpy, and I melt the butter in advance and drizzle it over at the end to make it go further, thereby reducing the fat.

2 pounds russet potatoes, peeled, cut into chunks

4 garlic cloves, chopped

1 bay leaf

1 teaspoon salt

½ cup whole milk or buttermilk (optional)

About 2 tablespoons melted unsalted butter

1. Combine the potatoes, garlic, bay leaf and salt in a large saucepan. Add water to cover. Cover and heat to boiling. Reduce the heat to medium and simmer until the potatoes are very soft, 20 to 25 minutes.

2. Place a strainer or a colander over a heatproof bowl, and drain the potatoes, reserving the liquid. Discard the bay leaf. Return the potatoes and garlic to the saucepan.

3. Mash the potatoes with a hand potato masher or a pastry blender, adding small amounts (about ½ cup) of the reserved cooking liquid and/or milk or buttermilk until the potatoes are of the consistency that you prefer.

4. To serve, spoon into a serving dish and drizzle with the butter.

Roasted Potatoes with Red Peppers, Onions and Rosemary

PREPARATION TIME: 10 MINUTES ✹ COOKING TIME: 45 MINUTES ✹ SERVES: 4 TO 6

HERE'S AN UNEXPECTEDLY simple combination, the result of my discovering a leftover roasted red pepper in my refrigerator. I added it to my favorite recipe for roasted potatoes and onions. This dish is delicious with roast pork or chicken.

4 russet or baking potatoes (about 1½ pounds), peeled, quartered lengthwise
4 small yellow onions (about ½ pound), trimmed, peeled, quartered lengthwise
4 garlic cloves, peeled
1 large red bell pepper, halved, stem and seeds removed, cut into 8 wedges
3 tablespoons extra-virgin olive oil
1 teaspoon dried or fresh rosemary leaves, plus sprigs for garnish (optional)
½ teaspoon salt
   Freshly ground pepper, to taste

1. Preheat the oven to 400 degrees F. Combine the potatoes, onions, garlic and red pepper in a large, shallow baking dish (approximately 13 x 9 inches). Drizzle with the oil and sprinkle with the rosemary leaves, salt and pepper.

2. Bake until the vegetables are browned and tender, about 45 minutes, carefully turning them occasionally so that they brown evenly. Garnish with sprigs of rosemary, if using, and serve.

Roasted Potatoes and Shiitake Mushrooms

PREPARATION TIME: 20 MINUTES ◈ COOKING TIME: 40 TO 45 MINUTES ◈ SERVES: 4

THIS IS A GOOD SIDE DISH with beef, lamb or chicken. Because shiitake mushrooms have such a meaty quality and earthy flavor, I also like this as part of an all-vegetable meal.

3 medium russet or Idaho potatoes, scrubbed (peeled or unpeeled), cut into 1-inch chunks

4 tablespoons extra-virgin olive oil
Salt and freshly ground black pepper, to taste

¼ pound large shiitake mushrooms, stems discarded, caps cut into 1-inch-thick pieces

¼ cup finely chopped fresh Italian (flat-leaf) parsley

2 teaspoons fresh thyme leaves, stripped from the stems, or ½ teaspoon dried

1 garlic clove, crushed through a press

1 tablespoon mild fruit-flavored red wine vinegar, such as raspberry, or more to taste (optional)

1. Preheat the oven to 400 degrees F. Combine the potatoes, 3 tablespoons of the oil, salt and pepper in a bowl; toss to coat. Spread in a single layer on a nonstick baking sheet.

2. Add the mushrooms to the bowl. Add the remaining 1 tablespoon oil and a little more salt and pepper; toss to coat and set aside.

3. Roast the potatoes until they are golden and crisp on one side, about 25 minutes. Carefully turn with a spatula; add the mushrooms and stir to combine. Bake until the mushrooms are tender and the potatoes are crisp, 15 to 20 minutes more.

4. Chop the parsley, thyme and garlic together. Sprinkle over the potatoes and mushrooms and toss to blend. Drizzle with the vinegar, if using; toss and serve.

Skillet-Browned Red Potatoes with Rosemary and Garlic

PREPARATION TIME: **10 MINUTES** ● COOKING TIME: **20 MINUTES** ● SERVES: **4**

SERVE THESE QUICK-COOKING potatoes as a side dish with meat or fish or as part of a main-dish salad. Whole cooked new red potatoes can also be used. Halve or quarter the cooked potatoes; omit step 1 and fry the potatoes in oil as described in step 2.

3	tablespoons extra-virgin olive oil
1½	pounds small new red potatoes, quartered or halved
2	garlic cloves, minced
1	teaspoon fresh rosemary leaves or ½ teaspoon dried
	Salt and freshly ground black pepper, to taste

1. Heat the oil in a large nonstick skillet until hot enough to sizzle a piece of potato; add the potatoes and stir to coat with oil. Cover and cook over medium to medium-low heat, stirring occasionally and adjusting the heat as needed, until the potatoes are tender when pierced with the tip of a knife, about 15 minutes.

2. Uncover and fry the potatoes over medium-high heat, turning so they brown evenly, about 5 minutes. Sprinkle with the garlic and rosemary; toss to coat. Remove the potatoes to a side dish with a slotted spoon or spatula. Season with the salt and pepper and serve.

VARIATION

Cumin-Scented Red Potatoes: Substitute cumin seeds for the rosemary and heat along with the oil in step 1. Omit the garlic and rosemary.

Favorite Oven-Baked Potatoes with Olive Oil, Garlic and Herbs

PREPARATION TIME: 5 MINUTES ● COOKING TIME: 30 TO 35 MINUTES ● SERVES: 3 TO 4

THERE IS NOTHING EASIER than popping a whole, unpeeled russet or sweet potato (pricked a few times with the tip of a knife so it doesn't burst) into the oven and coming back an hour later to find a luscious baked potato. Sometimes, however, we don't have an hour, and sometimes, we don't want a plain baked potato.

Halved or sliced potatoes cook in half the time, and when tossed with olive oil, garlic and herbs (I like thyme or rosemary), they are far more interesting.

3-4   sweet potatoes or russet potatoes

3   tablespoons extra-virgin olive oil

1   garlic clove, crushed through a press

½   teaspoon fresh thyme or rosemary
    or ¼ teaspoon dried
  Salt and freshly ground black
    pepper, to taste

1. Preheat the oven to 400 degrees F.

2. Peel and slice the potatoes ¼ inch thick. Or, if you prefer, leave them unpeeled, but wash and split them lengthwise.

3. Toss the slices in a bowl with the oil, garlic and thyme or rosemary. Add salt and pepper. Or, if using the halved potatoes, combine the ingredients in a small bowl and brush over the cut surfaces of the potatoes.

4. Arrange the potatoes in a single layer, cut sides down, on a nonstick baking sheet and bake until browned, about 20 minutes. Turn and bake until tender, 10 to 15 minutes longer. Serve hot.

Smothered Spinach

THE BEST WAY TO COOK spinach is to steam it with the clean rinse water still clinging to the leaves. The most important part of this recipe is the timing: do not overcook the spinach. It is delicious when just wilted.

2 pounds (or two 10-ounce bags) fresh spinach, stems trimmed, washed and rinsed

1 tablespoon extra-virgin olive oil or unsalted butter

½ garlic clove, crushed through a press

Salt and freshly ground black pepper, to taste

1. Place a collapsible vegetable steaming rack in a large, wide saucepan filled with about 1 inch of water. Heat the water to boiling. Stack the spinach on top of the steaming rack, cover and set the timer for 3 minutes. The spinach should be wilted and limp. Carefully lift the rack from the pan with a mitted hand. Discard the water and wipe the pan dry.

2. Add the oil and garlic to the pan, and heat over low heat just until the garlic begins to sizzle, about 1 minute. Remove the pan from the heat. Add the spinach all at once, and sprinkle with salt and a little pepper. Stir to blend and serve immediately.

WASHING SPINACH

MOST SUPERMARKETS CARRY CELLOPHANE BAGS of washed spinach that simply needs to be quickly sprayed and tossed in a colander. If you buy your spinach in loose bunches, it may need a few good washings to remove the sandy soil. This is how I do it: I fill the sink or a large bowl with warm water and add the spinach leaves as I snap off the long stems. I swish the spinach around, drain it and wash it in cool water. Then I taste a leaf or two. If I detect any grit, I wash again in a clean bowl of water.

Oven-Roasted Sweet Potato Slices with Orange and Fresh Thyme

PREPARATION TIME: 15 MINUTES ❋ COOKING TIME: 50 MINUTES ❋ SERVES: 4 TO 6

SWEET POTATO SLICES are delicious when roasted until golden brown. They won't become crisp like white potatoes, but they melt in your mouth. They are great with turkey, chicken, game or roast beef.

3-4   medium-sized sweet potatoes (about 2 pounds), trimmed, peeled, cut into ⅛-inch-thick slices

1   garlic clove, crushed through a press

2   tablespoons extra-virgin olive oil

¼   cup packed parsley sprigs

½   teaspoon fresh thyme, leaves stripped from the stems, or ¼ teaspoon dried

1   strip (about ½ x 2 inches) orange zest (use a vegetable peeler to remove)

Salt and freshly ground black pepper, to taste

1. Preheat the oven to 400 degrees F. Select a large nonstick sheet pan at least 14 x 10 inches. Combine the sweet potato slices with the garlic and the oil in a large bowl; toss to coat with the oil.

2. Bake, turning the potatoes once or twice as they begin to brown, about 40 minutes. Remove from the oven.

3. Meanwhile, finely chop the parsley, thyme and orange zest together; sprinkle over the potatoes. Sprinkle with salt and pepper. Return to the oven and bake for 10 minutes longer, or until the potatoes are tender, turning them once. Serve hot.

TOMATOES

My SUMMER IS COMPLETE when I've had a dip in the ocean, eaten fresh-picked corn to my heart's desire and enjoyed a warm, sun-kissed tomato right out of hand just a few feet from where it was picked. From late July through September, I take full advantage of the abundance of locally grown tomatoes, knowing that their robust flavor will soon be just a sweet memory.

For lunch, I eat a sliced-tomato sandwich with mayonnaise and a large basil leaf on a toasted English muffin, or I arrange the tomato slices on a plate, lightly sprinkle them with coarse salt and splash them with extra-virgin olive oil.

My favorite "shake" is made from a cut-up tomato, a cup of yogurt and a handful of ice cubes whirled in the blender, then served in a tall glass with a straw. I have been known to add basil and a little onion to the shake, call it soup and serve it from a bowl on a hot summer day. Another of my mainstays is a quick sauce of chopped tomatoes, olive oil, basil and garlic tossed with hot fresh pasta.

I also celebrate the season with a wonderful Italian bread-and-tomato salad called Panzanella (page 220). It is traditionally made with day-old bread soaked in water and squeezed dry. My variation uses thick slices of toasted whole-wheat sourdough. The bread soaks up the tomato juices, which are rich with the flavor of olive oil and fragrant with basil.

A less elaborate but equally luscious way to enjoy tomatoes is to leave them whole, top them with herbs and crumbs and slowly bake them in a pool of good olive oil.

Roasted Tomatoes with Herb Crumbs

USE ONLY THICK, JUICY slices of tomato for this rendition of bread-crumb-topped roasted tomatoes. I usually roast these in the oven while I grill fish or chicken.

1 garlic clove, halved

4 tablespoons extra-virgin olive oil

3 large tomatoes, trimmed, cored, cut into ¾-inch-thick slices (about 8 slices)
Salt and freshly ground black pepper, to taste

8 large basil leaves, torn into small pieces

1 cup coarse bread crumbs (made from day-old Italian bread)

1 teaspoon chopped fresh oregano or a pinch of dried

1. Preheat the oven to 375 degrees F. Rub a shallow 2- or 3-quart glass baking dish with the cut side of the garlic; reserve the garlic for the crumbs. Drizzle the baking dish with 2 tablespoons of the oil.

2. Arrange the tomato slices in a single layer in the baking dish. Sprinkle lightly with the salt and pepper and top with the basil leaves.

3. Crush the reserved garlic; toss with the bread crumbs, the remaining 2 tablespoons oil and the oregano. Sprinkle over the tomatoes, distributing evenly.

4. Bake until the crumbs are lightly browned, 20 to 25 minutes. Serve warm or at room temperature.

Warm Sautéed Tomato Slices with Melted Cheese

PREPARATION TIME: 10 MINUTES ✳ COOKING TIME: 5 MINUTES ✳ SERVES: 4

WHEN TOMATOES ARE plentiful and scrumptious, try this simple but hearty tomato side dish. It makes a meal when toasted bread is added to the pan juices and the warm cheese-topped tomatoes are served on top of the juice-soaked toast.

2 tablespoons extra-virgin olive oil

1 garlic clove, crushed through a press

8 thick (½ inch) slices tomato
   Salt and freshly ground black
      pepper, to taste

2 tablespoons slivered fresh basil

8 thin slices mozzarella cheese
   (fresh is best)

1. Heat the oil and garlic in a large skillet over medium-low heat until the garlic sizzles, about 2 minutes. Stir to blend. Add the tomato slices and turn to coat with the oil. Sprinkle with salt and pepper.

2. Top with the basil and the cheese, distributing evenly. Cover and cook for 2 minutes, or until the cheese melts. Use a spatula to transfer the tomato slices to a platter. Serve warm.

Winter Squash with Indian Flavors

THIS VEGETARIAN DISH is excellent served on a bed of basmati (or Tex-mati) rice as a main course. Look for the unsweetened dried coconut in health food stores. The sweetened coconut used in baking is too cloying for this slightly spicy Indian-inspired dish.

2	tablespoons unsalted butter
1	cup cubed (1 inch) yellow onion
1	tablespoon minced peeled fresh ginger
1	garlic clove, cut into thin slivers
2	teaspoons curry powder
½	teaspoon ground cumin
1	can (14½ ounces) whole plum tomatoes
1	medium acorn squash or small butternut squash (1-1½ pounds) peeled, seeded, cut into 1-inch cubes
1	cup frozen lima beans, partially thawed
1	cup sliced carrot (¼ inch thick)
½	teaspoon salt
¼	cup packed finely chopped unsweetened dried coconut
½	cup heavy cream
¼	cup finely chopped dry-roasted cashews, preferably unsalted

1. Heat the butter in a large, wide saucepan over medium heat. Stir in the onion, ginger and garlic. Cover the pan and reduce the heat to low. Cook until the onion is very soft but not browned, about 10 minutes. Uncover and stir in the curry and cumin; cook for 1 minute.

2. Add the tomatoes with their liquid and break them up with the side of a spoon. Stir in the squash, lima beans and carrot; season with the salt. Cook, covered, stirring occasionally, over low heat until the vegetables are tender, about 20 minutes.

3. Place the coconut and cream in a food processor, and process just until blended, about 20 seconds. To prevent the cream mixture from curdling, let the vegetables stand off the heat uncovered to cool slightly before adding the cream. Stir in the coconut-cream mixture. Sprinkle with the cashews. Serve hot. (If you reheat, do not boil.)

PREPARING WINTER SQUASH

INSTEAD OF STRUGGLING TO CUT AND PEEL winter squash before cooking, I bake it until softened and then cut it into pieces. Simply halve the squash, scoop out the seeds and place, cut side down, in a lightly oiled baking dish. Cover with foil, and bake until tender when pierced with the tip of a knife, 35 to 45 minutes, depending on the size of the squash.

Baked Squash with Parmesan, Onion and Bacon

PREPARATION TIME: 5 MINUTES ✺ COOKING TIME: 35 TO 40 MINUTES ✺ SERVES: 4 TO 6

SQUASH, LIKE POTATOES, bake more quickly if it is sliced first. Use a large, heavy knife, but watch your fingers, because it takes a little pressure to cut through the tough outer skin. Trim the stem and blossom ends before cutting each half into approximately ½-inch-thick half rings.

1   strip bacon, finely diced
1   cup thin wedges (¼ inch wide)
      sweet onion
1   large acorn squash (1½-2 pounds),
      halved lengthwise, seeded, each
      half cut into 4 half circles
      Salt and freshly ground black
      pepper, to taste
¼   cup grated Parmigiano-Reggiano

1. Preheat the oven to 350 degrees F. Combine the bacon and onion in a shallow 13-x-9-inch baking dish; toss to blend. Arrange the squash on top of the bacon and onion, slightly overlapping the slices. Cover tightly with foil and bake for 20 minutes.

2. Increase the oven temperature to 400 degrees. Uncover the baking dish, carefully turn the squash and onion mixture together; sprinkle with salt and pepper. Bake, uncovered, for 10 minutes, or until the vegetables begin to brown.

3. Sprinkle the cheese evenly on top. Bake until the cheese melts and the squash is tender, 5 to 10 minutes longer. Serve hot.

Orange Baked Squash

PREPARATION TIME: 15 MINUTES ❧ COOKING TIME: 1 HOUR ❧ SERVES: 4

WINTER SQUASH AND ORANGE are a natural combination, perhaps because they are both plentiful during the same season. The flavors couldn't be more different, but I love the fresh tang of orange with the soft sweetness of the squash.

2	small acorn squash or 1 butternut squash, washed
	Salt and freshly ground black pepper, to taste
1	tablespoon extra-virgin olive oil
½	cup packed fresh Italian (flat-leaf) parsley sprigs
1	strip (½ x 2 inches) orange zest
1	garlic clove

1. Preheat the oven to 400 degrees F. Select a large (2-quart) shallow baking dish.

2. Halve the squash lengthwise; cut off the stems and scoop out the seeds. If using the acorn squash, cut the halves into 1-inch wedges. If using the butternut squash, cut the halves crosswise and cut each section into wedges.

3. Arrange the squash skin side down in the baking dish. Sprinkle with salt and pepper and drizzle with the oil.

4. Finely chop the parsley, orange zest and garlic together. Sprinkle evenly over the squash. Cover with foil and bake until the squash is tender, about 1 hour. Serve hot.

Roasted Zucchini Vinaigrette with Basil and Mint

PREPARATION TIME: 10 MINUTES ❋ COOKING TIME: 10 TO 15 MINUTES ❋ SERVES: 4

BUY ZUCCHINI when they are small and the skin is taut and shiny. I usually wait until summer, but sometimes, I find zucchini in the supermarket that pass my test for freshness. Serve as part of an antipasto platter, as a vegetable or as a salad along with roasted peppers (page 276 or 278).

4 firm, unblemished zucchini, preferably small (1-1½ inches in diameter and 3-4 inches long), trimmed, or larger zucchini cut to size

½ garlic clove

3 tablespoons extra-virgin olive oil
Salt and freshly ground black pepper, to taste

1 tablespoon chopped fresh basil, plus 6-8 whole leaves, for garnish

1 tablespoon chopped fresh mint

1 tablespoon mild red or white wine vinegar

1 teaspoon balsamic vinegar

1. Halve the zucchini lengthwise if they are small. If they are large, cut them into lengthwise quarters. Cut them as uniformly as possible to ensure even cooking.

2. Preheat the oven to 450 degrees F. Select a large, shallow baking pan, preferably with a nonstick finish (a jellyroll pan is good). Rub the bottom of the pan with the cut side of the garlic; leave the garlic in the pan. Add 1 tablespoon of the oil to the pan; add the zucchini and turn to coat. Arrange the zucchini, cut sides down, in the pan.

3. Bake for 10 minutes. Carefully rearrange the zucchini halfway through the cooking, cut sides still down, so they begin to brown evenly. After 10 minutes, some of the zucchini will be golden and almost tender; remove these to a side dish. Continue to bake the remaining zucchini for 5 minutes more.

4. Arrange the zucchini, cut sides up, on a serving platter; sprinkle with the salt and pepper, chopped basil and mint. Whisk the remaining 2 tablespoons oil and the wine vinegar and balsamic vinegar; drizzle over the zucchini. Let stand at room temperature, basting occasionally with the dressing, until ready to serve. Taste before serving and add more vinegar, if needed. Garnish with whole basil leaves.

Roasted Zucchini with Red Onion Vinaigrette

PREPARATION TIME: 15 MINUTES ✸ COOKING TIME: 25 MINUTES ✸ SERVES: 4

A SPLASH OF VINEGAR adds sparkle to zucchini, which is a rather plain vegetable, even when fresh from the garden. This is a good place to show off your favorite fruit- or herb-scented vinegars. Serve as a side dish for grilled or broiled fish or meat.

2 tablespoons extra-virgin olive oil

1 large red onion, halved lengthwise and cut into ¼-inch lengthwise slices

1 strip (½ x 2 inches) orange zest

1 teaspoon fresh thyme leaves, stripped from the stems, or ¼ teaspoon dried

4 small zucchini (about 4 inches long), washed, trimmed, halved lengthwise

1 tablespoon red wine vinegar or apple cider vinegar

Salt and freshly ground black pepper, to taste

1. Preheat the oven to 400 degrees F. Combine the oil, onion, orange zest and thyme in a baking dish. Stir to blend. Bake until the onion begins to brown, about 15 minutes, stirring once or twice.

2. Add the zucchini, cut sides down, and spoon the onion mixture over the zucchini. Bake until the zucchini are tender, about 10 minutes. Remove from the oven and cool slightly.

3. Arrange on a serving plate and sprinkle evenly with the vinegar, salt and pepper. Serve warm or at room temperature.

Oven-Roasted Vegetable Plate with Herb Dressing

PREPARATION TIME: 15 MINUTES ❁ BAKING TIME: 1 HOUR 15 MINUTES ❁ SERVES: 4

I SERVE THIS PLATTER of oven-roasted onions, beets, carrots and asparagus as the first course of a spring or summer dinner. The vegetables can all be roasted well ahead of time and served at room temperature.

2 medium-sized sweet onions, trimmed, peeled, halved crosswise
Extra-virgin olive oil
Salt and freshly ground black pepper, to taste
2 medium-sized beets, leafy tops and roots trimmed
4 medium carrots, peeled, halved lengthwise
½ bunch asparagus, trimmed, washed

HERB DRESSING
⅓ cup extra-virgin olive oil
2 tablespoons fresh lemon juice
1 tablespoon chopped fresh dill
1 tablespoon chopped fresh basil
1 garlic clove, crushed through a press

1. Preheat the oven to 400 degrees F. Sprinkle the cut sides of the onions with 1 teaspoon oil, salt and pepper. Wrap each onion and beet in a small square of foil.

2. Arrange the carrots, cut sides down, in an 11-x-7-inch baking pan and drizzle with 1 tablespoon oil. Sprinkle with salt and pepper. Place the carrots, onions and beets in the oven. Roast until the carrots are lightly browned and tender, about 35 minutes, and the beets and onions are tender when pierced, about 1 hour.

3. Cool the beets and onions slightly before removing the foil. Slip off the skins and cut each beet in half crosswise through the center.

4. Increase the oven temperature to 450 degrees. Place the asparagus in a baking pan and drizzle with ½ tablespoon oil. Roast, turning once with a fork, until tender, about 15 minutes. Season with salt and pepper.

5. Arrange all the vegetables on a large platter.

6. Make the Herb Dressing: Combine all the ingredients in a small bowl. Whisk to blend, spoon over the vegetables and serve warm or at room temperature.

Roasted Summer Vegetables

PREPARATION TIME: 20 MINUTES ❦ COOKING TIME: 45 TO 55 MINUTES ❦ SERVES: 4 TO 6

THESE VEGETABLES can be oven-roasted, broiled or grilled. They are a delectable side dish with beef, chicken or seafood. Or coarsely chop them, season with red wine vinegar and serve as a salad. You can also toss them with a little more oil and a spoonful of grated Parmigiano-Reggiano and mix them with hot pasta.

2　large red bell peppers, quartered, seeds and stems removed, cut into ½-inch wedges

2　small or 1 medium eggplant, stems trimmed, quartered lengthwise

2　small zucchini, scrubbed, trimmed, halved, cut into ½-inch-thick diagonal slices

2　small yellow squash, scrubbed, trimmed, halved, cut into ½-inch-thick diagonal slices

2　medium-sized red onions, peeled, trimmed, cut into ½-inch wedges

4　garlic cloves, halved

3　tablespoons extra-virgin olive oil

1-2　medium tomatoes, cored, cut into wedges

2　tablespoons coarsely chopped fresh Italian (flat-leaf) parsley

2　tablespoons coarsely chopped fresh basil

1　teaspoon fresh thyme leaves, stripped from the stems, or ¼ teaspoon dried

1　tablespoon red wine vinegar (optional)
　　Salt and freshly ground black pepper, to taste

1. Preheat the oven to 400 degrees F. Select a large (11-x-14-inch) sheet pan. Add all the vegetables, the garlic and oil. Toss to coat. Spread the vegetables in a single layer. Roast, turning often and moving the vegetables from the center of the pan to the edges so they brown evenly, 45 to 55 minutes.

2. Remove from the oven and add the tomatoes, parsley, basil, thyme, vinegar (if using), salt and pepper; stir to blend. Serve immediately.

DESSERTS

FAST

WHEN YOU HAVE MORE TIME

Umberto's Oranges with Grand Marnier and Red Pepper

PREPARATION TIME: **10 MINUTES** ◆ CHILLING TIME: **30 MINUTES** ◆ SERVES: **4**

THIS IS THE PERFECT DESSERT after a seafood meal. The combination of acid from the oranges, sweetness from the orange liqueur and heat from the pepper is brilliantly delicious. I first tasted this dessert at a restaurant (now closed) called da Barone, in lower Manhattan.

> **PLAN AHEAD:**
>
> Allow 30 minutes for the oranges to chill.

4-5   large seedless oranges
1   tablespoon sugar
¼   cup Grand Marnier
     Cayenne (ground red pepper)

1. Using a thin, sharp knife, cut the peel and white pith from the oranges. Cut them crosswise into ¼-inch-thick slices. Arrange the oranges, slightly overlapping, on a large serving platter.

2. Sprinkle the oranges evenly with the sugar. Drizzle them with the Grand Marnier and dust lightly with the cayenne. Cover and refrigerate until ready to serve.

3. This is best chilled for at least 30 minutes. Serve with a knife and fork.

QUICK FRUIT DESSERTS

BECAUSE I PREFER FRUIT to a rich dessert after dinner, I have, over the years, come up with dozens of simple recipes showcasing fruits in season.

Peaches, strawberries or nectarines: Sweeten with sugar or honey and serve over frozen yogurt, sorbet or ice cream.

Raspberries or a mixture of raspberries, blackberries and blueberries: Serve over lemon ice, or sprinkle with sugar and serve with a pitcher of heavy cream.

Watermelon, cantaloupe or honeydew slices: Sprinkle with fresh lime juice, and serve with lime wedges.

Cherries: Place in a bowl of water and ice cubes, and serve directly from the bowl.

Sliced apples or pears: Serve with a wedge of fresh domestic goat cheese, Stilton, Brie, Gorgonzola, sharp Cheddar or Saga cheese, with a few oven-toasted (just until warm) walnuts or almonds on the side.

Plump dried dates, dried apricots, dried apple slices, whole cashews, Brazil nuts, almonds, hazelnuts, pecans or walnuts: Arrange on a platter, Middle Eastern style, and nibble on them with coffee.

Kiwifruit: Peel, cut into wedges, and arrange on a plate with large unstemmed strawberries.

Jumbo strawberries: Arrange on a thin layer of granulated sugar.

Strawberry sorbet (store-bought): Serve with chopped sweetened fresh strawberries.

Pineapple sorbet (store-bought): Serve with chopped kiwifruit.

Orange sorbet (store-bought): Serve with sugared raspberries and/or blueberries.

Assorted grapes (purple, green and red): Rinse, drain, place in a bowl and serve.

Sliced strawberries or sliced fresh pineapple: Place in a bowl, and splash with cold white wine.

Yellow watermelon: Cut into wedges, and top with blueberries or blackberries.

Sliced ripe peaches or nectarines: Place on a platter, sprinkle with sugar and lime juice, and top with blueberries.

Papaya with Lime Sauce

PREPARATION TIME: 15 MINUTES ● CHILLING TIME: 30 MINUTES ● SERVES: 4

HAWAIIAN PAPAYAS are in season midwinter, when local summer melons are but a distant memory. Lime juice adds a pleasant spark that heightens the sweet, mellow flavor of this pale orange fruit. This is a lovely dessert, a little different and just slightly exotic.

PLAN AHEAD:

Allow 30 minutes for the papayas to chill.

2 limes

2 tablespoons sugar, or more to taste

2 ripe papayas, halved, seeds scooped out, peeled, cut into thin wedges

Strawberries, blueberries or raspberries, for garnish (optional)

1. Cut the limes in half and juice 3 of the halves into a medium bowl. Cut the remaining half into thin slices. Add the lime slices and the sugar to the bowl; stir until the sugar is dissolved.

2. Add the papayas and carefully turn to coat with the syrup. Cover and refrigerate until ready to serve. Spoon the papaya slices and syrup into shallow bowls or onto dessert plates, distributing evenly. Garnish with a few berries, if using. Chill for at least 30 minutes. Serve chilled.

Nectarines in Mint Syrup

PREPARATION TIME: 10 MINUTES ● SERVES: 4

WHEN NECTARINES are at their juicy best (usually July through September), they make a perfect dessert because, unlike peaches, they don't need peeling. The rosy skins lend a pale pink color to the syrup of sugar, boiling water and mint leaves, making this especially appropriate to serve in a clear glass or white china bowl.

¼ cup boiling water
¼ cup sugar
2 tablespoons torn mint leaves
4-6 large nectarines, rinsed and dried
¼ cup crème fraîche (optional)

1. Combine the water and the sugar in a bowl; stir to dissolve the sugar. Add the mint leaves. Stir, pressing on the leaves with the back of the spoon to crush and release the juices.

2. Cut the nectarines into ½-inch-thick slices, and place in the syrup. Stir to coat. Refrigerate until ready to serve.

3. Spoon into dessert bowls and top each with a spoonful of crème fraîche, if using.

Sliced Peaches or Nectarines with Candied Ginger

PREPARATION TIME: 10 MINUTES ● SERVES: 4

PREPARE THIS RECIPE with ripe cantaloupe when peaches or nectarines are not in season—it is delicious with any of these fruits. This tastes best served at room temperature

6   large, ripe peaches or nectarines
      Juice 1 lime
2   tablespoons chopped
      crystallized ginger

1. Peel the peaches if the skins are thick and very fuzzy. Otherwise, simply wash and dry the fruit, rubbing the skins to remove the excess fuzz.

2. Cut the fruit into ½-inch-thick wedges. In a large bowl, toss the fruit slices and lime juice together. Sprinkle with the ginger. Cover and set aside at room temperature until ready to serve. To serve, spoon the fruit into individual dessert dishes or onto a serving platter.

Grandpa's Peaches in Red Wine

PREPARATION TIME: 10 MINUTES   ❋   SERVES: 4

THIS IS AN OLD FAMILY FAVORITE. My grandfather, Daniel Abbruzzese, showed me how to make this, carefully slicing the peach into a goblet, sprinkling it with a little sugar and adding just the right amount of wine from the gallon jug stored under the counter in a kitchen cabinet. This is delightful in its purity and simplicity.

4   large, ripe peaches, washed, peeled

2   teaspoons sugar

2   cups full-bodied red wine, such as Chianti or Zinfandel

1. Slice the peaches directly into 4 wine glasses.

2. Sprinkle each with about ½ teaspoon sugar. Divide the wine among the 4 portions. Serve with a spoon.

FIGS

WHEN FIGS ARE IN SEASON, usually early summer (June) and early fall (August to September), cut them up and serve over vanilla ice cream. Or quarter them and drape them with thin slices of prosciutto. I arrange them on arugula leaves and drizzle with olive oil. Or I eat them out of hand, preferably while sitting in the sun.

There are only a few varieties of figs available commercially in the United States, most of them grown in California. The Black Mission, probably named by the Spanish who first cultivated figs in the New World, is small and dark purple and has a deep, rich flavor. The Calimyrna (from Smyrna, Turkey, where the fig is purported to have been first cultivated) is another; it is plump, green and very juicy. The Kadota, which is also greenish, is longer than the Calimyrna but just as sweet and fragrant. With figs, ripeness is more important than variety.

A ripe fig is soft and squishy and gives the sensation of sweetness, without being sugary-tasting, when one takes a bite. Most figs are thin-skinned and don't need to be peeled, but if the skin seems thick, carefully peel it away, leaving a thin, white flannel-like membrane.

Raspberries and Fresh Figs

PREPARATION TIME: 10 MINUTES * STANDING TIME: 30 MINUTES * SERVES: 4

THIS IS AN ESPECIALLY SIMPLE but elegant dessert. I love the contrast of tart raspberry and sweet fig.

2   half-pint baskets raspberries
1   tablespoon sugar
4   large, ripe fresh figs, rinsed,
      stems trimmed, peeled
      if the skins are tough

1. Combine the raspberries and sugar in a bowl and toss to coat. Set aside at room temperature for about 30 minutes, or until the sugar dissolves.

2. Just before serving, remove 1 cup of the raspberries and any juices in the bottom of the bowl and puree in a food processor. Press through a sieve to remove the seeds. Divide this puree among 4 dessert plates and tilt the plates to spread a thin layer over the bottom.

3. Place a fig in the center of each plate. Using a sharp knife, quarter each fig, cutting from the stem end down but only partially cutting through the base.

4. Spoon the remaining raspberries onto the plates. Serve at room temperature.

PLAN AHEAD:

Allow about 30 minutes for the raspberries and sugar to sit before continuing with the recipe.

Summer Fruits in Lime Syrup

PREPARATION TIME: 15 MINUTES ❋ STANDING TIME: 20 MINUTES ❋ SERVES: 4

THIS RECIPE USES LIME JUICE in a quick syrup for a fresh fruit compote. Although lemon juice can be substituted, I like the distinctive taste of lime. It seems to add just the right amount of acid, especially if the fruit is just slightly underripe, or it can help brighten the flavor of perfectly ripened fruit. Use any combination of fresh fruits that you have on hand. I like to use at least three different kinds.

PLAN AHEAD:

Allow 20 minutes for the fruit to stand before serving.

1   pint fresh blueberries, blackberries, raspberries or strawberries, rinsed, stems removed, strawberries halved

3   ripe peaches or nectarines, washed, fuzz wiped from the peaches, cut into thin wedges, pits discarded

½   pound fresh sweet cherries (with stems) or 1 cup seedless grapes, removed from the stems

3   tablespoons fresh lime juice

3   tablespoons sugar

1. Combine the fruit in a large bowl. Add the lime juice and sugar and toss to blend.

2. Let stand at room temperature until ready to serve, at least 20 minutes.

Strawberries with Raspberry Puree

PREPARATION TIME: 10 MINUTES ● SERVES: 4

FROZEN RASPBERRIES are a staple in my freezer. True, they aren't fresh, but they sure are convenient. And although frozen raspberries can't compare to fresh in appearance, they retain their deep berry flavor and make a wonderful sauce. A simple puree of raspberries elevates a plain bowl of sliced strawberries, peaches or even melon from ordinary to special. If you have a few blueberries on hand, don't hesitate to add them to the strawberries.

1 package (10 ounces) unsweetened
    frozen raspberries, thawed
1 tablespoon sugar or honey,
    or more to taste
2 pints fresh strawberries,
    hulled and halved or quartered
1-2 teaspoons fresh lime juice

1. Combine the raspberries and sugar or honey in a food processor and puree. Press through a strainer to remove the seeds, if desired. (The sauce can be made up to 1 day ahead.) Taste and add more sugar or honey, if desired.

2. Place the strawberries in a large bowl; toss with the lime juice. Top with the raspberry puree; stir to blend. Refrigerate until ready to serve or serve at room temperature.

Rhubarb with Strawberries

PREPARATION TIME: 15 MINUTES ⊛ COOKING TIME: 25 TO 30 MINUTES ⊛ SERVES: 4

THE SECRET TO PERFECT (not stringy or mushy) rhubarb is not to stir during or after the cooking. This is good plain or served over vanilla ice cream.

½ cup sugar
½ cup water
1 pound fresh rhubarb, trimmed, cut into 1-inch lengths
1 pint strawberries, rinsed, hulled, halved
1 vanilla bean, split
Vanilla yogurt, for topping (optional)

1. Preheat the oven to 325 degrees F. Combine the sugar and water in a 2-quart baking dish or a deep casserole with a lid; stir to dissolve the sugar. Add the rhubarb and strawberries; stir just to coat with the sugar. Add the vanilla bean.

2. Cover the baking dish or casserole and bake until the liquid boils and the rhubarb is tender, 25 to 30 minutes. Uncover and cool to room temperature (do not stir). Refrigerate, if desired.

3. Serve at room temperature or chilled, plain or topped with vanilla yogurt.

VARIATION

Rhubarb in Ginger Syrup: Omit the strawberries and vanilla bean, and add 2 or 3 thin slices of fresh ginger to the sugar and water.

Sliced Strawberries with Honey

PREPARATION TIME: 5 MINUTES ✽ SERVES: 4

I USE HONEY TO POACH FRUIT or, as here, to sweeten a plain bowl of sliced strawberries. Honey is also good on sliced peaches or on a mixture of berries or other fruit. Use it sparingly at first, and then add more to taste. It is much sweeter than sugar and should not be substituted in the same amount.

1. Slice the strawberries directly into a serving bowl. Drizzle with the honey; gently stir to blend.

2. Serve immediately, or let stand at room temperature until ready to serve.

2   pints strawberries, rinsed,
         hulled, sliced
2   tablespoons honey, or to taste

Whole Strawberries in Vanilla Sugar

PREPARATION TIME: 5 MINUTES ● SERVES: 4

MAKE THIS when the strawberries are big and plump and have their hulls still attached.

To make the vanilla sugar called for in this recipe, split a vanilla bean and store it in a glass jar filled with the sugar for 1 or 2 weeks before using. The aroma from the bean will perfume the sugar. You can use plain sugar here instead, if you wish.

1-2   pint baskets large, ripe strawberries (hulls left on)
⅓   cup vanilla sugar or sugar

PLAN AHEAD:

If you want to sweeten the berries with vanilla sugar, make the sugar 1 to 2 weeks in advance.

Lightly rinse the berries and dry with paper towels. Spread a thin layer of sugar on a serving platter. Arrange the berries, hull ends up, on the platter. Serve at room temperature.

Melon and Berries with Lime Sugar Syrup

PREPARATION TIME: 10 MINUTES ✷ OPTIONAL CHILLING TIME: 30 MINUTES ✷ SERVES: 4

WATERMELON IS SIMPLICITY and perfection in one big sphere. Whether you eat it out of hand under the hot summer sun or serve it on cut-glass plates topped with a few choice summer berries, as in this recipe, watermelon never fails to please. Cut the watermelon into ½-inch-thick wedges or into a size that fits comfortably on your best dessert plates.

Select all or just one of the berries, depending on what looks good in the market. Lime and sugar perk berries up without masking their natural taste. I use this combination on seasonally fresh fruits all year long. (See photograph, page 40.)

1   pint blueberries, raspberries or strawberries (or a mixture)

    Juice 1 lime (about 2 tablespoons)

2   teaspoons sugar

4   slices watermelon (½ inch thick) or other melon

> **PLAN AHEAD:**
>
> If you want to serve this cold, allow 30 minutes for it to chill.

1. Combine the berries, lime juice and sugar in a bowl; toss to blend, then set aside.

2. Arrange the melon on a large platter or on 4 individual plates. Top with a spoonful of the berries and chill for 30 minutes, if desired, before serving.

Wine-Laced Watermelon

PREPARATION TIME: 10 MINUTES ❋ CHILLING TIME: AT LEAST 1 HOUR ❋ SERVES: 4

SERVE THIS WATERMELON icy cold on a beautiful platter. Use an inexpensive fruity, slightly sweet wine. I like white zinfandel, because it has a pretty pale pink color that reminds me of the watermelon.

8 triangular slices
    (½ inch thick) watermelon

1 cup white zinfandel, Chenin Blanc,
    Muscadet or other fruity white
    wine, chilled

2 cups dark, sweet cherries with stems,
    washed, dried (optional)

1. Arrange the watermelon on a serving platter. Drizzle with the wine. Cover and refrigerate for at least 1 hour, until it is very well chilled.

2. Garnish the platter with cherries before serving, if using. Serve on dessert plates, spooning the chilled wine onto each plate. Eat with a fork and knife.

PLAN AHEAD:

Prepare this before sitting down to eat and let chill for about 1 hour while you enjoy your main course.

Fresh Pear Compote

THIS IS THE RIGHT DESSERT for a winter evening after a hearty meal of bean soup or meat stew. It is also sublime with a wedge of sharp blue-veined Roquefort or Stilton cheese and some plain crackers.

4   large, ripe Bartlett pears, peeled, quartered, cored
1   tablespoon fresh lemon juice
1   teaspoon sugar
     Pinch ground cinnamon
¼   cup broken walnuts

1. Combine the pears, lemon juice, sugar and cinnamon in a large bowl; gently stir to coat.

2. Heat the walnuts in a small, dry skillet over low heat, stirring, until warm and fragrant, about 3 minutes.

3. Divide the pears among 4 dessert bowls, sprinkle with the warm walnuts and serve.

Pears Baked in Red Wine

PREPARATION TIME: 10 MINUTES ❋ COOKING TIME: 45 TO 55 MINUTES ❋ SERVES: 4

THESE PEARS ARE elegant to look at and simple to make. I often bake them for a crowd and then stand them on an enormous platter on a side board for everyone to admire. Sometimes called crinkly pears, they are not peeled.

1½   cups dry red wine

½   cup sugar

4   whole allspice

1   piece (about 2 inches) cinnamon stick

1   piece (about 2 inches) vanilla bean

1   bay leaf

4   large, firm, ripe Bosc pears, washed, dried

1. Preheat the oven to 350 degrees F. Select a baking dish large enough to hold the pears in one layer. (A 10-inch pie plate works well.)

2. Add the wine, sugar, allspice, cinnamon stick, vanilla bean and bay leaf to the baking dish. Stir just until the sugar is partially dissolved.

3. Cut a thin slice from the bottom of the pears so they will stand upright. Place in the wine mixture and spoon some of the wine over them.

4. Bake until the syrup has begun to boil and thicken, 45 to 55 minutes, basting the pears with the wine mixture two or three times during the baking. The pears are done when they are tender when pierced with a toothpick or skewer. Serve at room temperature with the wine syrup spooned over each serving.

Warm Rosy Applesauce

PREPARATION TIME: 10 MINUTES ● COOKING TIME: 12 TO 25 MINUTES ● SERVES: 4

THE QUALITY AND FRESHNESS of the apples you select will determine the final flavor of the applesauce. I like to mix and match some of my favorite varieties. I prefer the fruit's natural sweetness, so I rarely add sugar. But you might want to stir in a spoon or two of light brown sugar or a little maple syrup. For years, I have been baking applesauce in my microwave. I also make it on top of the stove. Here are both methods.

2   pounds (or more) fresh apples (Empire, Winesap, Cortland, McIntosh, Idared or other juicy, flavorful apples), washed thoroughly in 2 rinses of warm water, dried

1   cinnamon stick
    Sugar or maple syrup (optional)

1. Quarter the apples and cut out the stem, core and blossom end. Cut the quarters into thin wedges.

2. To cook in the microwave: Place the apples and the cinnamon stick in a 3-quart covered glass casserole with a lid. Microwave on high for 12 to 14 minutes, or until the apples are soft, stirring once after 10 minutes.

To cook on the stovetop: Place the apples and cinnamon stick in a large, wide saucepan; add ¼ cup water. Cook, covered, over medium-low heat, stirring often, until the apples are soft, about 25 minutes.

3. Cool the apples slightly. Remove the cinnamon stick, and set aside. Place a food mill over a large bowl and puree the apples through it. Discard the skins and solids. Return the cinnamon stick to the applesauce. Taste and add sugar or maple syrup, if desired. Serve warm, chilled or at room temperature.

VARIATION

Warm Applesauce Sundaes: Place about ½ cup warm applesauce in each of 4 dessert bowls. Top with softened vanilla ice cream and sprinkle with cinnamon sugar.

Baked Apples

PREPARATION TIME: 15 MINUTES ✻ BAKING TIME: 35 TO 55 MINUTES ✻ SERVES: 6 TO 8

IT WOULDN'T BE FALL without baked apples—a favorite dessert in our family. Although not fast to cook, they are easy to prepare.

6-8   large, flavorful apples
       (I prefer Romes)

4   tablespoons unsalted butter,
       cut into small pieces

¼   cup packed light brown sugar

¼   teaspoon ground cinnamon

2   tablespoons raisins
       Softened vanilla ice cream
       (optional)

1. Preheat the oven to 350 degrees F. Lightly butter a 13-x-9-inch baking dish. Cut a thin slice from the bottom of each apple so that it will stand up straight. Core the apples. Peel ½ inch of the skin from the crown. Arrange the apples, crown up, in the baking dish.

2. Using a fork, work the butter, brown sugar and cinnamon together until blended. Add the raisins. Stick clumps of the butter mixture down into the cored area of each apple, distributing evenly.

3. Bake the apples, basting frequently with the pan juices, until tender when pierced with a skewer, 35 to 55 minutes, depending on the variety. Watch carefully so they do not overbake.

4. Serve warm or at room temperature, with the pan juices spooned around each apple. Top with a spoonful of softened ice cream, if desired.

VARIATION

Baked Apples with Brandied Raisins: Soak the raisins overnight in ¼ cup brandy. Drain and reserve the brandy. Add the raisins to the butter mixture in step 2. Use the brandy to baste the apples while baking.

Poached Dried Apricots in Wine Sauce

PREPARATION TIME: 10 MINUTES ✦ COOKING TIME: 35 MINUTES

CHILLING TIME: ABOUT 2 HOURS ✦ SERVES: 4

I ALWAYS KEEP DRIED APRICOTS on hand. They are great for a snack or can be easily dressed up to make an elegant dessert.

2 cups dry white wine

2 cups water

1⅓ cups sugar

1 cinnamon stick (3 inches)

1 package (12 ounces) dried California apricot halves

1. Heat the wine, water, sugar and cinnamon stick in a medium saucepan, stirring to dissolve the sugar. Cover and cook over very low heat until the sugar is absorbed and the syrup is clear, about 10 minutes.

PLAN AHEAD:

Allow at least 2 hours to chill the apricots.

2. Add the apricots and simmer, uncovered, until they are soft and plump, about 25 minutes. Cool to room temperature. Transfer to a serving bowl, cover and refrigerate until very cold, about 2 hours.

3. To serve, ladle the apricots and syrup into dessert bowls, distributing evenly.

Dried Figs in Red Wine

PREPARATION TIME: 10 MINUTES ● COOKING TIME: 45 MINUTES

CHILLING TIME: 1 HOUR OR MORE ● SERVES: 4

THE INSPIRATION for this recipe was a half-empty bottle of wine abandoned on the kitchen counter and some forgotten (but very elegant) imported dried figs in the pantry. Make these ahead, and keep on hand for a quick dessert later in the week. Here, I use all figs, but a combination of apricots, pitted prunes and figs is also nice. If the dried fruit is very hard (as compared to moist), plump it in boiling water to cover for 1 hour, then drain, and simmer in the spiced wine syrup.

PLAN AHEAD:

Allow at least 1 hour to chill the figs.

2 cups dry red wine

1 cup water

⅓ cup sugar

2 whole cloves

2 whole allspice

1 cardamom pod

1 cinnamon stick (2 inches)

1 bay leaf

1 package (10-12 ounces) dried Calimyrna figs

Sour cream, crème fraîche or whole-milk yogurt, for topping

1. Combine the wine, water, sugar, cloves, allspice, cardamom, cinnamon and bay leaf. Heat to boiling, stirring, until the sugar is dissolved, about 5 minutes. Add the figs.

2. Cover and cook over very low heat, about 30 minutes. Uncover and continue to simmer for a little longer if necessary, until the syrup is slightly thickened and reduced, about 10 minutes. Refrigerate until chilled, at least 1 hour.

3. Serve topped with a spoonful of sour cream, crème fraîche or yogurt.

Fresh Plum Sauce

PREPARATION TIME: 10 MINUTES ❀ COOKING TIME: 15 MINUTES

OPTIONAL CHILLING TIME: 30 MINUTES ❀ SERVES: 8; MAKES 2 CUPS

I LIKE THIS ROSY PINK plum sauce with Sweetened Ricotta (page 334), topped with sliced fresh peaches or served over vanilla ice cream or frozen yogurt.

1½   pounds fresh red or purple plums, pitted, cut into chunks

¼   cup sugar, or to taste

2   teaspoons fresh lime juice, or to taste

1. Combine the plums and sugar in a medium saucepan. Heat over low heat, stirring; add a little water by teaspoonfuls if the plums do not release their juices. Cook, stirring, until the plums are softened, about 15 minutes. Cool slightly.

2. You may or may not want to puree the sauce. If the plum skins are small and the sauce is slightly chunky, you can leave it as is. Or, for a smooth result, transfer to a food processor and puree.

> **PLAN AHEAD:**
>
> If serving cold, allow 30 minutes for the sauce to chill.

3. Serve at room temperature or refrigerate for at least 30 minutes to chill before serving. Stir in the lime juice and more sugar, if desired.

Lemon Sauce

PREPARATION TIME: 5 MINUTES ❧ COOKING TIME: 5 MINUTES ❧ SERVES: 4; MAKES ABOUT 1 CUP

THIS LEMON SAUCE RECIPE is from my mother-in-law, Beatrice Simmons. She always served it with warm One-Egg Gingerbread (page 344). I like it with Baked Ricotta Pudding (page 336).

2   tablespoons cornstarch
½   cup sugar
    Pinch salt
1   cup hot water
    Juice and grated zest of 1 lemon
1   tablespoon unsalted butter
4   thin slices lemon, halved

1. Combine the cornstarch, sugar and salt in a small saucepan. Gradually add the water and stir until blended. Cook, stirring gently, until thickened, about 3 minutes. Stir in the lemon juice, lemon zest and butter.

2. Add the lemon slices and serve warm.

Blueberry-Lemon Sauce

PREPARATION TIME: 5 MINUTES ❋ COOKING TIME: 5 MINUTES

STANDING TIME: 5 MINUTES ❋ SERVES: 6 TO 8; MAKES ABOUT 1¾ CUPS

SERVE OVER ICE CREAM, lemon sorbet, angel food cake or frozen vanilla yogurt.

⅓ cup sugar

1 tablespoon cornstarch

1 pint (about 2 cups) blueberries, rinsed, sorted

½ teaspoon grated lemon zest

1. Stir the sugar and cornstarch together in a medium saucepan until thoroughly blended. Add the blueberries.

2. Heat the blueberries, stirring constantly, over medium-low heat until they soften and the mixture thickens, about 5 minutes. Remove from the heat.

3. Stir in the lemon zest and let stand for at least 5 minutes before serving.

Fresh Apricot Sauce and Vanilla Ice Cream Sundae with Toasted Almonds

PREPARATION TIME: 15 MINUTES ❈ COOKING TIME: 2 MINUTES ❈ SERVES: 4

APRICOTS ARE IN SEASON for only a short time. I devised this simple recipe for an apricot sauce that I can whip together quickly and enjoy before the season ceases for yet another year.

10	ripe apricots, rinsed, quartered, pits discarded
2	tablespoons sugar, or more to taste
1	tablespoon fresh lemon or lime juice, or more to taste
⅛	teaspoon almond extract
2	tablespoons sliced natural (with skins) almonds
1-1½	pints good-quality vanilla ice cream

1. Process the apricots, sugar, 1 tablespoon lemon or lime juice and almond extract in a food processor until smooth. Taste and add more sugar or lemon or lime juice, if needed. Transfer to a small bowl and let stand at room temperature until ready to serve.

2. Spread the almonds in a small, dry skillet. Heat over low heat, stirring, until they begin to turn golden, about 2 minutes. Remove from the heat.

3. To serve, scoop the ice cream into 4 dessert bowls or ice-cream glasses. Top with the apricot sauce and sprinkle with the almonds.

Fresh Fig Ice Cream

PREPARATION TIME: 5 MINUTES ❀ SERVES: 4

AS MUCH AS I LOVE ICE CREAM, I indulge only on special occasions. I feel the same way about fresh figs, except that unlike ice cream, which is always available, fresh figs have a limited season. But when they are ripe and lush, I serve them repeatedly—in salads, with ham, baked into a tart or simply mashed and stirred into ice cream. To make this recipe, you need the best vanilla ice cream you can find.

1-2   pints good-quality vanilla
         ice cream, softened
  4   large green or purple figs,
         rinsed, stems trimmed,
         peeled if the skins are tough,
         chopped (see page 306)

1. Scoop the ice cream into a bowl and add the figs. Using a wooden spoon, gently work the figs into the ice cream, mashing them slightly.

2. Serve the ice cream immediately while still soft, or freeze until ready to serve.

Crystallized Ginger Ice Cream with Red Plum Sauce

PREPARATION TIME: 10 MINUTES ● SERVES: 4 TO 6

FOLDING CRYSTALLIZED GINGER into rich vanilla ice cream is the ultimate ice-cream experience for me. This is especially delicious served with plum sauce, although sliced sweetened peaches or nectarines would be equally good.

PLAN AHEAD:

This recipe calls for Fresh Plum Sauce.

2 pints good-quality vanilla
ice cream, softened slightly
½ cup finely chopped
crystallized ginger
Fresh Plum Sauce (page 321)

1. Scoop the ice cream into a large bowl. Using a wooden spoon, gently work the ginger into the ice cream until blended. Serve the softened ice cream immediately or freeze until ready to serve.

2. Just before serving, spoon a little plum sauce into the bottom of the dessert bowls. Fill with generous scoops of the ginger ice cream. Top with more plum sauce.

Chocolate Ice Cream with Espresso Sauce

PREPARATION TIME: 5 MINUTES ❋ COOKING TIME: 6 MINUTES ❋ SERVES: 4

THIS RECIPE IS A SIMPLE rendition of chocolate cooked with heavy cream and flavored with instant espresso coffee, available in small jars in most supermarkets. I like to emphasize the chocolate by serving this thick, velvety sauce over the creamiest chocolate ice cream money can buy. But pairing it with butter pecan or vanilla ice cream makes a smashing dessert as well.

1. Combine the cream, chocolate chips and espresso in a medium saucepan. Heat, stirring, over low heat until the chips melt and the sauce is smooth, about 5 minutes. Boil, gently stirring, for 1 minute. Remove from the heat and cool slightly.

2. Serve the sauce warm or at room temperature over scoops of chocolate ice cream.

1	cup heavy cream
1	cup semisweet chocolate chips
2	teaspoons instant espresso powder
1-1½	pints good-quality chocolate ice cream

GRANITA

GRANITA IS A POPULAR ITALIAN ICE that is extremely refreshing and easy to make. It starts with fresh fruit or fruit juice sweetened with sugar or a sugar syrup. The sweetened mixture is placed in the freezer in a shallow pan and stirred, usually with a fork, as it slowly freezes. Because of its low sugar content and the method used to make it, the consistency is very grainy (*granita* means "grainy" in Italian). Every icy mouthful bursts with zingy flavor.

The mixture melts quickly once it is scraped out of the pan and into a dessert dish. To serve, spoon into chilled wine glasses. If the granita gets too hard, shave off portions with the side of an ice cream scoop or a large spoon. Serving the granita in wine glasses makes sipping the melted ice less awkward when you get to the bottom. Wine glasses that have been frosted for about 30 minutes in the freezer add a nice touch. Italians serve liqueur over granitas.

Strawberry Granita

PREPARATION TIME: 10 MINUTES ❁ COOKING TIME: 5 MINUTES

FREEZING TIME: 1½ HOURS ❁ SERVES: 6 TO 8

THERE IS NO GREATER TASTE of summer than a spoonful of fruit granita. Intensified by the cold, it is unadulterated by any other flavors.

> 1½   cups water
>
> ⅓   cup sugar
>
> 2   pints strawberries, rinsed, hulled, sliced
>
> 1   tablespoon fresh lime juice, or more to taste

1. Combine the water and sugar in a small saucepan and stir over medium heat until the mixture boils and the sugar dissolves completely, about 5 minutes. To quick-chill, pour into a large bowl (preferably metal, which will help the syrup to cool down faster) and place in the freezer.

2. Place the strawberries and ½ cup of the cooled syrup in a food processor and puree. Set a large strainer over the bowl with the remaining syrup and strain the puree, pressing down on it with a rubber spatula. Add 1 tablespoon lime juice. Taste and add more lime juice, if needed.

PLAN AHEAD:

Allow 1½ hours to freeze the granita.

3. Place the mixture in a 13-x-9-inch baking pan and freeze, using a fork to stir the slushy center into the almost frozen edges every 20 minutes or so, until the mixture is semifrozen, about 1½ hours.

4. To serve, scrape the granita into dessert bowls or frosted wine glasses.

Orange Granita

FRESH JUICE is preferred for this recipe, but if you don't have time to squeeze it, frozen is an acceptable substitute. This is also delicious when made with tangerine juice.

1   cup boiling water
⅓   cup sugar
2   cups orange juice
1   tablespoon fresh lemon or lime juice
1   teaspoon grated orange zest

PLAN AHEAD:

Allow 1½ hours to freeze the granita.

1. Stir the water and sugar together until the sugar dissolves, about 5 minutes. Add the orange juice, lemon or lime juice and orange zest; stir to blend.

2. Place the mixture in a 13-x-9-inch baking pan and freeze, using a fork to stir the slushy center into the almost frozen edges every 20 minutes or so, until the mixture is semifrozen, about 1½ hours.

3. Scrape the granita into dessert bowls or frosted wine glasses and serve.

Peach and Buttermilk Ice

PREPARATION TIME: 15 MINUTES ● FREEZING TIME: ABOUT 2 HOURS 15 MINUTES
MAKES: 1 QUART

I LIKE TO SERVE THIS TOPPED with sliced peeled fresh peaches and a few raspberries for color.

1½ cups buttermilk

½ cup sugar

1 tablespoon fresh lemon juice

2-3 cups chopped peeled, pitted peaches (about 6 large peaches)

1. Process the buttermilk, sugar and lemon juice in a food processor. With the motor running, add the peaches, a few at a time, until the mixture is pureed. Transfer to a shallow 9-inch baking pan.

2. Freeze the peach mixture until semifrozen, about 45 minutes. Using a fork, stir the frozen edges into the slushy center. Freeze until the mixture is semisolid. Break into chunks and puree in the food processor. Transfer to a plastic container with a tight-fitting lid and freeze, about 1½ hours. If the ice is frozen hard, let it sit out at room temperature for about 20 minutes to soften it before serving.

PLAN AHEAD:

Allow 2¼ hours to freeze the ice.

Caramelized Bananas with Rich Chocolate Fudge Sauce

PREPARATION TIME: 5 MINUTES ❋ COOKING TIME: 7 TO 10 MINUTES

SERVES: 4; MAKES 1 CUP SAUCE

THERE IS ALWAYS A BUNCH of bananas sitting in our fruit bowl—and a box of cocoa powder stored in the pantry. Who would have thought that these two unassuming foods could be transformed into such a sophisticated dessert? This is adapted from my friend Susan Westmoreland's recipe for a fudge sauce that she makes as a gift for my husband every Christmas. The sauce can be prepared ahead. It will keep for 1 month or more, refrigerated. At serving time, all you have to do is heat the bananas with just a little sugar and butter. This beats any banana split I have ever laid eyes on.

FUDGE SAUCE

½ cup unsweetened cocoa powder

½ cup packed light brown sugar

¾ cup heavy cream

1 tablespoon unsalted butter

2 tablespoons unsalted butter

2 firm, ripe bananas, peeled and cut into ¼-inch-thick diagonal slices

2 tablespoons packed light brown sugar

1-2 pints good-quality vanilla ice cream

1. **Make the Fudge Sauce:** Stir the cocoa, brown sugar and cream together in a small saucepan. Heat to boiling, stirring constantly, over low heat. Remove from the heat and stir in the butter. Serve warm or at room temperature. Or, to prepare in a microwave, combine the cocoa, brown sugar and cream in a 4-cup microwave-safe bowl. Microwave on high until boiling, 2 to 3 minutes, stirring once. Microwave for 30 seconds more, or until the sauce is very smooth. Set aside.

2. Heat the butter in a medium nonstick skillet over medium-low heat. Add the bananas and sprinkle with the brown sugar. Sauté, turning the bananas as they begin to brown and the sugar caramelizes, 5 to 8 minutes.

3. Scoop the ice cream into 4 serving dishes. Top with the bananas, dividing evenly; drizzle with the warm fudge sauce.

Rich Chocolate Pudding

PREPARATION TIME: 10 MINUTES ❋ COOKING TIME: ABOUT 15 MINUTES

OPTIONAL COOLING TIME: 15 MINUTES ❋ SERVES: 4

I HAVE NEVER OUTGROWN my childhood infatuation with chocolate pudding. At home, we had My-T-Fine brand—didn't every child of the fifties?—but somewhere in my early culinary education, I learned to make real chocolate pudding from scratch. Now I am hooked. This recipe is almost as easy as the packaged kind, and because I can select top-quality chocolate, the taste is much more deep, dark and dense. This is by far the most enthusiastically embraced dessert recipe in my classes.

Try some variations by adding a teaspoon of instant espresso coffee, substituting coffee for part of the milk, or adding a tablespoon of chocolate, orange or coffee liqueur or a little grated orange zest. I usually make the pudding plain, but if I don't hide it, it never survives until dinnertime. The best bet is to make it and serve warm.

¼ cup sugar

2 tablespoons cornstarch

2 cups hot milk

3 ounces semisweet or bittersweet chocolate, preferably imported, coarsely chopped

1 teaspoon vanilla extract

1. Stir the sugar and cornstarch together in a medium saucepan. Gradually stir in the milk. Heat, stirring constantly, until the sugar dissolves and the mixture begins to boil and thicken, about 10 minutes. Add the chocolate.

2. Cook over medium-low heat, stirring, until the chocolate is melted and the mixture boils and thickens, about 5 minutes. Remove from the heat; cool for 5 minutes. Stir in the vanilla. Pour into small custard cups. Serve warm or at room temperature.

Sweetened Ricotta

PREPARATION TIME: 10 MINUTES ❋ SERVES: 4 TO 6

RICOTTA CHEESE MAKES a lovely dessert when simply sweetened with confectioners' sugar, spiced with ground cinnamon or nutmeg and stirred together with a little heavy cream. Serve it plain in a wine glass, or in midwinter, spoon it into a cored ripe Bartlett pear. In spring, top with sliced sweetened strawberries; in midsummer, with sliced ripe peaches and rosy plum sauce.

The best ricotta for this dessert is the fresh whole-milk kind available at many Italian specialty markets, but supermarket brands (either whole-milk or part-skim) are an acceptable substitute.

1¾	cups (15-ounce container) ricotta
¼	cup confectioners' sugar
1-2	tablespoons heavy cream, or as needed
½	teaspoon vanilla extract
¼	teaspoon ground cinnamon, or as needed
¼	teaspoon grated orange zest (optional)

Combine the ricotta, confectioners' sugar, 1 tablespoon cream, vanilla, ¼ teaspoon cinnamon and orange zest, if using. If a smoother or looser consistency is desired, add more cream, 1 tablespoon at a time. Whisk or stir to blend well. Taste and adjust the seasonings, adding more cinnamon if you like. Refrigerate until ready to serve. The ricotta can be made up to 1 day before serving.

Sweetened Ricotta with Fresh Peaches or Nectarines and Plum Sauce: Make Fresh Plum Sauce (page 321). Peel 4 large, ripe peaches and cut into thick wedges; or cut up nectarines and toss in a large bowl. Add 1 tablespoon sugar and 1 tablespoon fresh lime juice. Divide the fruit among 4 dessert dishes. Add the sweetened ricotta, dividing evenly and top with a spoonful of the plum sauce.

Sweetened Ricotta with Fresh Strawberries: Stem and slice 1 pint of strawberries. Toss in a large bowl with 1 tablespoon sugar and 1 tablespoon lime juice. Divide evenly among 4 dessert bowls, and spoon the sweetened ricotta on top, dividing evenly. Garnish each with a dusting of cinnamon.

Sweetened Ricotta with Bartlett Pears: Use ½ recipe of sweetened ricotta. Just before serving, peel and halve 2 large, ripe Bartlett pears. Place in a bowl and toss with 2 tablespoons fresh lemon juice. To serve, place a pear half on each of 4 dessert plates. Using a measuring teaspoon, scoop the core from each half. Add a spoonful of the sweetened ricotta and top each with a dusting of ground nutmeg.

Baked Ricotta Pudding with Lemon Sauce

PREPARATION TIME: 15 MINUTES ❈ BAKING TIME: 30 MINUTES

COOLING TIME: 20 MINUTES OR MORE ❈ SERVES: 4

IN ITALY, BAKED PUDDINGS are made with ricotta and have a texture similar to a ricotta cheesecake. These puddings can be made individually, as here, or in a small shallow baking dish. Serve this with lemon sauce, or place a tablespoon of fruit preserves or jam (strawberry, apricot or raspberry) in the bottom of each soufflé or custard cup, and bake with the pudding.

> **PLAN AHEAD:**
>
> This recipe calls for Lemon Sauce.

1½	cups whole-milk or part-skim ricotta
¼	cup plus 1 tablespoon sugar
2	tablespoons all-purpose flour
½	teaspoon grated lemon zest
½	teaspoon vanilla extract
	Pinch ground cinnamon
1	large egg yolk
2	large egg whites, at room temperature
	Pinch salt
	Lemon Sauce (page 322)
4	thin slices lemon, halved, for garnish
	Sliced strawberries, for garnish (optional)

1. Preheat the oven to 350 degrees F. Position a rack in the center. Lightly butter four 6-ounce soufflé or custard cups. Set them in an 11-x-7-inch baking dish.

2. Puree the ricotta, ¼ cup sugar, flour, lemon zest, vanilla, cinnamon and egg yolk in the bowl of a food processor; transfer to a mixing bowl. Set aside.

3. In a separate bowl, beat the egg whites and salt until foamy. Gradually add the remaining 1 tablespoon sugar, beating until soft peaks form. Gently fold the egg-white mixture into the ricotta mixture.

4. Spoon the mixture evenly into the prepared soufflé cups. Add boiling water to the baking pan to a depth of 1 inch. Bake the puddings until they are puffed and golden, about 30 minutes.

5. Remove the puddings from the oven. Cool slightly in the water bath, about 20 minutes. Lift from the water and place on a rack. Loosen the edges with the tip of a knife and invert onto individual serving plates. Top with lemon sauce, placing a thin slice of lemon on each pudding. Garnish with strawberries, if desired.

MANGOS

ALTHOUGH I KNOW HOW to cut up and serve a mango neatly, I usually end up standing over the sink, slurping and dripping to my heart's content. A peeled and diced mango is a delicious addition to fruit salad, green salad or salsa. Mango makes a sublime sorbet when pureed and strained (if it is stringy), stirred into a simple syrup and frozen in an ice-cream maker.

How to Cut a Mango

Stand the mango on one side, and using a sharp knife, cut it just off center so the knife grazes the side of the large, flat center pit. Repeat on the other side of the pit. If the mango flesh is free of strings, serve cut sides up with a spoon to scoop the flesh from the skin. If the flesh appears to be stringy, slice off the skin and cut the flesh into large cubes.

An easy way to eat a whole mango is to score the flesh with the tip of a knife, stopping just short of the thick leathery skin. Then, using your thumbs, press against the rounded (skin) side of the scored mango and literally turn the fruit inside out so that the flesh opens into a crown of cubes. Eat the cubes right off the skin, or cut them away with the tip of a knife.

Mango and Rice Pudding with
Toasted Coconut and Pistachios

PREPARATION TIME: 15 MINUTES ❊ COOKING TIME: 30 MINUTES ❊ SERVES: 6 TO 8

FOR THIS RECIPE, use a soft or sticky variety of rice, such as California medium-grain (often sold as Japanese), Spanish or Italian.

3	cups water
1	cup medium-grain rice
½	teaspoon salt
1	cup plain whole-milk yogurt
½	cup heavy cream, or more as needed
⅓	cup sugar, or to taste
1	teaspoon vanilla extract
⅛	teaspoon almond extract
½	cup flaked sweetened coconut
¼	cup finely chopped skinned pistachios or sliced natural (with skins) almonds
2	cups peeled, pitted, diced ripe mangos (about 2 large)

1. Combine the water, rice and salt in a large, wide saucepan. Heat to boiling over high heat. Stir once. Reduce the heat to low, cover and cook over low heat until the rice is very soft and tender but still moist, about 25 minutes. Uncover and let stand for 5 minutes.

2. Meanwhile, combine the yogurt, cream, sugar, vanilla extract and almond extract in a bowl and stir to blend. Let stand at room temperature, stirring occasionally to dissolve the sugar, about 10 minutes.

3. Preheat the oven to 350 degrees F. Spread the coconut at one end of a baking sheet and the pistachios or almonds at the other end. Bake in the oven just until lightly toasted, about 5 minutes. Cool.

4. Add the warm rice to the yogurt mixture, and stir to blend. Fold in the mangos. To serve, spoon into dessert dishes and top each with the toasted coconut and nuts. This is best served warm. The pudding will stiffen upon standing. Thin with a little more cream or with yogurt thinned with a little milk, if desired.

Apple and Ginger Crisp

PREPARATION TIME: 10 MINUTES ❈ BAKING TIME: 35 MINUTES ❈ SERVES: 4

MAKE THIS PLAIN with brown sugar and add raisins, dried cranberries or tiny currants. If you are a crystallized-ginger fan, as I am, chop some and add it instead of the raisins. Or jazz up the raisins by soaking them in brandy first. This is the easiest of baked desserts and can be varied in countless ways.

4-5 large apples (Granny Smith or Golden Delicious; Jonathan, Winesap, Rome, Royal Gala, Northern Spy or other crisp baking apples in season), quartered, peeled, cored, thinly sliced

1 tablespoon fresh lemon juice

2 tablespoons plus ½ cup packed light brown sugar

1 tablespoon minced crystallized ginger, raisins, currants or dried cranberries

1 cup quick-cooking (not instant) oats

⅓ cup all-purpose flour

¼ teaspoon ground cinnamon

6 tablespoons unsalted butter, melted Softened vanilla ice cream or frozen yogurt (optional)

1. Preheat the oven to 350 degrees F. Place the apples into a 9-inch pie plate or other small, shallow baking dish. Add the lemon juice and 2 tablespoons of the brown sugar; toss to blend. Sprinkle with the ginger, raisins, currants or cranberries.

2. In a medium bowl, blend the oats, the remaining ½ cup brown sugar, flour and cinnamon. Drizzle with the butter, and using a fork or fingertips, mix until crumbly. Sprinkle evenly over the fruit.

3. Bake until the top is browned and the fruit is tender, about 35 minutes. Serve with softened vanilla ice cream or frozen yogurt, if using.

Peach and Blueberry Crisp with Toasted Almonds

PREPARATION TIME: 20 MINUTES ❋ BAKING TIME: 50 MINUTES ❋ SERVES: 6 TO 8

I MAKE THIS CRISP all the time in July and August, when peaches and blueberries are in season. To save time, substitute nectarines for the peaches, since the skins don't need to be peeled. In midwinter, this crisp topping of oats, brown sugar, flour and butter perfectly complements apples and pears. Just slice hard fruits thin so that they will cook in the same time it takes to brown the crisp topping. Serve warm, topped with heavy cream, ice cream or frozen yogurt. (See photograph, page 88.)

½ cup whole natural (with skins) almonds, coarsely chopped

8 large peaches

2 tablespoons plus ⅓ cup all-purpose flour

2 tablespoons plus ½ cup packed light brown sugar

½ teaspoon ground cinnamon

1 pint (2 cups) blueberries, rinsed, sorted, drained on a paper towel

1 cup quick-cooking (not instant) oats
Pinch salt

6 tablespoons unsalted butter, softened
Heavy cream, vanilla ice cream or frozen vanilla yogurt

1. Preheat the oven to 350 degrees F. Spread the almonds in a shallow pan and bake until lightly toasted, about 10 minutes. Set aside to cool; leave the oven on.

2. Half fill a large saucepan with water and heat to boiling. Have ready a large bowl half filled with cold tap water and a few ice cubes. Place the peaches in the boiling water and let sit for 3 minutes in the simmering water to loosen their skins. Transfer the peaches to the cold water. Let sit for 2 minutes. Lift the peaches out of the water and slip off the skins. Cut the peaches into large wedges and discard the pits.

3. In a large bowl, combine the 2 tablespoons flour, 2 tablespoons of the brown sugar and cinnamon; stir to blend. Add the peaches and stir to coat. Spread the peaches and blueberries in a shallow (13-x-9-inch) rectangular baking dish.

4. In a separate bowl, combine the toasted almonds, oats, remaining ⅓ cup flour, remaining ½ cup brown sugar and salt; stir to blend. Add the butter and work it into the oat mixture, using a fork or fingertips, until crumbly. Sprinkle evenly over the peaches.

5. Bake until the top is browned and crisp and the peaches are bubbly, about 35 minutes. Serve warm, topped with cream, ice cream or frozen yogurt.

Strawberry Shortcake

PREPARATION TIME: 15 MINUTES ● BAKING TIME: 30 TO 35 MINUTES ● SERVES: 6

MY FAVORITE SHORTCAKE is warm, slightly crunchy and very, very tender. This recipe for a shortcake biscuit is from the late James Beard.

SHORTCAKE BISCUIT

1¾ cups all-purpose flour

¼ cup plus 1 teaspoon sugar

1 tablespoon baking powder

½ teaspoon salt

1 cup heavy cream

TOPPING

2 pints small, ripe strawberries, hulled, sliced

½ cup sugar

2 tablespoons fresh lime or lemon juice

Heavy cream

1 tablespoon confectioners' sugar

1. Preheat the oven to 400 degrees F. Generously coat a 9-inch metal pie plate or a round cake pan with butter.

2. Make the Shortcake Biscuit: Sift the flour, ¼ cup sugar, baking powder and salt into a medium mixing bowl. Gradually pour in the cream while tossing the mixture lightly with a fork, just until the dough comes together. (The dough should be lumpy; do not overwork it or the cake will be tough.) Turn the dough into the buttered pan and gently pat it evenly with floured fingers to fit (the top will be lumpy). Sprinkle with the remaining 1 teaspoon sugar.

3. Bake the shortcake until the top is golden brown and the edges are crisp, 30 to 35 minutes. Cool slightly on a wire rack, then transfer to a serving plate.

4. Meanwhile, Make the Topping: Combine the strawberries, sugar and lime or lemon juice. Cover and let stand at room temperature to allow the fruit to release its juices, about 20 minutes.

5. Beat the cream and confectioners' sugar with an electric mixer until soft peaks form.

6. While the shortcake is still warm, cut it into wedges and place a wedge on each dessert plate. Spoon the strawberries and their juices over the cake, and top with a spoonful of the whipped cream.

BISCUIT VARIATIONS

Brown Sugar Shortcake: Substitute packed light brown sugar for the granulated sugar. Sieve 1 teaspoon brown sugar over the top before baking. This is excellent with any fruit topping.

Toasted Hazelnut Shortcake: Stir ¼ cup ground toasted hazelnuts into the dry ingredients after sifting. This is especially good with peach topping.

Citrus Shortcake: Stir 1 teaspoon *each* grated orange and lemon zest into the dry ingredients after sifting. This is especially good with strawberry topping.

Spiced Shortcake: Sift ½ teaspoon ground cinnamon, ¼ teaspoon ground nutmeg and a pinch of ground allspice with the dry ingredients. This suits any fruit topping.

TOPPING VARIATIONS

Three-Berry Topping: Substitute 1 cup *each* raspberries and blackberries and 2 cups blueberries for the strawberries.

Peach or Nectarine Topping: Substitute 2½ pounds ripe peaches or nectarines, sliced into ½-inch-thick wedges for the strawberries. For added flavor and color, don't peel the peaches or nectarines; just rinse and wipe dry with a kitchen towel.

One-Egg Gingerbread

PREPARATION TIME: 15 MINUTES ❀ BAKING TIME: 35 TO 45 MINUTES ❀ SERVES: 8

THIS IS A SIMMONS FAMILY recipe from my husband's maternal grandmother. It is an old-fashioned gingerbread, adapted slightly, with butter substituted for the shortening of the original.

> **PLAN AHEAD:**
>
> This recipe calls for Lemon Sauce

½   cup (1 stick) unsalted butter, at room temperature

½   cup packed light brown sugar

1   large egg

1   cup dark molasses

2½   cups all-purpose flour

1½   teaspoons baking soda

2-3   teaspoons ground ginger

½   teaspoon ground cloves

½   teaspoon salt

1   cup boiling water

Lemon Sauce (page 322)

1. Preheat the oven to 350 degrees F. Lightly butter a 9-inch square pan or a round cake pan.

2. Cream the butter and brown sugar with an electric mixer until very light. Beat in the egg until blended. Gradually beat in the molasses, scraping the sides of the bowl.

3. Sift the flour, baking soda, ginger, cloves and salt together onto a piece of waxed paper. Slowly stir into the molasses mixture, just until blended. Do not overmix. Gradually stir in the water.

4. Pour into the prepared pan and bake until a toothpick inserted into the center comes out clean and the edges of the cake begin to pull away from the sides of the pan, 35 to 45 minutes. Cool on a wire rack.

5. Serve the cake warm or at room temperature with the warm lemon sauce.

Index

(Numbers in boldface indicate photographs.)